From the Center of Tradition

From the Center of Tradition

CRITICAL PERSPECTIVES ON LINDA HOGAN

EDITED BY
Barbara J. Cook

University Press of Colorado

© 2003 by the University Press of Colorado

Published by the University Press of Colorado
5589 Arapahoe Avenue, Suite 206C
Boulder, Colorado 80303

All rights reserved
Printed in the United States of America

 The University Press of Colorado is a proud member of
the Association of American University Presses.

The University Press of Colorado is a cooperative publishing enterprise supported, in part, by Adams State College, Colorado State University, Fort Lewis College, Mesa State College, Metropolitan State College of Denver, University of Colorado, University of Northern Colorado, and Western State College of Colorado.

The paper used in this publication meets the minimum requirements of the American National Standard for Information Sciences—Permanence of Paper for Printed Library Materials. ANSI Z39.48-1992

Library of Congress Cataloging-in-Publication Data

From the center of tradition : critical perspectives on Linda Hogan / Barbara J. Cook, editor.
    p. cm.
"Selected Works by Linda Hogan": p.
Includes bibliographical references (p.) and index.
    ISBN 0-87081-737-X (alk. paper) — ISBN 0-87081-738-8 (pbk. : alk. paper)
    1. Hogan, Linda—Criticism and interpretation. 2. Women and literature—United States—History—20th century. 3. Chickasaw Indians—Intellectual life. 4. Indians in literature. I. Cook, Barbara J.
    PS3558.O34726Z66 2003
    818'.5409—dc21
                                                   2003008791

Design by Daniel Pratt

12 11 10 09 08 07 06 05 04 03   10 9 8 7 6 5 4 3 2 1

CO-WINNER OF THE 2002 COLORADO ENDOWMENT FOR THE HUMANITIES PUBLICATION PRIZE

 The CEH Publication Prize annually supports publication of outstanding nonfiction works that have strong humanities content and that make an area of humanities research more available to the Colorado public. The CEH Publication Prize funds are shared by the University Press of Colorado and the authors of the works being recognized.
    The Colorado Endowment for the Humanities is a statewide, nonprofit organization dedicated to improving the quality of humanities education for all Coloradans.

To Ron and Shannon Leigh
For all your love and support

CONTENTS

	Introduction *Barbara J. Cook*	1
1	From the Center of Tradition: An Interview with Linda Hogan *Barbara J. Cook*	11
2	"How Do We Learn to Trust Ourselves Enough to Hear the Chanting of Earth?": Hogan's Terrestrial Spirituality *Katherine R. Chandler*	17
3	Hogan's Historical Narratives: Bringing to Visibility the Interrelationship of Humanity and the Natural World *Barbara J. Cook*	35
4	Storied Earth, Storied Lives: Linda Hogan's *Solar Storms* and Rick Bass's *The Sky, the Stars, the Wilderness* *Ann Fisher-Wirth*	53
5	Linda Hogan's "Geography of the Spirit": Division and Transcendence in Selected Texts *Benay Blend*	67
6	Rhetorics of Truth Telling in Linda Hogan's *Savings* *Jennifer Love*	81
7	Circles Within Circles: Linda Hogan's Rhetoric of Indigenism *Ernest Stromberg*	97

Contents

8	Visioning Identity: Ways of Seeing in Linda Hogan's "Aunt Moon's Young Man" *Barbara J. Cook*	109
9	"The Inside of Lies and History": Linda Hogan's Poetry of Conscience *Ernest Smith*	121
10	Standing Naked Before the Storm: Linda Hogan's *Power* and the Critique of Apocalyptic Narrative *Michael Hardin*	135
11	Dancing the Chronotopes of Power: The Road to Survival in Linda Hogan's *Power* *Carrie Bowen-Mercer*	157
	Biographical Information and Chronology —Linda Hogan	179
	Bibliography	181
	Contributors	185
	Index	189

From the Center of Tradition

INTRODUCTION

Barbara J. Cook

> They walk inside me. This blood
> is a map of the road between us.
> I am why they survived.
> The world behind them did not close.
> All around me are my ancestors,
> my unborn children.
> I am the tear between them
> and both sides live.
> —Linda Hogan, "Tear"

"I want to tell you my story," Chickasaw author Linda Hogan writes in her recent book of recollections, *The Woman Who Watches Over the World: A Native Memoir*. She continues, "This is what Indian people say. And our stories do not begin with us as individuals" (78). Hogan's writing tells the stories of Native peoples on this continent in a way that enables a reader to see the stresses of individual lives encompassed in the broader stories and events of history. She writes from a cultural ecotone,[1] a zone that draws strength from her mixed-blood heritage—Chickasaw and Anglo. Hogan considers her work "traditionally centered,"[2] however, even though it does not focus only on her Chickasaw traditions. Rather, she seeks to tell the stories of Native people's experiences in the world and to encourage others to view the world—especially the natural world—from the perspective of traditional Native ways of knowing. Hogan's writing is often at the intersection of environmental matters and the historical and ongoing treatment of American Indians, thus linking environmental justice and social justice issues.

Although Linda Hogan earned an M.A. in creative writing from the University of Colorado in 1978, she began her prolific writing career as an adult

Barbara J. Cook

with no experience as a writer and little experience reading literature. In an interview with Bo Schöler she says that while she was working with physically challenged children, she began to write on her lunch hours: "[S]omething about the process of doing that writing tapped into my own life in a way I wouldn't have done without the writing" ("A Heart Made out of Crickets" 107). Hogan's first poetry collection, *Calling Myself Home* (1978), reveals that connection and her love for the history, landscape, and oral tradition of her Oklahoma Chickasaw roots. She also drew on those family stories and tribal histories for her first novel, *Mean Spirit*, published in 1990. With the publication of *Mean Spirit*, Hogan quickly moved to the center of the Native American Renaissance. She has since published two other novels that draw on Native traditions outside her own Chickasaw culture: *Solar Storms* (1995) and *Power* (1998). Both novels are fictionalized narratives based on actual events in recent Native history. Her body of work also includes poetry, short fiction, nature essays, and nonfiction essays on environmental issues written for mainstream organizations such as The Nature Conservancy and the Sierra Club. Hogan's works center around community and the traditional indigenous view of and relationship to the land, animals, and plants—an interconnected, reciprocal relationship between the human and the nonhuman world.

Her novels are not specific to her Chickasaw ancestry but rather draw on her self-described "traditional, indigenous perspective of the land and human relationship with the land" (*Western Voices Interview*). Native literary studies critics such as Craig S. Womack have called for "tribally specific literatures and critical perspectives" (225), but Hogan points out that non-Indian people "seem to be able to go into any territory and use it as theirs to write about, but Indian people can't do that. . . . And non-Indian readers expect us to somehow explain our culture to them" (*Western Voices Interview*). As she considers herself "primarily an environmental writer, [she] find[s] that to be unfair" (*Western Voices Interview*). Hogan also points to the intrusions tribal people have endured into their personal cosmologies, and by providing a more pan-Indian Native view she is being protective of those sensibilities. Womack also argues that "Native literary aesthetics must be politicized" (11). Hogan has shown support for this type of argument through her writing and interviews. She said in a *Western Voices Interview* with Brad Johnson:

> I've found that talking about issues somehow doesn't create change in the world, but if I can take of the issues, political issue, or a tribe that is being devastated because of development, or land that's being devastated because of development—and I put it into a story, it has more of an impact. People read it and they get it because it's not a political diatribe; they find characters that they can relate to and care about and they see a story from inside their own body, inside their own selves, instead of hearing about it and going back to their daily lives.

Introduction

This stated goal places her not only within the Native American Renaissance but emphasizes that her work, as well as that of other Native American writers, is at the center of the contemporary literary canon. As Womack further argues, "Without Native American literature, *there is no American canon*" (7; his emphasis).

The wide-ranging study of Hogan's work shows this is certainly true of her work. Her texts are studied in a variety of university classes ranging from literature courses focusing on American fiction and American Indian writers to more interdisciplinary classes in women's studies, ecofeminist ethics, and environmental studies. Numerous critical essays and conference presentations have focused on Hogan's writing, including a single-author issue of *Studies in American Indian Literatures* in 1994. Her writing has been discussed from a range of theoretical approaches including ecocritical, postcolonial, feminist studies, American Indian studies, and narrative theory. Given her central role in contemporary American literature, a collection of essays on her work is long overdue.

This collection places Hogan's work at the center of current discussions in American literature and shows that, as Carter Revard argues, "the true values of America are just as vividly and richly present in the 'ethnic' as in the classic" (162).[3] Rather than focusing on a single facet of her writing, these chapters reflect the variety of approaches currently employed in discussing her work and suggest productive avenues of continued study not only for Hogan's work but for work by other Native American authors as well. Because of the pan-Indian theme in much of Hogan's work, critical readings often incorporate more generalized observations about Native peoples than readings of more tribally specific literatures do. The chapters also locate Hogan's work within the larger conversation of contemporary literature. For instance, several chapters approach her work from various perspectives within the relatively new but flourishing field of ecocriticism. One of those chapters makes an explicit comparison between Hogan's work and that of Rick Bass, a central figure in the contemporary American nature-writing canon. Further, the collection reflects the variety within Hogan's own literary production, as it includes articles on her fiction, poetry, short stories, and essays—often drawing from more than one genre to support a point. Thus the diversity of critical approaches mirrors the diversity of Hogan's work.

This collection begins with my recent interview of Hogan, "From the Center of Tradition." The chapters that follow reflect the most current and productive critical commentary on Linda Hogan's texts and provide a useful foundation for discussion of those works.

In "'How Do We Learn to Trust Ourselves Enough to Hear the Chanting of the Earth?': Hogan's Terrestrial Spirituality," Kate Chandler explores Hogan's articulation of forgotten connections between nature and spirit. Drawing on

Barbara J. Cook

essays written at different times and for various publications that are collected in *Dwellings: A Spiritual History of the Living World,* Chandler finds a unifying link and consistent worldview expressed by Hogan. As Chandler points out, this forgotten connection is a lament heard from many contemporary sources—environmentalists, philosophers, theologians, anthropologists, and sociologists. She argues that Hogan focuses on resolution and that she relies on language that is sensitive to land and realigns "story with ceremony" in each of her essays.

Hogan's union of spirit and nature in this group of essays creates what Chandler calls "land-language" that "demonstrates genuine respect for the land, assumes our interconnectedness with organizing ecosystems, acknowledges our role in relation to other life forms"; a language that "we live more than [we] speak." Such a blend of spirit and nature begins with an ecology of mind that includes caring for and listening to the earth. This caring and listening become the language of story and ceremony—a step that draws humans closer to nature in a spiritual and interactive way.

The second chapter in the grouping of environmentally focused approaches is "Hogan's Historical Narratives: Bringing to Visibility the Interrelationship of Humanity and the Natural World." In this chapter I examine Hogan's narrative strategies, which tell a cultural/tribal story while also calling attention to environmental justice issues that have affected local communities in devastating ways. Both *Mean Spirit* and *Solar Storms* are centered in historical events. Hogan begins with the history and creatively embellishes it in a multiplicity of ways. Her rhetorical techniques include anthropomorphism of the landscape and the natural world, a shifting reality, and a story line that juxtaposes changes in landscape with changes in members of her fictional communities. In this close reading it becomes apparent that Hogan insists upon the interrelationship of the treatment of land and peoples. These texts vividly demonstrate that interrelationship and reveal the historical politics that have created the link between socially and environmentally destructive policies.

Ann Fisher-Wirth also incorporates an ecocritical approach in her chapter "Storied Earth, Storied Lives: Linda Hogan's *Solar Storms* and Rick Bass's *The Sky, the Stars, the Wilderness.*" She situates the work of Bass and Hogan within the larger context of environmental literature, drawing on ecocritic Michael Branch's argument that the two dominant forms this literature takes are the jeremiad and the elegy. Fisher-Wirth argues that a third "impulse in environmental writing mitigates the darkness of the first two." She identifies that impulse as one that expresses the particulars of rapture—"an impulse to be subsumed in the present . . . [a narrative that] can intermingle bittersweetly with anger and mourning, affirming the abiding presence of the sacred and envisioning human life in harmony with, learning from, and honoring the natural world." Fisher-Wirth sees Bass's novella *The Sky, the Stars, the Wilderness* and the central section of Hogan's *Solar Storms* as "particularly eloquent manifestations of this vision."

Through her exploration of these two works, Fisher-Wirth underscores the patterns of elegy, jeremiad, and rapture within each author's narrative. Although she draws parallels between the two, Fisher-Wirth also clearly finds differences in their approaches to political history, private property, and the natural world. In contrast to the tenets of mainstream deep ecology and the sense of loss of connection to the land in Bass's novella, Hogan voices the stories of Native women who have "lost virtually everything *but* their mysticism; the path to [the waters of their homeland] is marked with suffering and dispossession far beyond anything Bass's narrator ever imagines." Whereas Bass concentrates on the changes in the land and natural species wrought by development and increased water usage along the Balcones Escarpment of central Texas, Hogan writes of the environmental destruction that also targets minorities. Fisher-Wirth contrasts these two writers' stories as each reflects the "storied earth" and "storied lives" in their own way, thus identifying and contrasting differing ways of knowing and understanding the world.

In "Linda Hogan's 'Geography of the Spirit': Division and Transcendence in Selected Texts," Benay Blend also calls attention to Hogan's "storied land." Blend connects this idea of historical landscape to Hogan's creation of identity from the "act of remembering domestic, geographic, cultural, and discursive spaces . . . the map that exists inside tribal thoughts and traditional knowledge." Blend draws on poetry, essays, and fiction to argue that Hogan inhabits a place "between," a borderland space that incorporates tribal traditions and the effects of colonization—both internal and external. For Blend, a central theme of Hogan's work is an exploration of cultural hybridity within a "borderlands," as identified by Gloria Anzaldúa. This is a "literal and figurative terrain that by its very nature encourages the integration of ancient and modern cultural beliefs."

Although Hogan draws on these cultural beliefs, she also achieves her own sense of individual identity by integrating her personal history with a sense of greater tribal and human history. Through this transcendence of "boundaries between herself and others and between humans and their environment," Blend argues, she creates an individual environmental ethic based on a "ritual or ceremonial understanding of human life." Thus Hogan demonstrates a "terrestrial intelligence" that calls for political as well as personal transformation.

Jennifer Love's chapter, "Rhetorics of Truth Telling in Linda Hogan's *Savings*," applies an ecofeminist approach that probes Hogan's philosophy of language and the unspoken communication that occurs—and sometimes fails—between humans and nonhuman species such as plants, animals, and nonanimate nature. Love explores the "troubled or failed communication between plants/animals and humans" that she finds articulated in Hogan's poetry collection, *Savings*.

Barbara J. Cook

She argues that although in some ways the poems "resist, rather than inscribe, the ideal of a common language," Hogan also allows the "Western-entrenched hierarchy between nature and culture" to persist. Ultimately, the dualism Hogan's poems reflect in this volume shows the "perhaps insurmountable persistence" of the power of the nature-culture divide.

Tracing the tropes of honesty and truth in *Savings* within the framework of a Western rhetorical tradition and the American Indian tradition of oral storytelling and in ecofeminist rhetorical theory, Love finds Hogan "is calling for rhetorical, ecologically sensitive action," urging us to rethink the relationship between human and nonhuman nature and to open up to the possibilities of interspecies communication. In *Savings*, Hogan "both invokes and unsettles Western philosophies of truth telling and interspecies relationships" and offers rhetorical avenues to the possible reconstruction of those philosophies.

In "Circles Within Circles: Linda Hogan's Rhetoric of Indigenism," Ernest Stromberg considers Hogan's rhetoric from another perspective—that of articulation of identity within literary representations of Native Americans by Indians and non-Indians. As Stromberg points out, Native American authors and critics such as Elizabeth Cook-Lynn and Craig Womack question the relationship between literary productions of Indian identity and "ongoing struggles by specific Indian communities to assert their political sovereignty and insist upon their treaty rights." Additionally, for critics Cook-Lynn and Womack, Hogan transgresses the boundaries of "sovereignty of specific tribal literary traditions" by writing narratives rooted in tribal cultures outside her specific Chickasaw heritage. Womack argues that this pan-Indian writing represents an "Indian genericism . . . that obscures concrete tribal and land relationships."

Stromberg utilizes Hogan's work to explore the issues these critical positions imply and at the same time examines "the extent to which Hogan's novel[s] advance the] nationalist and separatist agendas" of Womack and Cook-Lynn. In "Hogan's acts of literary trespass," Stromberg finds she articulates an indigenist commitment "both to the specific tribes she writes about and to pan-Indian concerns and values"—a literary activism that challenges the dominant culture's version of history and the policies that have emanated from that history that are detrimental to American Indians.

In "Visioning Identity: Ways of Seeing in Linda Hogan's 'Aunt Moon's Young Man,'" I analyze Hogan's use of metaphorical language of looking and seeing, which helps her young protagonist understand her identity within a mixed-blood tribal culture. This imagery recalls the feminist connotation of the gaze, a patriarchal, controlling, objectifying of the other—the female. Hogan seemingly reverses this idea and instead explores the attempt by the women of the community to control each other. In this community the women rather than the men act as spectators and voyeurs. The dichotomy Hogan creates with this move reflects the negativity of attempted control through the gaze but allows for a more positive possibility—"observation as a key to one's development."

Hogan appropriates images such as mirrors, windows, crystal, and the inner eye in ways that create reflections from within as well as outside the individual. Each of these reflections contributes to the protagonist Sis's awakening to identity and the possibility of relationships within communities as well as between individuals. Sis comes to realize that her identity and those relationships are enhanced by an "adherence to traditions of their [individuals'] ancestors." These traditional ways of seeing and knowing enable her to escape the controlling gaze of the community of women influenced by dominant cultural ideals, to escape a fragmented self-identity, and to recover a place within an ordered, balanced world.

In "'The Inside of Lies and History': Linda Hogan's Poetry of Conscience," Ernest Smith finds a tension between the struggle to shape a self-identity that is whole and integrated and the struggle to achieve that integration through establishing a relationship with community. This tension of communal and individual includes tensions of the political-lyrical and the epic-personal as well. Smith argues that Hogan is a poet of conscience whose "awareness of history is always ecological and global" and whose work involves an interweaving of "both human connections or reconnections with the natural world and vital elements of the self." In Hogan's work these elements of self are often centered in "Native and communal heritage," and the voices from the past are "clearly audible, a legacy to be absorbed." Smith finds these voices from the past are often a "sequence of snapshots of the self . . . not stages to be moved through and left behind but vital components of the whole personality." Smith's chapter provides close readings of Hogan's poetry that clearly illustrate these arguments.

Michael Hardin's chapter, "Standing Naked Before the Storm: Linda Hogan's *Power* and the Critique of Apocalyptic Narrative," takes the collection in an entirely different direction. In discussing Hogan's latest novel, Hardin argues that she critiques the Judeo-Christian apocalyptic narrative—a "product of binary thinking [functioning] within a victim-oppressor structure" that invites the oppressor to cite that narrative "as divine justification for [the] conquest and oppression of 'Evil.'" *Power* calls into question "the religious and secular elements . . . and the dualistic thought processes that underlie" apocalyptic narratives, "specifically as they are used against the American Indian." In setting up his argument, Hardin gives a historical overview of how this type of story has been employed in the past, specifically by Christopher Columbus and other Spanish explorers. As Hardin points out, Hogan mentions both Juan Ponce de León and Alvar Núñez Cabeza de Vaca in the novel; and by "locating her narrative in Florida, a region conquered by the Spanish, Hogan can participate in both American Indian and Latin American literary traditions."

Barbara J. Cook

Hardin invokes other comparisons, such as the historical writings of John Cotton, Jonathan Edwards, William Bradford, and Father Bernabe Cobo and the fiction of Gabriel García Márquez. He also asserts that *Power* joins other contemporary American Indian writing that "openly confront[s] and subvert[s] the apocalyptic nature of the Europeans, both Spanish and English." *Power*'s message can be compared to that in *Indian Killer* by Sherman Alexie and that in *Crown of Columbus* by Michael Dorris and Louise Erdrich. For Hardin, Hogan is reclaiming agency for Native Americans by subverting and ultimately purging the apocalyptic tale that accompanied conquest of the Americas.

In "Dancing the Chronotopes of Power: The Road to Survival in Linda Hogan's *Power*," Carrie Bowen-Mercer also finds the possibility of hope, agency, survival, and power in this novel. Bowen-Mercer says the truths of Hogan's narrative are found in the historical fact woven "into her fictional account of the struggling Tiaga on a diminished section of swampland in northern Florida. Poisoned fish and unsafe drinking water are the truths of Hogan's novel." As Hogan ponders "the intersections of lives and cultures and times and spaces," she questions the linear time lines of history as Euro-Americans know it. Bowen-Mercer delves into these time and space relationships (and the differences in Native and Euro-American understandings of those relationships) through the metaphor of chronotopes as defined by Mikhail Bakhtin. For Bakhtin the chronotope is a time-space matrix that is emblematic of "the most immediate reality." Bowen-Mercer suggests that "not only does the chronotope imply reality as lived, but it also suggests the immediacy of its lived reality. In other words, the chronotope is relative; it changes depending on its context; it is emblematic of a particular space-time; it is history." The chronotope also "draws relations between the world and its art," opening a space for the literary critic to question linear concepts of time and space. She sees Bakhtin's chronotope as a trickster figure, as does critic Gerald Vizenor, and through this lens she views Hogan's protagonists Ama and Omishto as gaining power by means of a trickster-like shifting of time and space and a revisioning of history.

The themes that draw these chapters together include a focus on the natural world and also on the historical and contemporary consequences for Native peoples of governmental actions and decisions. The chapters draw on Native literary critics such as Vizenor, Womack, and Louis Owens but also find literary theorists such as Anzaldúa, Bakhtin, Foucault, John Berger, and Laura Mulvey useful in reading and understanding Hogan's work. Following these chapters is a brief chronology of Linda Hogan's literary awards and a Bibliography that includes most of Hogan's major texts and interviews, as well as a selected list of secondary sources. These lists are not meant to be exhaustive but are included to aid scholars in further studying her work.

Introduction

I would like to thank University of Oregon professors Louise Westling and Suzanne Clark who encouraged me to begin work on this collection while reminding me not to neglect another project already under way. The Center for the Study of Women in Society enabled me to have the time for both projects when it awarded me the Jane Grant Dissertation Fellowship for 2001–2002. I will be forever grateful for the organization's support. Thanks also to my colleagues and friends, Ce Rosenow and Tina Richardson, who have lived through each step of this project with me. Sandy Crooms and the rest of the staff at the University Press of Colorado have been wonderful to work with, and I appreciate all their patience and help. Most of all, I want to thank Linda Hogan not only for her wonderful writing but for her willingness to talk to me about her work.

Notes

1. An ecotone is a transition zone between two adjacent ecological communities, such as desert and mountain, containing species of both zones as well as other transitional species. Within this rich habitat is a complex interplay of contrasting plant and animal communities that support each other, intermingle, or adapt and change (Krall 4). The zones where these differences within the natural world come together "are the richest of habitats" (4). I am using ecotone as a cultural metaphor that draws on the ecological definition to call attention to the social and cultural zone from which Native American and other mixed-blood writers emerge. In this zone, diversity strengthens the cultural life of a region such as Hogan's Southwest and thus contributes to its people's survival. Ecotone as a cultural metaphor gives us a way to understand the acculturation that has occurred in a multiplicity of directions and therefore created a variety of contexts out of which conflict and change emerge. Hogan's writing reflects both the conflict and the possibility for change.

2. "From the Center of Tradition: An Interview with Linda Hogan," Chapter 1 in this volume.

3. Revard compares individual Native American poems by Simon Ortiz and Louise Erdrich to classic texts such as Milton's "On the Late Massacre in Piedmont" and Robert Frost's "Never Again Would Bird's Song Be the Same" as illustrations of this argument in "Herbs of Healing," in *Family Matters, Tribal Affairs*.

Works Cited

Hogan, Linda. "A Heart Made out of Crickets: An Interview with Linda Hogan." By Bo Schöler. *Journal of Ethnic Studies* 16 (1988): 107–117.

———. "Tear." In *The Book of Medicines*. Minneapolis: Coffee House Press, 1993. 59–60.

———. *Western Voices Interview with Linda Hogan*. By Brad Johnson, 2 March 1998 <http://www.centerwest.org/voices/hogan-interview.html>.

———. *The Woman Who Watches Over the World: A Native Memoir*. New York: W. W. Norton, 2001.

Barbara J. Cook

Krall, Florence R. *Ecotone: Wayfaring on the Margins.* Albany: State University of New York Press, 1994.

Revard, Carter. *Family Matters, Tribal Affairs.* Tucson: University of Arizona Press, 1998.

Womack, Craig S. *Red on Red: Native American Literary Separatism.* Minneapolis: University of Minnesota Press, 1999.

FROM THE CENTER OF TRADITION
An Interview with Linda Hogan

BARBARA J. COOK

THIS INTERVIEW WAS PLANNED FOR EARLY JUNE 2002; but the wildfires began raging in Colorado, and we mutually agreed that we would conduct our discussion via e-mail. This electronic process was preceded by several phone conversations during which Linda Hogan was very gracious. We shared stories about our children, our work, and our everyday lives, including her horses and her new puppy and our daughters.

BC: Can you talk about the spiritual and political united in your work? How does that create a space for change, transformation?

LH: For Native peoples there is no difference. Decisions are made based on the spiritual, and they may be political decisions. In *Solar Storms,* for example, the traditional people have to fight in court for the termination of the dam that would destroy their land, their traplines, and their future grandchildren. This was based on the true event—the Hydro-Quebec energy grid. They showed up without warning to tell people to leave their homes, as they were going to bulldoze them, and the Natives had no paper ownership. Since the people knew all the plants, animals, even the purposes of insects, they made a museum exhibition to show people all that was sacred to them, and they won in court. It took twenty years and monumental environmental impact statements. But the land was loved, is loved, is spirit. That is why they wouldn't sell it.

BC: Your three novels are based on actual events. Do you see them as a series? Why start from a historical event?

LH: No, I don't see the novels as a series. I just have been closely aware of the issues facing us, and so I have used those events. They are still fiction.

The canoe trip in *Solar Storms* was fictionalized. I had to go over maps, portage areas, waterways, and go up there and do it myself to write it. What a wonderful thing. What muscle after carrying all that stuff for days and days. But these are the things that concern us the most, that we care about, and they are our way of survival.

With *Mean Spirit,* much of it was family history, but I completely fictionalized the place. It is in reality a grassland, but I made it much more like the area around my family allotment lands. This bothers people, but it is fiction and that is hard to accept. The murders are real, as are the names of the killers. Some of the children of survivors knew the killers. They were let out of jail early, and two women in Ponca City told me they had lived near them all their lives and not known.

I pick these events and make them stories because only then will people listen. If I carry a sign, I am ignored. So I do it in the work.

BC: Does Oklahoma influence the way you approach other locales? Florida and Canada are so different from each other and Oklahoma. Why other biosystems?

LH: Each biosystem is held in the stories. Ceremonial literature contains an entire ecosystem, what is now called a textbook for knowledge. American Indian knowledge systems have been ignored until recently. And for each book I had to read and study all of the literatures, the stories, and I interviewed people for *Power.* I interviewed the attorney of the man who originally killed a panther. It was not like in the book at all. He killed it late at night—drinking, poaching—then took it to a number of other people's houses to get a photo, then took it home and barbecued it. When the wildlife and police officials arrived, they found parts of other endangered animals. There was a four-year effort to charge him and put him in jail, but he was acquitted. I read the court transcripts in Florida. He was the chief of the Seminole, James Billie, and he now passes out info about the Endangered Species Act but keeps two declawed panthers for tourists to see.

In addition to all this, I love the land. I love the glades and the mangrove swamps. Just as I love the land in Oklahoma. This means I learn it.

BC: You changed the narrative quite a bit in *Power*.

LH: I can't control what my books do. I know there are writers who work with outlines, but for me the books seem dictated from something within even if they are first based on interest and research.

BC: You have mentioned being involved in Native Science Dialogues in the past. I am fascinated with Husk and his interest in tracking scientific discoveries that only reinforce traditional tribal beliefs. Michael Horse and the Hog Priest seem to begin to develop that idea. Can you talk about the connections?

LH: What has been most interesting to me about Native science, or I call it indigenous traditions, is that it does account for and hold scientific theory. The new Gaia theory credited to white scientists is old knowledge on this continent. We know everything has a purpose and deserves to be. We understand astronomy. How else could people have been so brilliant to make the sun dagger and other observation points? We know agriculture and had to teach European arrivals about planting. I always wonder what happened in Europe that made such a hole in the knowledge system. Study that time in history and you find people who watched torture for entertainment—people who had deforested and worn the land thin on their continent. After how many years of habitation. What happened that there was no one observant enough? That is the question.

As for the science dialogues, Native people gather to talk about such knowledge systems and the unique way of thinking that so differs from that of non-Indian people. I do, however, recognize that there have been shifts in this—that some non-Indians are thinking, yes, this world is alive; that some Native peoples are now in imitation or for economic reasons are breaking spiritual laws. There are traditions and laws that are beyond human. Just because it is drawn up on a piece of paper doesn't make something right, legal, ethical.

I consider my own work to be traditionally centered.

BC: In a *Frontiers* article from the 1980s you said you don't identify as a feminist because "what affects the women also affects the entire community."[1] Yet much of your work seems based in a feminine tradition. Some ecofeminist theory is grounded in concern for community. Would you say you see yourself as an ecofeminist?

LH: *Frontiers*: I forgot all about that interview. There was a lot of conflict in those days, and I'll tell you that for us, we were in despair, poverty, and with little recognition as people. We have had a very long history to re-

Barbara J. Cook

cover from. When feminists went to the reservation and took off their shirts for equal rights or invaded the Yaqui reservation looking for Don Juan, it just didn't go over very well. Our struggles were separate from theirs. And the right to not wear a shirt was hardly an issue at all when we were watching enforced sterilization of our women, all children born in one time frame given up for adoption, hunger, etc. This, truly, was a continuation of genocide. And when people wanted to lay claim to our spiritual identity without having the knowledge systems to back it, that was another theft.

However, much has changed in the many years intervening, and I am more of a feminist mind now. I especially think of it in terms of economics, work, and the ever-increasing number of violent crimes. Even the ones on television are primarily women. And when two women like Thelma and Louise fight back, the movies become threatening to the men! What is this? I saw it with Terry Tempest Williams, and afterward, to tell the truth, we were very noisy in the car. I had no idea that the movie would be so berated by the male critics. This says something to me.

BC: You have mentioned anthropologist Michael Harner's work in the past. He has established a network of classes on soul loss and shamanism. Although he approaches this respectfully, isn't it appropriation?

LH: You mention Michael Harner. One night he was traveling through and stopped at the Indian center where I was in Minnesota, and he asked us to come in the room a minute. Then he tried to drum everyone's spirit animals. All the people were too polite to even laugh. But as soon as there was a break, no one returned. I do think what he does is appropriation, yet some of his background may be grounded in scholarship. I no longer like to judge people because there are worse crimes than trying to drum spirit animals; for instance, people killing herds of animals, such as in the North with Hydro-Quebec. I'd rather the administrators of those types of projects be like Harner.

For instance, with Maria Sabina,[2] she lived in absolute poverty while she was being "sold" here in books, films, and textbooks. Other poets tried to imitate her. She tried not to become bitter as she aged, but she did say that everyone had lived off of her and there she was at home, nothing more than a dog to pee on.

BC: Your work is filled with images of glass, mirrors, and crystal. Do they signify something for you? Are they placed as signifiers? How do they function?

LH: I had no idea I wrote about glass, mirrors, and crystal. Maybe if you gave me an example. Well, I suppose in *Solar Storms* the broken mirror reflected a broken face. But that is only a superficial reading of the story. One of the things that happens with readers is that they focus on something of significance to their own reading and ask me about it and why I did it, said it, created it, and I just simply can't account for it. Like I said, I am a student of the book being written. When one of the characters in *Solar Storms* died, I was very unhappy with that because it wasn't, in my mind, the way it should have worked out. When a writer writes, if she is doing it well it is from magic, another place and world.

BC: I guess as literary critics we want to find special meaning in all of the metaphors.

You have talked about the stages of development a writer goes through; you have written in a variety of genres and on a variety of topics. Do you feel pushed to try something new each time?

LH: Pushed to try new things: no, I never do feel pushed. Mostly I just desire time to write. I have so much to write. That is the only push. Most of my time goes to business, etc., and very little to writing. I am always loving whatever it is I am working on. Right now I am on hold. Well, I wouldn't call it hold exactly. I write every moment I can. I am working on two novels, and one is very heavy, a Vietnam vet whose daughter comes to find him and ends up living on a fishing boat with his former girlfriend, another legal-ecological novel. But then, too, I am working on one about a girl who takes off with a circus and her life as a trick rider. What I would really like is for them to come out at the same time so everyone would be confused about what kind of writer I am!

BC: What else are you working on now?

LH: I have finished a book of poems and not yet sent them out. I don't know why. They are in final draft. It just doesn't seem like the right time yet. A writer has to trust those feelings. So there they are in my oven where I keep my work, since it would (I hope) be the last place to burn in a fire. Most writers I know use their freezers. Unfortunately, I don't have one. I have a 1937 refrigerator. If I want ice I have to buy it and bring it in and put it in a cooler in my tiny kitchen. The place I live is quite amazing and quaint and historic. However, the whole place is incredibly small.

Until you go outdoors! I can handle a miniature home because I live in a forest valley, a house I always wanted to buy, the house where Bush in *Solar Storms* lived. Luck. Fate. Whatever. One day I was walking my dog, and the realtor was putting a sign up and I got in his car, rode to his office, and bought it. Then I was shocked at myself. Buyer's remorse. But here I am with my beautiful mares.

Barbara J. Cook

Speaking of them, it is time to go hose them off so they can roll around in the ground and be cool and clay-covered.

Notes

1. Interview, "Native American Women: Our Voice, the Air," *Frontiers* 6, no. 3 (1982): 1–4.

2. Maria Sabina was a Mazatec healer and shaman, a native of Huaulta de Jimenez in Oaxaca, Mexico. She became renowned after a *Life* article (13 May 1975) discussed the participation of two men from New York in a *velada,* a nocturnal mushroom ceremony. The mushroom was the *psilocybe caerulescens var mazatecorum.* The article and ensuing publicity inspired Dr. Timothy Leary, among others, to try the mushroom, ushering in the "Psychedelic Revolution" of the 1960s. Sabina became famous, and her small village was besieged by people seeking her spiritual guidance and hoping to "trip" with her. Her home was later burned, and she was banished to the outskirts of town. Sabina died in 1985 at age ninety-one.

"HOW DO WE LEARN TO TRUST OURSELVES ENOUGH TO HEAR THE CHANTING OF EARTH?"
Hogan's Terrestrial Spirituality

KATHERINE R. CHANDLER

ENVIRONMENTALISM, NATIVE AMERICAN CULTURE, THEOLOGY, FEMINISM, social justice—Linda Hogan's writings range widely in issue as well as genre. Viewing these concerns as inseparable, Hogan consistently directs attention to the principle that weaves them together: spirituality. Significantly, this is the quality she considers most lacking in today's world. *Dwellings: A Spiritual History of the Living World* (1995) is her most developed discourse on the undividable relationship among the human, the natural, and the spiritual. Although this is a collection of discrete essays, the essays are associated by their "lessons learned from the land" (12). Hogan's preface to *Dwellings* explains that her work "connects the small world of humans with the larger universe, containing us in the same way that native ceremonies do, showing us both our place and a way of seeing" (12). Throughout the book Hogan demonstrates that it is possible to revive an "ecology of mind . . . that returns us to our own sacredness" (60), and this essay explores how Hogan demonstrates that reawakening process for readers. Hogan's aim is to decipher the language of a spiritual universe within the natural world; my aim is to examine how Hogan reaches into the natural to attain the spiritual.

Katherine R. Chandler

Hogan opens with a fundamental question: Why have many of us "forgotten the mystery of nature and spirit, while for tens of thousands of years such things have happened and been spoken [of] by our elders and our ancestors"? (17). Believing that humanity's diminished relationship with the natural world is a significant cause of the lack of peace many feel, she describes in "The Feathers," her first essay, mystifying incidents in her life associated with eagle feathers. Logically, we do not understand how an eagle feather kept in a box can be the means by which a lost valuable is located, but Hogan experiences such an occurrence and concludes that the power is a form of "sacred reason . . . linked to forces of nature" (19). Clearly, her Chickasaw heritage influences the directions in which Hogan turns, but she does not limit her search for answers to her own traditions. She investigates a wide range of twentieth-century sources and offers her observations with a wide audience in mind.

Explanations about why modern cultures have forgotten connections between nature and spirit are familiar, repeatedly articulated by contemporary philosophers, anthropologists, theologians, sociologists, and environmentalists, including Hogan. In "A Different Yield"—her essay meditating on listening, language, and variant means of communication—Hogan cites the work of psychologist C. A. Meier as evidence that the "whole of western society is approaching a physical and mental breaking point," adding that the "result is a spiritual fragmentation that has accompanied our ecological destruction" (52). Working toward reestablishing healthy connections with the natural world, Hogan does not flinch when claiming those connections are sacred. The question, difficult even for her to answer, is, How *do* we access a spiritual realm?

Helpfully, in *Dwellings* Hogan's ponderings do not remain at the level of lament. Her major focus is on resolutions for the troubling results. As she investigates the trying territory of personal, familial, and tribal losses, she relies on language to help her sort it through. Peggy Maddux Ackerberg concludes that Hogan turns to writing about these issues because of "the nourishing and ordering effects of words and language" (11). With the essays in *Dwellings* serving as moments set apart, as places in which to contemplate, as words that imagine, Hogan commences revising her own attitudes and practices. She considers solutions and portrays processes. Reflecting on topics as diverse as the Anasazi, DNA, and NASA—as well as those generated by what she encounters in nature, including snakes, caves, and porcupines—Hogan claims we are "the wounders" of ourselves, our culture, and the natural world. Rather than merely pointing a finger, though, Hogan asserts that we are also "the healers" (151). Her deep concern for nature and her view of wilderness as "sanctuary" provide Hogan with starting ground for embracing a philosophy of life that includes a spiritual dimension. The ways in which Hogan initiates her developmental process—listening to and learning from the earth—are not, however, techniques commonly taught in our schools or homes. Fortunately, the essays in *Dwellings* reveal how Hogan perfects her ability to learn about the spirit by listening to the land.

Drawing closer to nature is the initial way Hogan reaches for the sacred, but she also turns to two other sources for spiritual enlightenment: stories and ceremonies. Of course, nature, stories, and ceremonies intersect and overlap in spiritual settings in many ways, but I separate them for discussion. Also, this three-part schema I suggest is not found in Hogan's book. Since each essay can stand on its own—most having appeared individually in journals, magazines, or anthologies—they are not presented in *Dwellings* as a cohesive assemblage. Instead, they are linked by reemerging themes and a consistent worldview. Although *Dwellings* does not provide a developed philosophical system, it presents Hogan's most direct statements of her values and beliefs. I have gathered ideas from throughout the compilation and totalized a system of thought that is implicit in *Dwellings* but not straightforwardly formulated by Hogan.

Hogan is not alone among those who perceive the value of turning to nature, stories, and ceremonies as avenues to comprehend the spiritual. Among others, a range of contemporary environmental writers—including Gary Snyder, Marilou Awiakta, Barry Lopez, and Terry Tempest Williams—examine other cultures to derive patterns of imparting spiritual knowledge and principles of interaction with the natural world. Hogan, however, accentuates the compelling effect created by merging stories with ceremonies. We can see through her essays that for her, that merger simultaneously evokes the integration of nature and spirit. Hogan's ultimate destination is a terrestrial, not a celestial, spirituality. Her search for a life force is centered on earth. By employing language sensitive to the land and realigning story with ceremony (37), Hogan further develops an ecology of mind she considers vital to survival. Indeed, each essay is a ceremony of its own, marking the significance of seemingly mundane events. Thus *Dwellings* distinguishes itself from her other writings as Hogan's most deliberate invitation to readers to step outside routines, ponder ramifications, and reconsider what motivates our daily dealings with each other and with the world.

Nature

Hogan first looks to nature for signs of the spiritual, believing the words of an Indian elder that natural laws are evidence of "ways above ours" (45). In keeping with the terrestrial character of her spirituality, birds, bats, and blue racers populate the pages of *Dwellings*. Since technological advances, mechanized lifestyles, and postmodern sophistications distance us from the natural world, Hogan's search is for a means to lessen and eventually eliminate that disconnection.

Katherine R. Chandler

The process of connecting with nature to experience the spiritual is difficult. Hogan's vision is shared by John Daniel who observes that "nature's being is only partly what it shows. Its greater part, and greater beauty is always past what human eyes can understand" (45). The terrestrial call is subtle; thus Hogan's effort is to discover ways to heed it. As the protagonist of her novel *Solar Storms* views it, those seeking but not finding a spiritual dimension in their lives might wonder if they are unable to hear the call because they have the "inarticulate souls" ascribed to many in contemporary society (181). Hogan admits to not always being adept at hearing the call, in part because of unmindfulness, in part as a result of lack of knowledge. She begins with increasing efforts to be heedful. Contrary to what readers might expect, however, the sacred ways Hogan speaks of are not uncomfortably otherworldly or distantly mystical. To Hogan, respect is paramount for "our spiritual and psychological well-being" (45), and genuine respect for all forms of life is an attitude not everyone in our society practices but one with which all are familiar. Volunteering at the Birds of Prey Rehabilitation Foundation, described in her essays "Dwellings" and "Waking Up the Rake," is one way Hogan experiences how even close association with animals assists in cultivating such approaches to living. Birds teach her about the value of silence and watching and listening, of effort and repetition and cycles, of intuition and awe and order (150–151).

Not all of these attitudes, skills, concepts, and practices are found in the language of rationality with which our culture tends to be more comfortable, but they are understandable, and this is how Hogan speaks of approaching the spirit. Echoing Thoreau, Hogan views our means of communication as "a language of commerce and trade, of laws that can be bent . . . a language that is limited, emotionally and spiritually" (45–46), a barrier to the "terrestrial call" she perceives is "the voice of God, or of gods, the creative power that lives on earth, inside earth" (85). In "Walking" she laments not being able to read the sunflower's "golden language" (156–157), and in "The Bats" she wonders how we can hear the nocturnal mammals' "world alive in its whispering songs," how we can "get there from here . . . to the center of the world, to the place where the universe carries down the song of night to our human lives" (26, 28). Hogan is convinced that if we adapt observational techniques long utilized by earlier cultures, we will be able to listen and feel our way toward deeper understanding of the spirit evident in nature.

Developing a greater sensitivity to our complex natural world is another way Hogan reaches toward a deeper understanding of the ineffable. Indeed, it is her life work. Hogan is not a dilettante or a vague hypothesizer; she draws from experience. Although *Dwellings* can be seen as Hogan commencing a philosophy, her fiction and poetry are enactments of those principles in image and story. Omishto, the young narrator in *Power,* for instance, concludes her tale by achieving a consciousness that echoes Hogan's thinking: "I know this; this earth, the swamp, it's the same thing as grace, full of the intelligent souls of cat, deer, and wind. I am stronger in nature. There is something alive here and generous" (231). In Hogan's poetry as well, whether she is praising a daughter or lamenting harsh words, nature pervades her images. Hogan's key principles also manifest themselves throughout her memoir *The Woman Who Watches Over the World*, in which relying on and giving back to the earth are as central as valuing memory and wisdom. "What can I say without touching the earth with my hands?" (132), she states, employing a Pablo Neruda line to summarize the practices that are evidence of her principles. If respect for and knowledge of the earth are prerequisites for living, learning, and speaking by the spirit, Hogan's oeuvre manifests that her commitment is complete, with the essays in *Dwellings* providing the most straightforward articulation of that commitment.

Story

In addition to exploring these principles through her relationship with nature, Hogan reaches for the terrestrial spirit in stories she has heard. As the anecdotes in her essays demonstrate, narratives help listeners and readers experience—thus better understand—sacred responses to and from the natural world. In the essay "Creations" she indicates that ideological tales told by a technological culture have contributed to the unhealthiness of both land and people; she also claims that "[w]e need new stories . . . a new narrative that would imagine another way, to learn the infinite mystery and movement at work in the world" (94). Edward O. Wilson envisions a similar cultural landscape, one that illuminates what Hogan implies; he sees our world "drowning in information, while starving for wisdom" (269). Hogan asserts that stories can provide wisdom, and although she does not quote Wilson, his sense that "[p]eople need a sacred narrative" lends credence to Hogan's view, especially as a scientist who recognizes that individuals "must have a sense of larger purpose" (264). Hogan's quest manifests ways we can reach for larger purposes. Her quest also motivates her search for new tales and myths, a search that leads her to old stories, to *her* old stories.

For Hogan, an invaluable resource for sacred stories comes from rituals she participates in from her tribal heritage. They provide her with answers to the difficulties with which she struggles. She writes about these tales in "All My Relations," "A Different Yield," "Creations," and "The Snake People," discussing how traditional stories have provided her with ways to access what she senses as spiritual. Hogan writes about how narratives taught her the danger of severance from and the benefits of reverence for the natural world. They also prompt her to investigate other cultures' stories in an effort to better see the world. Creation, kinship, and renewal myths, for instance, remind her of central life principles. "In nearly all creation accounts," Hogan relates, "life was called into being through language, thought, dreaming, or singing, acts of interior consciousness" (81). Quoting and paraphrasing from the *Popul Vuh*, Hogan recounts the Quiche Maya creation story, specifically the narrative about the wooden people. As the story goes, the wooden people became hollow and lacked compassion for other forms of life, thereby creating "their own dead future out of human arrogance and greed" (80–82). Whether Hogan accepts the *Popul Vuh* as true is not at issue; she does not suggest that readers believe in its sacredness, just as she does not insist that they ascribe sacred status to Native American stories such as those of Kachina or Coyote.

What Hogan does advocate is gleaning the value of sound principles and age-tested wisdom from earlier eras and other cultures. We can turn to Claude Levi-Strauss for conceptual terminology here—mythical tales by which people seek a comprehensive perspective of the world and ethical ideas about how to live "totalize" rather than compartmentalize a view of the universe. Myths move listeners to think of concerns and questions larger than themselves. Whereas contemporary readers comprehend narrative's unique ability to expand the scope of listeners' perspectives by engaging them sensorily as well as emotionally and intellectually, Hogan invites readers to consider ways in which stories can also instruct spirits. Contemporary culture tends, with our twenty-first-century skepticism, to categorize myths with a dismissal similar to fairy tales, but in "A Different Yield" Hogan directs readers to a key quality: myths' unique ability to allow us to "hear the world new again" (51).

Finding myths "a high form of truth," Hogan considers them "the deepest, innermost cultural stories of our human journeys toward spiritual and psychological growth" (51). Seeing that "we have been split from what we could nurture" and "what would fill us" by current cultural attitudes and habits, Hogan adapts techniques from aboriginal ways and wisdom to suggest healthier philosophies and practices (82). From the Bushman, she better comprehends the damage done by "far-hearted," self-concerned thinking (45); from the Sufi, the value of working hard and living one's beliefs (149); from the Quiche Maya, the fostering of "care-taking" attitudes (82). As Hogan visits the Yucatan looking for historical and cultural connections between the Chickasaw and the Maya, she recognizes that whether one calls the creative force God or something without religious connotation, that power is still one anyone can invoke. "Sometimes beliefs are inventions of the mind," she writes. "Sometimes they are inventions of the land. But how we interpret and live out our lives has to do with the religious foundations and the spiritual history we have learned" (85). Even if some twenty-first-century cultures lack a widely accepted sacred language or framework, Hogan believes those without religion cannot afford to deny the possibility of the existence of the spirit. With *Dwellings*, Hogan provides readers with a means for recognizing and reconciling nature and spirit.

Hogan's Terrestrial Spirituality

In her search for powerful stories, Hogan does not ignore wisdom from Western traditions or contemporary expertise. *Dwellings* is filled with references to artists, writers, priests, psychologists, scientists, a Nobel Prize–winning peacemaker, and a Nobel Prize–winning biologist. Significantly, Hogan quotes the specialists' anecdotes rather than their scientific studies. When she writes about her experiences with animals in "A Different Yield," "Deify the Wolf," and "Waking Up the Rake," Hogan records tales told by those who have devoted their lives to working with beasts or birds. When pondering the perplexing power of creating and organizing the universe, she quotes, among others, renowned anthropologist and Darwinian expert Loren Eiseley, whose metaphorical writings manifest that he, too, recognizes the power of stories. Hogan's retelling of their stories illustrates the truth of William Kittredge's formulation: "It's important to recognize that the natural world isn't valuable to us until we inhabit it emotionally. . . . We need stories about intimacy and connection. And we need to know details, specific things. Storytelling can give us that" (28).

Hogan also incorporates stories of her own in *Dwellings*; and because they are derived from her experiences with the natural world, they are especially vivid. Through the brief anecdote that comprises "Porcupine," readers face along with her the decision she must make when she finds dead the life-battered porcupine seen for years along the dirt road: pause to honor, or hasten away because of "busyness" (145). Hogan offers readers the voice of someone deliberating over a choice; what, she asks, carries significance in our lives? This idea has been echoed by Robert Coles who states that "[n]ovels and stories are renderings of life. . . . They can offer us kinsmen, kinswomen, comrades, advisers—offer us other eyes through which we might see, other ears with which we might make soundings" (159–160). In most cases the anecdotes record occasions when nature provides her with spiritual insight, as in the essay "Dwellings" where she reflects on the abodes of humans, animals, birds, even spirits. She observes bees at work building clay hillocks from dirt and spittle and comes to understand that they are flying according to maps invisible to us, maps maintained by a "circling story" repeated among the bees (118). Twenty-first-century America, however, has lost its "circling story." Hogan sets out to remedy that loss, retelling ancient tales and creating new ones, accomplishing what philosopher Max Oelschlaeger observes—that such stories help preserve us. "Culture can be described in various ways," Oelschlaeger says, "but clearly it is a web of talk, a continuous conversation about how to live" (68). Such is the web of talk Hogan feels is most significant and currently most bankrupt.

Stories are instrumental in keeping what is significant with us. Hogan recognizes this truism, a belief with which Terry Tempest Williams concurs: "Story bypasses rhetoric and pierces the heart. Story offers a wash of images and emotion that returns us to our highest and deepest selves, where we remember what it means to be human, living in place with our neighbors" (3). If we extend "neighbors" to include beavers, aspens, and mountain streams, we can better understand how a writer such as Hogan offers us perspectives that take us beyond the boundaries of human sight, sounds, and directions. Stepping outside our human realm is also a step outside a focus solely on ourselves. Of course, we share with writer and self-acclaimed observer David Brendan Hopes an interior focus—"With nature . . . I do not seek intimacy, but understanding, and not of it, but of me" (ix). Self-knowledge is important, but Hogan admonishes us to broaden beyond a focus on self. When Hogan tells a story she extends outward the sphere of learning in which she circles. Hogan folds into stories her experiences with nature, and their power emerges from a deepening understanding of not only ourselves and others but of the inexpressible spirit of a living world.

Hogan's emphasis is on the value of making reflective narratives a part of one's life—an emphasis she demonstrates more than asserts. As she points out in "The Kill Hole," in which she retells the story of Ishi, the one remaining Yana Indian found in California in 1911, stories tell us "what kind of people we are" and illuminate "the world of civilization and its flaws" (111). In this essay alone, Hogan retells many stories—Jane Goodall on humor in gorillas, de Kooning on art painted by elephants, and sign language experts on chimpanzees' communication skills, as well as stories from the Anasazi, Mimbres, Yanas, Iroquois, and Mandan about mending the direction life takes through the "hole"; rather than a focus on the spirit escaping at death, she highlights the spirit emerging with life. Throughout the stories embedded in her essays, Hogan demonstrates that telling and retelling are crucial if we are to remember who we are and learn how we are to live—both also key purposes for participating in ceremonies.

Ceremony

Along with nature and narrative, Hogan views ceremony as essential for accessing what I have termed terrestrial spirituality. Ceremonies provide her with the most specific means to retrieve such a spirituality. Hogan's interest is in perspectives and purposes grander than self; and sacred or special observances provide the kind of physical, emotional, and mental setting that cultivates larger concerns. A change in attitude and activity makes accessing the spirit more likely; and ceremonies allow one to quiet, to focus, and to nurture a more comprehensive perspective. From watching and listening to her Chickasaw elders, Hogan comes to realize why such occasions invite the spirit to be present. "There is a still place, a gap between worlds, spoken by the tribal knowings of thousands of years," Hogan explains in "The Feathers," and "when we are silent enough, still enough, we take a step into such mystery, the place of spirit" (20). Hogan's means, however, are not limited by a specific set of beliefs; the ceremonial occasion need not be religious for a "gap between worlds" to show itself if one maintains a ceremonial attitude.

Since few events in our contemporary culture encourage us to be still or silent, making the effort to formally observe time in a calm, removed setting constitutes a kind of ritual. Hogan is convinced that quiet is needed if one is to step into the mystery. What Hogan senses and attempts to counter, Sandra Ingerman confirms in her study of alternative methods of healing, *Medicine for the Earth*: "Creating personal ceremonies and ritual is not part of our culture, and we are not taught about their power or how and why they are created. Ceremony and ritual remain mysterious to us, and things we don't understand we tend to fear" (224). But, as Ingerman points out, "[c]eremonies and ritual are used to honor, celebrate, heal, and transmute" (224); and through direct experience Hogan comes to understand their astonishing effectiveness. Even public ceremonies provide space for reflecting; one can feel the power of collective focus of attention. Intensity conveyed by speakers and experienced by listeners marks these events as different. The words spoken during ceremonies—at times stories, at times chants, at times songs—guide participants to reflect on matters of significance, and that ritualized language quiets both external and internal chatter. Hogan emphasizes that the sincerity with which these special occasions are approached and conducted further ensures that significance lingers.

As Hogan describes her participation in various ceremonies, two purposes come clear: renewing one's own health while simultaneously restoring healthier connections with others. Whether for one person or for a group, the ceremonies Hogan practices bring readers into a larger circle. Hogan characterizes those participating in the sweat lodge ceremony described in "All My Relations" as sitting together in aloneness but remembering their part in an "immense community" (40). "In a sweat lodge ceremony, the entire world is brought inside the enclosure. The soft odor of smoking cedar accompanies this arrival. It is all called in" (39). Hot lava stones represent the heated core of the earth, water comes from the nearby creek, willow branches move overhead, and the sound of thunderclaps and bird songs penetrates the structure. This is a "place of immense community and of humbled solitude" (40). The ceremony's purposes include restoring, renewing, and restructuring the human mind by remembering "that all things are connected" (40).

Hogan is writing against the limited individualist approach Kathleen Norris describes as pervasive among modern culture's popular interpretations of spirituality:

> Modern believers tend to trust in therapy more than in mystery, a fact that tends to manifest itself in worship that employs the bland speech of pop

Katherine R. Chandler

> psychology and self-help rather than language resonant with poetic meaning—for example, a call to worship that begins: "Use this hour, Lord, to get our perspectives straight again." Rather than express awe . . . we focus totally on ourselves. (71)

A focus totally on ourselves is not Hogan's vision. In relating the story of the sweat lodge ceremony, Hogan emphasizes that the ceremony's purpose is to remind participants that "all things are connected" (40). That is the intention of bringing into the enclosure symbolic representations of the "entire world"—"to put a person back together by restructuring the human mind . . . by a kind of inner map, a geography of the human spirit and the rest of the world" (40). Humility, balance, and reverence are the healing principles, and Hogan clarifies that it is only after the formal occasion, when a person changes his or her "vision of earth" and enters into "compassionate relationship to and with our world," that the real healing occurs (40–41).

Remembering to see the larger whole is a primary purpose Hogan attributes to many ceremonies, but that conceptual vision is often instigated by sensory signals. Hogan indicates in *Dwellings* that she enters into ceremonial occasions with both her mind and her body alert. Relying on the assurance of family traditions, Hogan mentally and physically prepares before participating in any traditional ceremony. Indeed, preparation is indispensable. She twists tobacco prayer ties or retrieves sensory memories from childhood, such as breezes whispering through a cornfield. In our modern fast-paced society, the tendency is to omit preparatory stages, but Hogan convincingly demonstrates that using the body to help prepare the mind is a necessary step to access the spirit. As Hogan lowers her body into the healing water of an underground spring, the physical sensations she records in "The Caves" remind her of vulnerability and mortality. The smell of iron in the water is a preparatory greeting at the cave entrance, whereas the aromas of frying potatoes and baking bread accompany her preparation for another ceremony. Smells assist her by instantaneously returning her to prior ceremonial occasions. The importance of smells is borne out by David Rains Wallace who affirms that "[s]mells lie deeper than our remembering, thinking neocortex. . . . Yet smells are related to thought in profound ways" (1–2). For Hogan, the fragrance of smoking cedar in a lodge or musty air in a cave transports her to earlier times when she experienced other ways of knowing. Hogan demonstrates throughout *Dwellings* how our bodies sense that kind of knowing, hearkening to terrestrial spiritual energies that most of us conceptually never knew, now ignore, or have forgotten.

The notion of ceremonies to which Hogan refers in *Dwellings* includes the primal memory in our bodies' cells that assists us in remembering "the source of our living . . . the sacredness of all life" (83). Even if our minds are focused elsewhere, our bodies know the world through unconscious habits. There is a material nature to spirit, Hogan believes, and in ceremonies our senses are as crucial as our concentration. Much as we remember by smell, we remember moments of significance through other physical sensations. The contour of the rounded stone she uses while grinding corn kernels in an ancient metate, described in "A Different Yield," manifests to her how our senses respond to languages of natural elements even if we do not intellectually accept that such languages exist (60–62). This idea is explored by David Abram in his study of perception and the sensual foundations of language. Abram reports that shamans first "know" through their senses because "the sensuous world itself remains the dwelling place of the gods" for indigenous cultures: "It is not by sending his awareness out beyond the natural world that the shaman makes contact with the purveyors of life and health, nor by journeying into his personal psyche; rather, it is by propelling his awareness laterally, outward into the depths of a landscape at once both sensuous and psychological" (10). Hogan is cognizant of and respects such capabilities. One Native healer provides her with a personal ceremony that involves walking on a moonlit night where the songs of insects and a nighthawk accompany her (17–18). Through the vehicle of the ritual, she feels her physical senses facilitating her mind in a process of realigning body with spirit.

Hogan's ceremonies, both those in which she participates and those she creates through her written reflections, are her primary means of stepping outside daily attitudes to discover how she wants to live when she reemerges. Since her essays not only depict but enact the process, they themselves prove life-changing. "Waking Up the Rake" describes Hogan cleaning cages for the Birds of Prey Rehabilitation Foundation and demonstrates how even daily activities, accompanied by appropriate attitudes, can be turned into rituals from which we learn something spiritual—if, of course, we seek those rituals. Indeed, reading *Dwellings* can become a ceremonial act in itself, for Hogan's essays are at moments poetic enough to suggest a form of ritualistic chanting.

> Raking.
> It is a labor round and complete, smooth and new as an egg, and the rounding seasons of the world revolving in time and space. (153)

Even as commonplace a task as raking can grow to be something more than mundane.

> There is an art to raking, a very fine art, one with rhythm in it, and life. (153)

Repetitive tasks, she discovers, are indicative of natural cycles. For Hogan, raking becomes something to prize.

Katherine R. Chandler

> In this place, there is a constant coming to terms with both the sacred place life occupies, and with death. (151)

To understand a language that speaks in terms of the spirit, we take note of what we ordinarily avoid or pass by.

> Work is the country of hands, and they want to live there in the dailiness of it, the repetition that is time's language of prayer, a common tongue. Everything is there, in that language, in the humblest of labor. (154)

To understand an intuitive language, we need humility as well as respect.

> There are human lessons to be learned here, in the work. . . . And it is true, in whatever we do, the brushing of hair, the cleaning of cages, we begin to see the larger order of things. (151)

Repetition of mundane tasks also reminds us of the interconnectedness of life. But to achieve this—and this is key—Hogan prepares:

> There is a silence needed here before a person enters the bordered world the birds inhabit so we stop and compose ourselves before entering their doors, and we listen to the musical calls of the eagles, the sound of wings in air, the way their feet with sharp black claws, many larger than our own hands, grab hold of a perch. Then we know we are ready to enter. (150)

"Then we know we are ready to enter." Hogan's essays provide rituals and take readers inside quiet spiritual interludes through which we can learn to "trust ourselves enough to hear the chanting of the earth" (28).

With *Dwellings*, Hogan prepares readers to enter sacred circles. She recognizes a hunger among many not of Native American descent to learn and feel and remember in such ways. She witnesses tourists observing corn dances at Zia Pueblo pick up pieces of old, broken clay pots. She explains in "Dwellings" that Natives know to leave the potsherds to disintegrate to earth once again after the ceremonial dance, but "younger nations . . . have little of their own to grow on" and find in the clay pieces "a lifeline to an unknown land" (123). The tourists also long for something Hogan does not discuss in this instance. For some, the tactile connection with their piece of clay will recapture for them the sensory memory; if only for a moment, touching that bit of shaped, fired earth evokes the spirit of the witnessed ceremony. Other contemporary nature writers sense this desire, and evident in current environmental literature is the "peace" Ann Zwinger finds in the "singing air," the manzanita medicine songs Gary Snyder conjures, and the "solace of open spaces" Gretel Ehrlich seeks (Zwinger 214; Snyder, *Turtle Island* 27; Ehrlich 14). "Space has a spiritual equivalent," Ehrlich states, "and can heal what is divided and burdensome in us" (14). For those hungry for the spiritual, being carefully aware when engaged with the physical, natural world provides powerful ceremonial-type experiences. By refocusing attention, ceremonies offer a means to return health to ourselves, the land, our nation, our world.

Ecology of Mind and Land Language

Throughout *Dwellings* Hogan clarifies that she is searching for the "ecology of mind" that allows the merging of rationality, intuition, and faith (60). All are needed to access a terrestrial spirituality. She also perceives they are crucial not only for our survival but for the survival of healthy eco- and social systems. In a usage differing from Gary Snyder's in *The Practice of the Wild*, Hogan claims we need to develop this ecology of mind by finding what will help us "step over boundaries of what we think" (38).[1] In a twist on contemporary opinion, Hogan claims that an ecology of mind is "a way of thought older than measured time, less primitive than the rational present" (19).

Charging that "[o]thers have tried for centuries to understand the world by science and intellect but have not yet done so, not yet understood animals, finite earth, or even their own minds and behavior" (19), Hogan employs terms uncomfortable to some who seek answers solely through science and rational means. She verbalizes what some scientists have finally begun to admit: "The more they seek to learn the world, the closer they come to the spiritual, the magical origins of creation" (19). Biologists David Suzuki and Peter Knudtson provide persuasive supporting evidence of Hogan's notion, having proposed a "sacred ecology" based on their merging of knowledge from respected scientists with wisdom from aboriginal cultures. Suzuki and Knudtson, among others with scientific backgrounds, concede that "knowledge gained through science is unique and profound, yet also extremely limited. Not only does the Newtonian worldview fail to comprehend the complexity of life on earth, we have barely begun to understand its dimensions" (xliii). Hogan's "ecology of mind" recognizes the necessity of involving ourselves in the natural world with an attitude of participatory reverence rather than viewing it with distanced objectivity. Science is valuable, but academic inquiry cannot be our only source for comprehending ecological principles.

Hogan aligns an ecology of mind with what is central to her concept: "a tongue that speaks with reverence for life" (60), a language I term *land language*. This is not a language the land speaks, like the sounds of mountain water for which Wallace Stegner is known, "the small talk of side channels, the whisper of blown and scattered spray" (41–43). Listening to the land is an important component of deep ecological understanding, but Hogan advocates a language extending beyond pleasures we find in the sounds of nature. A land language demonstrates genuine respect for the land, assumes our interconnectedness with organizing ecosystems, acknowledges our role in relation to other life-forms.

Katherine R. Chandler

In terms of language, Hogan summarizes what she has learned from consciously engaging with nature, from stories told by elders, and from participating in ceremonies: "[T]here are communications that take place on a level that goes deeper than our somewhat limited human spoken languages" (57). We are knowledgeable about the ways humans, animals, and plants communicate through gesture, look, and scent but are unclear about other ways life-forms convey difficult-to-articulate feelings. Hogan provides examples in a number of essays, discussing in "A Different Yield" specific instances of documented communications between humans and animals. She also describes Nobel Prize–winning biologist Barbara McClintock's scientific methodology, which included listening to the corn plants she studied. Love and respect are keys for understanding this language, a means of communicating that reaches beyond sign systems: "It is not only the vocabulary of science we desire. We want a language of that different yield. A yield rich as the harvests of earth, a yield that returns us to our own sacredness, to a self-love and respect that will carry out to others" (60). A land language is a language of bearing and being.

Hogan encourages a language most frequently accessed in more intimate, reflective settings, yet she believes we need to extend it outward to embrace the whole of life. If, as Hogan claims, ceremonies include "not just our own prayers and stories . . . but also the unspoken records of history, the mythic past, and all the other lives connected to ours, our families, nations, and all other creatures" (37), the stories in *Dwellings* provide keys to hearing the chanting and relearning the vocabulary of the land. For Hogan, stories are foundational bricks in the sense described by Kittredge when he writes, "If you want to build a brick house, you build it brick by brick by brick by brick. And our storytellers are laying in bricks. Eventually I think we'll have a new house, but it's going to take a while" (28). The laying in continues, for more recently she has written that "[t]he cure for soul loss is in the mist of morning, the grass that grew a little through the night, the first warmth of sunlight, the waking human world infused with intelligence and spirit" ("The Great Without" 24). Or, to shift metaphors, storytelling for Hogan is using language like raking. "The word *rake* means to gather or heap up, to smooth the broken ground," Hogan reminds readers. "That's what this work is, all of it, the smoothing over of broken ground, the healing of the severed trust we humans hold with earth" (*Dwellings* 153). Land language is a language to be lived.

In most theologies, words are meaningless if not accompanied by works; similarly, Hogan reminds us that we draw closer to perceiving the subtle language spoken to the spirit when we change our "vision of earth" and enter into "compassionate relationship to and with our world" (40–41). Indeed, relationship is a land language's central tenet. Nature writers such as Hogan are misread if interacting with "nature" is understood solely in terms of preservation or management—reintroducing wolves to Yellowstone, for instance. Our inherent human qualities as well as our condition are inseparably entwined with elements of the natural world, and Hogan sees that "deep-moving . . . currents . . . pass between us and the rest of nature" (57). A land language is therefore a language we sense and feel and on which we act.

Hogan does not fully describe how a language of this nature would operate, but John Hay illustrates the process Hogan implies. Hay writes of encountering ravens that "tease me, in my rare meetings with them, toward recognition of a speech we have hardly begun to translate" (44). Hay's subsequent description re-creates methods and attitudes that Hogan promotes.

> One [raven] flew quite close to me one day as I was standing next to a spruce tree on the Maine coast. It swished past me on stiff and silky feathers, carrying a mouse in its bill. I sense enchantment in its character. The field guides fail to mention that. Perhaps we are afraid to stray too far beyond accepted nomenclature and the scientifically proven. We may sense too much of our suppressed anarchy to trust in merely intuitive equations, with their essences and vague parallels, but with the will to be haunted, I am leaving an open space for ravens. (44–45)

Hay's anecdote illustrates awe and humility, willingness to learn, paying attention, listening—attitudes, observations, and behaviors Hogan's *Dwellings* advocates. But Hogan also indicates the need to step outside of typical contemporary routines. We need to "make our own songs to contain these things, make ceremonies and poems," Hogan states, "searching for a new way to speak, to say we want a new way to live in the world, to say that wilderness and water, blue herons and orange newts are invaluable . . . in themselves" (46). Along with heightened sensitivity to nature, stories, and ceremonies, Hogan advocates employing language in ways antithetical to Wall Street and Independence Avenue.

According to Hogan, if we are to live in a living system employing living wisdom—an ecology of mind—our framework must include all interactions of all beings in all of their environment. In addition, our approach must be one of caring. In his book advocating an ecumenical approach to environmental issues, Oelschlaeger asserts an idea supportive of Hogan's view: "[A] new metaphor—caring for creation—can engender a psychologically satisfying (emotionally evocative, powerful), religiously distinctive, and scientifically plausible ethic for our time" (37–38). The metaphor is appealing; the mission, daunting. Increasing numbers desiring healthier ways of living, though, are considering the sacred power to which Hogan refers. One of that number, educator and essayist Scott Russell Sanders, also writes in terms of caring—evidence that Hogan's vision is not inaccessible.

> In America lately, we have been carrying on two parallel conversations: one about respecting human diversity, the other about preserving natural diversity. . . . Our effort to honor human differences cannot succeed apart from our effort to honor the buzzing, blooming, bewildering variety of life on earth. . . . If we care only for human needs, we betray the land; if we care only for the earth and its wild offspring, we betray our own kind. (271)

Hogan contends similarly that a different frame of mind needs to be adopted for life survival past the twenty-first century. Caring, Hogan demonstrates, is central to achieving such goals and to understanding the world of which we are a part. "What we really are searching for is a language that heals this relationship," Hogan states, "one that takes the side of the amazing and fragile life on our life-giving earth" (59). Humility drives this statement, an acknowledgment that there is, or could be, something quite the opposite of more than a century of accepted philosophies—something greater than human beings.

The essays in *Dwellings* demonstrate that if we focus our attention outward, become more intuitively perceptive, attend to our senses, then listen in ways not necessarily auditory, we *will* understand more about the natural world and its spirit. To diminish our estrangement from that greater creative power, we need caring and humility along with respect. To sit, to listen, to seek from those who are wise and from those—even the earth—to whom we have not been listening is Hogan's pattern for understanding a larger order.

Additionally, Hogan reaches for a language that "takes hold of the mystery of what's around us and offers it back to us, full of awe and wonder. It is a language of creation, of divine fire, a language that goes beyond strict borders of scientific inquiry and right into the heart of the mystery itself" (59). Native healers have traditionally been called "interpreters," Hogan mentions, "because they are the ones who are able to hear the world and pass its wisdom along" (50). Linda Hogan can be seen as an interpreter—she has listened to and lived the language of the land, written it, and passed along its wisdom and its terrestrial spirit.

Note

1. Gary Snyder employs "ecologies of mind" in a more comprehensive sense. When speaking of wild systems, he reminds us of the darker side of natural processes, what can be seen as "irrational, moldy, cruel, parasitic." As he states, "Life in the wild is not just eating berries in the sunlight." Snyder uses this phrase to indicate all phases and characteristics of natural systems (*Practice* 110–111).

Works Cited

Abram, David. *The Spell of the Sensuous: Perception and Language in a More-Than-Human World*. New York: Random House, 1997.

Ackerberg, Peggy Maddux. "Breaking Boundaries: Writing Past Gender, Genre, and Genocide in Linda Hogan." *Studies in American Indian Literatures Series 2,* vol. 6, no. 3 (1994): 7–14.
Brice, Jennifer. "Earth as Mother, Earth as Other in Novels by Silko and Hogan." *Critique* 39, no. 2 (1998): 127–138.
Coles, Robert. *The Call of Stories.* Boston: Houghton Mifflin, 1989.
Daniel, John. *The Trail Home.* New York: Pantheon, 1992.
Ehrlich, Gretel. *The Solace of Open Spaces.* New York: Penguin, 1985.
Hay, John. *The Immortal Wilderness.* New York: W. W. Norton, 1987.
Hogan, Linda. *Dwellings: A Spiritual History of the Living World.* New York: W. W. Norton, 1995.
———. "The Great Without: Humanity's Dislocation from Nature." *Parabola* 24 (1999): 21–25.
———. *Power.* New York: W. W. Norton, 1998.
———. *Solar Storms.* New York: Scribner, 1995.
———. *The Woman Who Watches Over the World: A Native Memoir.* New York: W. W. Norton, 2001.
Hopes, David Brendan. *A Sense of the Morning.* Minneapolis: Milkweed Editions, 1999.
Ingerman, Sandra. *Medicine for the Earth.* New York: Random House, 2000.
Kittredge, William. "Salvation Through Storytelling." *Orion Afield* (Autumn 2001): 26–28.
Norris, Kathleen. *Amazing Grace: A Vocabulary of Faith.* New York: Riverhead, 1998.
Oelschlaeger, Max. *Caring for Creation: An Ecumenical Approach to the Environmental Crisis.* New Haven: Yale University Press, 1994.
Sanders, Scott Russell. "Voyageurs." In *The Nature of Nature: New Essays from America's Finest Writers on Nature.* Ed. William H. Shore. New York: Harcourt Brace, 1994.
Snyder, Gary. *The Practice of the Wild.* New York: Farrar, Straus and Giroux, 1990.
———. *Turtle Island.* New York: New Directions, 1974.
Stegner, Wallace. *The Sound of Mountain Water.* Garden City, N.Y.: Doubleday, 1969.
Suzuki, David, and Peter Knudtson. *Wisdom of the Elders: Sacred Native Stories of Nature.* New York: Bantam, 1992.
Wallace, David Rains. *Bulow Hammock: Mind in a Forest.* San Francisco: Sierra Club Books, 1988.
Williams, Terry Tempest. *Red: Passion and Patience in the Desert.* New York: Random House, 2001.
Wilson, Edward O. *Consilience: The Unity of Knowledge.* New York: Alfred A. Knopf, 1998.
Zwinger, Ann. *Wind in the Rock.* Tucson: University of Arizona Press, 1978.

HOGAN'S HISTORICAL NARRATIVES
Bringing to Visibility the Interrelationship of Humanity and the Natural World

BARBARA J. COOK

> For my people, the problem has always been this: that the only possibility of survival has been resistance.
> —Linda Hogan, *Solar Storms*

WITH THE 1969 PUBLICATION OF THE PULITZER PRIZE–WINNING NOVEL *House Made of Dawn*, Kiowa writer N. Scott Momaday marked the beginning in literary history of the American Indian Renaissance. The rich offering of novels and poetry written by American Indians since that time has focused on tribal struggles, culture and traditions, indigenous views of American history, and a search for identity[1] and healing by the narratives' mixed-blood protagonists. In their writing, American Indian writers offer a worldview that challenges Western culture. Indians present "a holistic, ecological perspective, one that places essential value upon the totality of existence, making humanity equal to all elements but superior to none and giving humankind crucial responsibility for the care of the world we inhabit" (Owens 29). Underlying this perspective is a strong connection to place and landscape. Sometimes this link to the land addresses environmental justice issues that have affected local indigenous communities in devastating ways. Writers such as Linda Hogan employ a shifting sense of time and space and mystical characters that disrupt and destabilize mainstream expectations.

Barbara J. Cook

In this chapter I argue that Hogan's writing draws on a traditional understanding of the interconnections within our world. She establishes the interdependence of land, animals, and humans and draws attention to historic acts of destruction driven by corporate and government decisions and human greed and indifference to the environment.

Hogan's Historical Narratives

In the preface to *Dwellings: A Spiritual History of the Living World,* Linda Hogan (Chickasaw and Anglo) notes that the essays have grown "out of my native understanding that there is a terrestrial intelligence that lies beyond our human knowing and grasping" (11). Hogan writes "out of respect for the natural world, recognizing that humankind is not separate from nature" (12). Her essays and poems reflect the traditional view of the world she believes she was born with and the importance she places on the interconnections of humans and the natural world. It is in her fiction, however, that Hogan most forcefully delineates the interplay between human actions and impact on the land, animals, and vegetation. In her three novels she selects actual historical events and offers the reader insight into the repercussions of those events on individual communities. In doing so, she is acting on her belief that she has "to do something stronger than history to reach the emotions of the readers" (Hogan, "Interview" 116). To tell the stories, she begins with the history and embellishes "it to create and put the imagery to work" ("Interview" 117).

Hogan utilizes rhetorical techniques such as anthropomorphism of the landscape and the natural world, a shifting reality, and a story line that juxtaposes changes in landscape with changes in members of her fictional community. These techniques make visible the interrelationship of humanity and the natural world. Although critics have recognized *Solar Storms* (1995) as a powerful environmental novel, her first novel, *Mean Spirit* (1990), shows the communal effects loss of land and political manipulation of the resources of the remaining land can have. Hogan also draws a portrait of the earth and nature in active resistance as the Osage community attempts to disappear into the margins of the white world. They become "shadow people" as they struggle for survival, wanting "nothing more than to be left alone and in peace" (40). Meanwhile, the earth rebels.

Fire and Violence of a *Mean Spirit*

Fire permeates *Mean Spirit.* Homes are burned, oil wells explode, gas fires rumble underground, while at the same time Michael Horse and the Hill people keep their tribal ceremonial fires burning. Horse tells us that "[a]nyone who ministers to a fire . . . would learn very quickly that the world lives in a fire" (255). In this novel fire is regenerative as well as destructive. For instance, Belle

Graycloud is grateful that although in many places the land was "shorn and bare from the grazing of cattle and buffalo . . . [w]here the fires had burned . . . the charred land was again sending forth new shoots of life" (242). There is the possibility of hope, renewal, and—ultimately—survival. As the earth is wounded by drilling in the Oklahoma oil fields, the landscape changes and wildlife retreats into the hills with the traditional Indians, who strive to remain far away from the politicized economic changes.

Drawing on stories from her childhood as well as historical documents, Hogan chronicles in fictional form the historic saga of the development of the oil-rich Oklahoma Indian territory. She grew up immersed in the stories of the Oklahoma oil boom of the 1920s but chose to write about a fictional community not her own. Anchored in her southwestern landscape, Hogan tells a compelling story of the Osage tribal community and its struggles to maintain its culture and land against overwhelming government forces and local white greed for the rich oil resources in Indian country. Even as Hogan documents this loss of culture, she records the changes to the land that are a result of drilling for oil and establishing a new oil-driven economy.

In telling this story, Hogan draws our attention to the importance of telling history from an indigenous perspective by weaving Horse's journal entries throughout *Mean Spirit*. Although seen by the white population of Watona as "useless notebooks," the journals record a loss of culture and a changing ecosystem, as well as murders and fires. Horse is known to be a "good judge of people" (12), and he is central to the narrative. He is also a dreamer and has what others call a sixth sense, although, as he notes, that perception was "easy to lose when shiny cars honked on the dirt roads, and fine china plates were being thrown up in the air and shot down like clay pigeons" (40). He initially ignores the truth of the Indian community's deteriorating situation and sees it "coming only a little at a time" (40). Or perhaps this lack of notice was a result of his failing sixth sense, evidenced by the torrents of rain during what Horse had predicted to be a two-week dry spell.

Nevertheless, Horse continues to record the events of the community, and he realizes that "[i]t was a fatal ignorance we had of our place; we did not know the ends to which the others would go to destroy us" (341). The Osage could not comprehend the power of oil riches to corrupt. When the perpetrators of the murders are finally brought to trial, Horse listens daily to the testimony and proceedings and questions the sanity of the court system. After all, as he sees it, right or wrong "is such a simple thing, only a matter of whether a wrong has been done, or someone harmed" (341). But there are books other than his "filled with words, with rules about how the story can and cannot be spoken. There is not room enough, nor time, to search for the real story that lies beneath the rest" (341). Hogan attempts to tell the "real story." She sees fiction as "a vertical descent . . . a drop into an event or into history or into the depths of some kind of meaning in order to understand humans, and to somehow decipher what history speaks, *the story beneath the story* [emphasis added] ("Interview" 125).

Continuing to write, Horse escapes with his notebooks and the people's sacred fire to the Hill Indians' settlement and yearns for the old traditional ways of living. He notes the cries and moans of the earth and the thoughts that came to him while watching his fire intermingle with the fire of the Hill Indians. He turns to "writing a new chapter of the Bible" and asks the startled Hog priest (Father Dunne) if he knows "how he could get this chapter added to the whole book" (*Mean Spirit* 273). Asserting that the Bible is full of mistakes, he wants to correct them with his Gospel of Horse:

> "For instance, where does it say that all living things are equal?"
> The priest shook his head. "It doesn't say that. It says man has dominion over the creatures of the earth."
> "Well, that's where it needs to be fixed. That's part of the trouble, don't you see?" (273)

These words have the ring of Hogan's convictions. Finally, the journals become more than documentation. They become a treatise of Linda Hogan's body of work, her personal view of humanity and nature. Horse begins with simple rules for life such as "[t]ake care of the earth and all her creatures" (359). He tells the community that the oral transmission of these ideas is not enough; "they don't believe anything is true unless they see it in writing" (361). He begins, "Honor father sky and mother earth. Look after everything. Life resides in all things, even the motionless stones. Take care of the insects for they have their place, and the plants and trees for they feed the people. . . . [A]ll life is sacred" (361–362).

Horse is the observer and interpreter of what is happening to the land and the people. He records the loss of the last bit of the people's strength during the trials: "The land is ravaged and covered with scars and so are the broken people" (341). As people bring their bad dreams—which were "becoming as common as gas fires at the drill sites"—to Horse for interpretation, he reminds them that the "earth was being drilled and dynamited open. Disturbances of earth, he told them, made for disturbances of life and sleep. . . . In half a year there had been seventeen murders in just their small booming corner of Oklahoma" (39). A link exists between the wounding of the earth by incessant drilling and the calculated destruction of a community. This parallel is accentuated by the active resistance of the earth. While the Osage struggle for survival, Hogan gives the earth an agency that violently resists the devastation brought on by economic greed. The community struggles as it copes with the new wealth and unaccustomed availability of commodities such as shiny new cars, elaborate houses, and crystal trinkets. The revenues from the underground minerals separate them from their customary sustainable economy and their work ethic. Hogan shows us a culture being destroyed from within and, because of the serial killings and fraudulent practices, also from the outside. Hogan clearly locates the root of the dual destruction in governmental actions.

Under the Dawes Act (General Allotment Act of 1887), Native Americans were individually given 160 acres of land to farm. This governmental action, breaking up communal landownership by Indians, had at least a dual purpose. It offered a quicker road to assimilation into white culture and created more land availability for the white settlers, homesteaders, and ranchers. But Hogan does not allow such an easy identification of white versus Osage or good versus evil. She creates characters who blur the lines and leave the reader unsure of motivation. For instance, the sheriff, Jess Gold, appears throughout to be a friend of Benoit and appears to treat Belle and Moses Graycloud fairly. He is revealed in the end to be one of the serial murderers. In another example, we are never sure about Tate, Ruth's husband, who photographs every event. Moses finally kills him because Tate shoots Ruth, Moses's sister. Nola's husband, Will, on the other hand, appears to represent the system's greed, since his father is appointed Nola's legal guardian and controls her fortune. He collects and sells Indian artifacts in apparent disregard of the way Nola and other members of the community would view those actions. He does, however, appear to love Nola and wants to protect her interests. As Patrick Murphy points out, Hogan refuses "to grant the reader a simple dichotomy of innocent and good versus evil and corrupt . . . [and] encourages recognition of the complexity of the systems of domination on the one hand, and the diversity of forms of resistance and levels of awareness on the part of the oppressed on the other" (184).

These complexities are also played out by the various factions of the Osage community. Grace and Nola Blanket represent a link to the traditional and somewhat mystical Hill people. Grace has been sent by that community to learn the ways of the white world so the community can protect itself and, it hopes, stop the damming of the Blue River. Grace selects "barren, useless land" that no one else wants, only to find that "black undercurrents of oil moved beneath that earth's surface" (8). That oil discovery and "the sacrifice of Grace," whose murder begins the novel, stop the planned construction of the dam because "all the dark wealth" was first to be removed from the underground oil reserves (10). These massive reserves create a mélange of greed, murder, and fraud and extend the original goals of cultural extermination. What had once been a war aimed at extinguishing a race became a war waged with the earth (14).

In contrast to the war the white world wages with the earth, Belle Graycloud represents a traditional worldview as she attempts to live among the white and mixed-blood community. She retreats to her cellar for comfort rather than to the isolation of the Hill community. For her, "The earth is my marketplace" (16). She cares for her bees and chickens, gathers watercress and wild onion from along the creek, and plants corn in the traditional way. In a way, Belle represents what Hogan calls the "gap in time between one Indian way of life [reflected by the Hill people] and another where girls were sassy and wore satin ribbons in their hair" (22). Belle sees the murders as just "part of the madness cropping up like Johnson grass in dry, barren towns that grew rich overnight, part of what happened in poor old places where some gambler struck paydirt" (40). The white community does not see Belle's land as a marketplace; it is rather "without improvement" (80). She does not fence it off or burn the brush, and she leaves the trees standing. These actions are of no value, and the land is seen as not being utilized properly. Eventually, Belle's land is leased out by the Indian agent as a stockade for buffalo and cattle. Since she did not improve it, the agent decided it was "best not to leave the land lying idle" (213). It only takes a few days, however, for the buffalo to destroy the grassland, pulling "the tall grass up by its roots" and leaving the land bare, unable to regenerate (213). Hogan drives home the lack of understanding of sustainable land practices.

But evidence of the earth's restlessness is seen everywhere. A large crater 50 feet deep and 500 feet across reminds everyone of the gas well blowout that "swallowed five workmen and ten mules" (53). Once rich with tall grass and trees, the land is now "burned black" (53). The destruction of the land is ubiquitous. Pumps work noisily day and night on the "bruised fields," and blue flames are pervasive: "The earth bled oil" (54). The land is subjugated by the oilmen in their "steel-toe boots" as they pull "the great chains back and forth and, inch by inch, dr[ive] the pipes down and into the earth" (148). The earth moans and roars with rage, "complaining through an open mouth" as the gas rumbles underground (148). Later, after another explosion, China watches it burn and roar "like God's wrath" as it "melted the earth, melted the metal derrick," and she knows "the earth had a mind of its own" (185–186). The fires continue underground, the land rumbles "like an earthquake," and "trees burn . . . from the root upward" (187). Horse identifies this earthly destruction as "the rage of mother earth" (189). In addition to the penetration of the earth, other actions are devastating to the ecology of the region; new grasses have been introduced, each with its own consequences. The bluegrass was designed to fatten the cattle more quickly, but the Johnson grass causes the most devastation with its "roots so strong they spirited away the minerals and water from other trees and plants, leaving tracts of land barren-looking" (54).

Explosions become common as new wells blow out at the drilling sites, and a "faint roar of the gas fire could be heard burning in the distance" (75). As the

Indians are increasingly denied their government royalty checks, Benoit explodes: "They are stealing our lives! We've got to fight them. Why do you just take it" (63). But most of the Indians realize the dangers of dealing with government clerks and "know from the history itself, that it was smart to keep silent on the affairs and regulations of Washington, to be still and as invisible as possible. They might be cheated, but they still had life, and until only recently, even that was not guaranteed under the American laws, so they remained trapped, silent, and wary" (64). But as the murders continue and the wells explode and the fires burn, the people begin breaking apart "like the earth just did" (75). People begin to change, become opposites, "as if the earth's polar axis had shifted" (171). Hogan is presenting a continuum. Human actions have ecological consequences that in turn have effects on individuals and communities.

The effects extend to wildlife, insects, and birds. "Hot tongues of fire" (103) burn an ancient forest. As the fire burns close to Belle's home, she hears "the mournful sound of coyotes. The land pulled into itself, and the air was tense and restless. Birds were screaming in their nests" (103). The fire is difficult to put out, and it continues to burn "like a torn ragged edge of red cloth moving along the horizon" (104). Plants and animals are lost in the fire, which seems to be the impetus for a frightening mass movement of crickets. Thousands of dark crickets "moved like a single mind up the staircase . . . [and] filled [Nola's] room like [a] spreading dark stain of blood" (105). Although this depiction seems entirely unreal, Hogan recalls a similar story her father tells from his childhood ("Interview" 129).

No matter how bad their landscape is becoming, they are told it is even worse south of Watona, a nearby town: "The land's dead. They're boiling rocks for soup" (135). But the murders increase, and devastation of the ecosystem continues. Belle comments on the Hell of environmental destruction that surrounds the Blue River: "In places the banks were black from oil seepages like the one in Belle's spring, and there were rusted oil drums stuck in stagnant pools along the area, and swampy, polluted places where insects thrived" (274). A coyote paws at the earth, trees are killed by bagworms, fields are burned black or "overgrazed by hungry cattle the world-eaters raised. It was a desolate sight" (274). Belle begins to see rain as the crying of the sky (276).

Even Belle's bees reflect the disturbances. One day after finding many of her bees dead or dying, she faints from heat exhaustion, and the bees turn on her. She is saved by one of the mysterious watchers sent from the Hill community to watch over Nola. When the buffalo and cattle are placed on Belle's land, they upset the bees again, which in turn sting one of the hens, killing her. After Belle moves her bees farther from the cattle, more of her land is leased out, and the cattle move ever closer. Belle can only watch as she listens to the "loud angry hum of bees" (305). At this point Belle is shot; the bees attack Jess Gold, the sheriff; and Belle is charged with involuntary manslaughter for keeping vicious bees. The drive to utilize every inch of land ends in destruction and death.

Hogan gives the reader the tools to see that dominant ideologies support greed and lead to evil. Not content with the oil money, oil entrepreneur John Hale sponsors eagle hunts and brings easterners west "in plush new trains in order to shoot eagles out of the balmy Oklahoma sky" (57). Belle is enraged when she discovers 317 carcasses of sacred golden eagles. Her attempts to take out revenge on the hunters lead to her arrest rather than to protection of the eagles. Belle is again witness to the careless attitude toward wildlife when she encounters a group of young men excitedly shooting the bats at Sorrow Cave. Believing the bats carry rabies, they are after the "one-dollar bounty per 'flying rat'" (277). War is declared once again, and the frightened animals "scream with terror" (277). Belle is able to stop the shooting temporarily with help from the community. Both the Hill people and the townspeople assist, and they find another cave entrance that allows the bats to escape.

In depicting the saving of the bats, Hogan shifts from the hopelessness of the meaningless destruction of eagles early in the novel to the possibility of survival through communal action. The town also makes a communal turn to traditional spirituality. The spiritual leaders serve as a link to the more traditional ways of the Hill people. Belle, Horse, the Hog priest, Joe Billy, Stace, and others continually make the trek to the Hill settlement seeking refuge and solace. Finally, fearing the insanity of the townspeople's madness will "form itself like a turn wind in the air and travel up the red clay pathway to their own world," the Hill people decide to hide the path to their settlement (302). Nature helps protect the traditional way of life found in the Hill settlement. It covers the trail, taking back the land and separating the Indians from the white world. Hogan alludes to this protective stance of nature early in the novel. To escape the heat of their houses, many Indians set up their beds in gardens, pastures, and fallow cornfields; and "given half a chance, the vines and leaves would have crept up the beds and overgrown the sleeping bodies of people" (3). As Yonka Kroumova Krasteva notes in her discussion of *Mean Spirit,* the vegetation around the Indians sleeping in their gardens "seems to want to reclaim them and bring them back to their traditional environment, which they actually return to at the end of the novel" (49).

Hogan ends *Mean Spirit* on what a reader could construe as a note of hopelessness—"the land had gone dry and the insects had become more shrill and desperate sounding" (343), and the Osage are driven from their land because of fraud, lies, and fear. But Hogan has created a community that has reconsidered its identity in light of traditional values. Earlier in the novel, Elder Ona Neck had responded to Horse's reading from his Book of Horse with a laughing ironic cry of "[g]ive me liberty or give me death" (362). The Osage community has sought liberty through rekindling a traditional worldview. The Grayclouds represent the departure of that community in search of a better future and a safer landscape. Belle carefully collects her bees, which have returned home, and realizes they, "like everything else, wanted only to live. That was all they wanted, to live and continue" (365). She could be talking about the Indians as well. Although "the world had turned under and over," they are "left to go on, to survive" (344). As the Grayclouds leave, they look back at "the reddened sky" and know "they carried generations along with them, into the prairie and through it, to places where no road had been cut before them. . . . The night was on fire with their pasts and they were alive" (375). They have survived, and their culture continues.

Solar Storms and a Passage Through Water

Water is the natural element given agency in Hogan's second novel, *Solar Storms*. But water is not the only participant in dynamic resistance. Unlike the tribal community in *Mean Spirit*, Hogan depicts a northern community of Cree, Inuit, and mixed-blood Indians that actively resists corporate and governmental practices that threaten its culture and traditional way of life. She based the novel on the construction of the James Bay–Great Whale hydroelectric project in Quebec; however, although she does not identify that location in the novel, the setting is clearly the Boundary Waters between Minnesota and Canada. This is a deliberately ambiguous move by Hogan. The setting is both Quebec and the Boundary Waters and at the same time neither. In an interview in the *Missouri Review*, conducted while she was writing *Solar Storms*, Hogan says she "was creating a completely fictional community, and yet the story is really about the truth" ("Interview" 122). For Hogan, the creation of a fictional community is her response to "an unspoken rule that we [Indian writers] have to stay within our own tribe and our own territory in ways others don't" (Hogan in Johnson 2). One of the constraints that creates this position is that non-Indian readers expect Native American writers "to somehow explain [their] culture to them" (Johnson 2). Hogan also points out:

> I'm sensitive to how it feels to be a tribal person and to have the intrusions of others into your intimate connection with your own tribe and land, even if it's a more pan-Indian native view. So one of the things that I have been doing is fictionalizing the tribes that I'm writing about so nobody feels they're being invaded once again. (Johnson 2)

Although *Solar Storms* blurs the participants and enlarges the setting to tell a dramatic story, Hogan draws on the reality the indigenous inhabitants of James Bay faced and on their resistance to the project. The project was launched in 1971 to provide electricity for New York City without prior notification to the people it would affect. Hogan carefully details the effect of the Quebec project on the region's population, focusing on the negative impact on the indigenous people. I believe in chronicling the Anglo-European drive to control nature and an Indian community's struggle against that drive, Hogan is offering in *Solar Storms* a positive possibility for the future and a sensibility influenced by her Oklahoma childhood.

Linda Hogan's *Solar Storms* tells the story of Angel, a mixed-blood Cree-Inuit who, after growing up in a series of foster homes far removed from her traditional roots, returns to her tribal home in search of healing. She finds not only her matrilineage—her great-grandmother Agnes, her great-great-grandmother Dora-Rouge, and her step-grandmother Bush. She finds much more in a mixed indigenous community with strong ties to the land and its cooperative struggle for social and environmental justice. Hogan uses the town of Adam's Rib and the land of the Fat Eaters to reflect a recent development within the environmental movement: environmental or ecological justice.[2] When Agnes and Dora-Rouge return to their Canadian homeland to reconnect with their ancestors, they find development threatening to destroy the land and the way of life. They work to protect their ancestral homelands by nonviolent methods—such as petitions, community meetings, legal injunctions, and blockage of roads to prevent the movement of bulldozers—and ultimately gain temporary control over the development.

In *Solar Storms* Hogan focuses on the indigenous community and tells the story not only of a young woman's journey to the land of her ancestors and her healing process but of a tribal community's fight for survival and ecological justice. As Nicholas Low and Brendan Gleeson point out in *Justice, Society, and Nature*: "The struggle for justice as it is shaped by the politics of environment, then, has two relational aspects: the justice of the distribution of environments among peoples, and the justice of the relationship between humans and the rest of the natural world" (2). Hogan not only explores the relationship between humans and the rest of the natural world, she poignantly examines how justice has often been ignored in governmental decisions affecting one particular non-white community in Canada. Angel's battered and scarred body stands for the people and the land ravaged by Anglo-European practices. Her disfiguration and abuse are a result of the historical trauma suffered by her mother, Hannah. Angel's body is a result of generations of abuse and only heals slowly. The land has also been plundered for many generations and will only heal slowly, if at all.

In writing about environmental justice, Hogan emphasizes the historical contrasts and growing similarities between indigenous and Western worldviews and questions the place of science within those knowledge systems. In her interview with Rachel Stein, Hogan refers to the Native Science Dialogues she participates in "where non-Indian thinkers and indigenous thinkers get together and talk about Western science and how it fits into the traditional world view. We talk about similarities and differences in the knowledge systems" (114). The vehicle she uses for this discussion in *Solar Storms* is her character John Husk; however, I believe she begins to explore these ideas in *Mean Spirit*. At one point the Graycloud family gazes through Ben's telescope at the vastness of the universe, and Ben tries "to study the constellations of the white world," believing that was the key to whites' thinking (194). Ironically, he focuses on "Libra, the unbalanced scale of justice" (194).

In setting up the contrasts, Hogan presents an exchange between the Hill people and Father Dunne. When the Hill people explain that they feed the ants so they won't bother their other food, Father Dunne says that never occurred to him, "looking incredulous at his own ignorance" (271). This story could be right out of David Abram's *Spell of the Sensuous*.[3] Since *Mean Spirit* predates Abram's book, it would seem this is a direct example of a non-Western worldview fitting into logic within the Western paradigm. Later, Hogan depicts Father Dunne's wonder when, after being bitten by a rattlesnake, he decides "to think like a snake and see things from its point of view" (262). In that effort he becomes "one with the snake" and feels his "own snaking spine and double tongue" and realizes that "the snake is our sister" (262). Upon hearing the story one of the children responds, "Yes, so what new thing did you learn?" His mother tells him, "Don't be rude" (262).

Husk would seem to be the culmination of these ideas in Hogan's writing. In this character Hogan links Western scientific worldviews and indigenous ways of knowing. Husk loves science and keeps "stacks of magazines and books that divulged the secret worlds of atoms and galaxies, of particles and quarks" (*Solar Storms* 35). But he also knows the more traditional views: that humans and animals had made a covenant to care for one another and that animals felt pain. He wants to prove, through science, that the world is alive "to confirm what he knew was true" (62); "even the tools and the fishhooks were alive" (81). Hogan wants to show the overlap of new Western scientific discoveries and ancient traditional systems of knowledge. Husk reads that bees communicate by dancing (35) and says later, "[N]ow they're finding out that insects are intelligent" (91). In describing the forces and power of nature, Angel reflects, "Husk, who saw everything in terms of science, told me once how metal bridges were taken down, collapsed by the song of wind. A certain tone, a certain itch of wind" (102). We are told that Bush is like the traditional people and knows the world was alive and that all creatures were God. In this effort to contrast systems of knowledge, a parallel is drawn instead when Husk reminds us that "some things were so obvious the scientists couldn't even see them" (139). To Husk, science also confirms the indigenous cyclical worldview of time and space: "Einstein believed time would bend and circle back to itself" (64).

Barbara J. Cook

The interrelationships of humans and the natural world, the idea that all is alive and what affects one affects the other, are only beginning to be understood by mainstream thinkers. Jim Tarter argues that writers such as Silko, Hogan, Ursula Le Guin, and Gary Snyder offer prospects "that people on this continent will learn from the land and its spirits, that this process is happening now, and sooner or later—it could be a while—we will eventually return to the old ways" (144).[4]

Some argue that returning to the old ways includes a return to matriarchy, and one result of Hogan's focus on Angel's foremothers and other women as leaders of the indigenous resistance is that *Solar Storms* has variously been called an affirmation of Paula Gunn Allen's "gynocratic principles"[5] and of other environmental justice movements led by women.[6] I would argue that Hogan's work does represent a deeply involved stance that would be easy to label as feminist; however, in her novel Hogan explores the connections between humans and animals and the environment from an American Indian perspective. Although this view is not superficial, it also refuses to be strictly feminine. For instance, Husk, Tommy, and Tulik are men who have respectful relationships with animals and landscape. Even LaRue, who—psychically wounded by war—initially lives outside those boundaries of respect, comes to understand the connection between humans and nature. One of his customers shoots the last of a species and declares he has taken it. Angel observes, "Take, I thought then, what a strange word it is. To conquer, to possess, to win, to swallow. . . . He [LaRue] cried for the animal, for us, our lives, and for the war he'd endured and never told about. He changed after that, inch by inch" (339–340).

Thus, rather than a strictly ecofeminist text, *Solar Storms* reflects concerns most often expressed by the multicultural activists of the environmental justice movement, such as the "broader struggle against social forms which produce environmental injustice, biospheric destruction and the maldistribution of environmental risk" (Low and Gleeson 3). So although Hogan believes the possibility of crossover knowledge is there, for her a division still exists. Her narrator acknowledges developers' disregard for the land but also explores the connections among the environment, the animals, and the people on both sides of the confrontation. Angel reflects on one of the village meetings:

> And when the officials and attorneys spoke, their language didn't hold a thought for the life of the water, or a regard for the land that sustained people from the beginning of time. They didn't remember the sacred treaties between humans and animals. . . . [T]hinking about the lengths to which they would go, my mind drifted off to water, to wetness itself, and how I'd wanted so often to hold my breath and remain inside the water that springs from earth and rains down from the sky. Perhaps it would tell me, speak to me, show me a way around these troubles. Water, I knew, had its own needs,

its own speaking and desires. No one had asked the water what it wanted.
Except Dora-Rouge, that is, who'd spoken with it directly. (279)

Dora-Rouge makes a compact with a force of nature so the women can survive when they face a river crossing at flood stage. At that point Dora-Rouge talks to the river and asks for safe passage. A more Anglo-centric worldview would not allow for this possibility, but Hogan presents it as a real option. Hogan's narrator, Angel, considers the position of the opposing forces: "Later I wondered how these men, young though they were, did not have a vision large enough to see a life beyond their jobs, beyond orders, beyond the company that would ultimately leave them broke, without benefits, and guilty of the sin of land killing" (288). Negotiation with nature and an attempt to understand the opposition are representative methods of mediation. Hogan's mediatory approach represents her personal worldview. Hogan has expressed the idea that "all cruelty is needless. All fighting" and any kind of destruction to the land are to be avoided (Hogan in Bruchac 133). She considers herself an environmental writer but feels many people who write about the wilderness and the environment do not "look at the inner wilderness and what motivates people to be destructive" ("Interview" 122). She says "everything is connected, that I'm part of the destruction: we all are" ("Interview" 122).

This concept of interconnectedness is found in the writings of many Native American authors. As Jennifer Brice points out in her essay "Earth as Mother, Earth as Other in Novels by Silko and Hogan," a fundamental difference exists between the fiction of white Americans and that of Native Americans: "[W]hites are taught . . . to see the land as separate from themselves, whereas Native Americans believe the land is the same as themselves" (127). Another way to view this difference is to understand that the white European literary tradition comes from "the white European history of colonization [in contrast to] Native American writing[, which] arises from the experience of dispossession" (Brice 127).

In *Solar Storms* Hogan's consideration for the interconnectedness of humanity is again expressed when the young policemen are forced to confront the activists as they block a road to the construction site. Angel recognizes that the policemen have no courage and are afraid, much as the Indian community is; but "they were afraid of what no money, no home, no job might mean" (288). Angel contemplates how men could go against nature:

> I would wonder for years—I still wonder—what elements, what events would allow men to go against their inner voices, to go against even the cellular will of the body to live and to protect life, land, even their own children and their future. They were men who would reverse the world, change the direction of rivers, stop the cycle of life until everything was as backwards as lies. (288–289)

Hogan's portrayal of the humanity of everyone involved in the dispute presents her belief in the interconnectedness of all living things and the dichotomy in the conflict. Additionally, for Hogan, the land itself is also alive and part of the web of life, capable of exacting its own revenge. Traveling northward, Dora-Rouge, Bush, Agnes, and Angel encounter a river landscape not on their ancient tribal maps or in their stories and memories. This is a river changed by commercial development: "If they'd diverted the Big Arm River, as the man said, it would mean that certain waters ahead of us might be closed, others flooded. . . . [W]e'd already seen some of the flooding, mudflats where other rivers had failed to empty into their destinations" (192). The river is roaring past "so loud it sounded like earth breaking open and raging" (192). Dora-Rouge listens and understands: " 'It's angry,' said Dora-Rouge. [Angel] leaned toward her to hear. 'The rivers are angry. Both of them' " (192). Having gone too far to turn back—"Not too far in distance alone, but too far inside ourselves"—Dora-Rouge talks "to the churning river, the white and muddy foam of it, the hydrogen and oxygen of it," and convinces it to let the women pass (193).

This art of negotiation with nature underlies Hogan's novel. Her characters attempt negotiation not only with the rivers but with other forces as well—for example, with the developers who threaten their land. Negotiation, nonviolent demonstrations, and legal maneuvers are the tactics Hogan depicts. In her novel it is the developers and politicians who are initially unwilling to negotiate. As Angel points out, they only see the Indians as "dark outsiders whose lives had no relevance to them. They ignored our existence until we resisted their dams, or interrupted their economy, or spoiled their sport" (283). When faced with resistance, the developers and politicians do not recognize it as nonviolent: "Reversing the truth, they would call us terrorists. If there was evil in the world, this was it, [Angel] thought. Reversal" (283). Hogan's distaste for violence is reflected throughout *Solar Storms,* and in interviews she has spoken against using violence to protect the land:

> [A]s long as I can remember in my life, I have always been against violence. . . . I think that war and peace have been my occupation and my preoccupation for as long as I can remember. Spirituality necessitates certain kinds of political action. If you believe that the earth, and all living things, and all the stones are sacred, your responsibility really is to protect those things. I do believe that's our duty, to be custodians of the planet. (Hogan in Coltelli 79)

As Hogan indicates in her interview with Laura Coltelli, although she believes it is our responsibility to protect the earth and all living things, she does not see the necessity of violence, and her characters do not resort to violence even when they are in direct confrontation with the developers. For example, when the tribal community has no success with meetings and negotiation, it prepares to take the next step by stopping the progress of construction. The community identifies the railroad as the target, for "[i]ts purpose was not . . . human transportation, but to carry the land and trees away. Sometimes it sounded like an earthquake as the train passed by, carrying our world" (*Solar Storms* 304). The community members decide to block the tracks with whatever they can find, "pieces of pipe and dark gray stones . . . a rusted-out old truck . . . clutter and old oil barrels" (304). This action does bring the train to a halt, if only temporarily.

Hogan's form of activism, as well as her writing, stems from the community: "My writing comes from and goes back to the community, both the human and the global community" ("Aunt Moon's Young Man" 115). The tribal community works together as a group rather than as individuals. Angel comments on the cohesiveness: "In those days we were still a tribe. Each of us had one part of the work of living" (*Solar Storms* 262). Angel learns about community and loss of their way of life through her grandmothers' stories. She realizes that she "had come from a circle of courageous women and strong men who had walls pulled down straight in front of them until the circle closed, the way rabbits are hunted in a narrowing circle, but some lived, some survived this narrowing circle of life" (107). During their fight to protect the river, their land, and their culture, Angel longs for "a story for what was happening to us now, as if a story would guide us" (302). Instead of stories of the tribal community's survival, the media are filled with false stories making the Indians the enemy—reversing the reality. With irony, Angel notes, "and, we the enemy, sat there on quiet nights, warm with hope and no bitterness among us" (302). At one point, however, Angel contemplates violence as she walks toward the soldiers with a rock in her hand. She is gently stopped by Bush and realizes what "a single thrown rock would have done. Just one rock" (324).

Reversal of the story by the media is representative of the coverage environmental justice activists often receive, and Hogan eloquently depicts the difficulty in attempting to define their positions to the public. Although Hogan acknowledges the possibility of violence by the tribe, she depicts a community that returns to wholeness through its nonviolent fight in a struggle that enables its members to respect themselves again. In the process they recover the spirituality of their ancestors as they remember the old stories and songs. Angel, who during the novel heals from the psychic and physical scars inflicted by her mother, is an individual representative of the healing of the tribal community as it attempts to heal from the scars inflicted by the developers on the land and the river. Angel's healing is brought about through the strength of the community and the spiritual link to ancestors, stories, animals, and healing plants.

As Angel moves toward healing, there is a parallel restoration of tribal self-respect and wholeness. These struggles involve everyone and everything and suggest Hogan's web of interrelationships. *Solar Storms* is the story of the fight for survival of all parts of that web—Angel, tribal community, land, plants, and animals. Hogan's goal in her writing is political, but she is not interested in what she labels a "political diatribe." In an interview with Brad Johnson, Hogan asserts:

> I've found that talking about issues somehow doesn't create change in the world, but if I can take one of the issues, political issues, or a tribe that's being devastated because of development, or land that's being devastated because of development—and I put it into a story, it has more of an impact. . . . People read it and they get it . . . they find characters that they can relate to and care about and they see the story from inside their own body, inside their own selves. (3)

The effectiveness of Hogan's writing invites the reader to make that deep connection with the characters and thus opens up the Native American world to non-Natives, allowing us to "get it." Hogan expresses the effectiveness of this approach in a poem from her *Book of Medicines*: "The closed bundles of healing / are beginning to open" (84). Additionally, Hogan constructs an individualized story of a community that energizes a cold impersonal term such as environmental justice. The struggle of this personalized indigenous community reflects the distinctive organizational form of the environmental justice movement, the network. As John Dryzek notes, within the networks "local groups relate to each other without any national leadership or bureaucratic structure" (178). He argues that within this "alternative environmental movement" is an eclectic group of tactics: "Like the mainstream it engages in litigation and lobbying, but it is also more comfortable with confrontation tactics involving demonstrations, blockades, sit-ins, and boycotts" (178). The fictional community in Hogan's text engages in most, if not all, of these strategies.

As Hogan's protagonist moves from individual resistance to immersion in community, her resistance seeks a mediation and focuses on a Native American worldview in which community is so integrated with nature that it is gender balanced. It becomes a statement of interdependence as Native American men and women struggle against the oppression of the dominant culture. This commitment to communal action is a central element of the environmental justice movement.

Low and Gleeson have pointed out that "[s]ocial change on the scale which may well be necessary for the global society to carry on the task of finding and delivering justice in and to the environment is likely to proceed in a somewhat piecemeal and incremental way" (3). Hogan's work is indicative of the growth of awareness of ecological politics and provides one of those incremental pieces necessary to effect transformative social change.

Notes

1. Louis Owens and many other scholars of Native American literature argue that the search for identity is at the core of texts written by American Indians. Owens argues that "[t]he recovering or rearticulation of an identity, a process dependent upon a rediscovered sense of place as well as community, becomes in the face of such obstacles a truly enormous undertaking. This attempt is at the center of American Indian fiction" (5).

2. For more on the connections among environmental justice, environmental racism, and grassroots resistance movements, see Robert D. Bullard, *Confronting Environmental Racism: Voices from the Grassroots* (Boston: South End, 1993); Bullard, *Unequal Protection: Environmental Justice and Communities of Color* (San Francisco: Sierra Club, 1994); Bullard, *Dumping in Dixie: Race, Class, and Environmental Quality* (Boulder: Westview, 2000); Dryzek, *The Politics of the Earth: Environmental Discourses* (New York: Oxford University Press, 1997); Luke W. Cole and Sheila R. Foster, *From the Ground Up: Environmental Racism and the Rise of the Environmental Justice Movement* (New York: New York University Press, 2001); Low and Gleeson, *Justice, Society, and Nature: An Exploration of Political Ecology* (London: Routledge, 1998); and Richard Hofrichter, *Toxic Struggles: The Theory and Practice of Environmental Justice* (Philadelphia: New Society, 1993).

3. Abram tells the story of his Balinese hosts leaving rice on palm fronds at the "corners of various structures" to feed the "house spirits," or what he later learned were ants, so the family's food would not be attacked by the numerous ant colonies that surrounded their compound. "Placed in regular, repeated locations at the corners of various structures around the compound, the offerings seemed to establish certain boundaries between the human and ant communities" (11–13).

4. For more on new scientific beliefs that seemingly substantiate indigenous belief systems, see Abram, *The Spell of the Sensuous: Perception and Language in a More-Than-Human World* (New York: Vintage, 1996); J. E. Lovelock, *Gaia: A New Look at Life on Earth* (Oxford: Oxford University Press, 1979); Brian Greene, *The Elegant Universe: Superstrings, Hidden Dimensions, and the Quest for the Ultimate Theory* (New York: Vintage, 1999); Thomas S. Kuhn, *The Structure of Scientific Revolutions* (Chicago: University of Chicago Press, 1962); and Lynn Margulis, *Symbiotic Planet: A New Look at Evolution* (New York: Basic, 1988).

5. Roseanne Hoefel has drawn this parallel utilizing Allen's *Grandmothers of the Light: A Medicine Woman's Sourcebook* (Boston: Beacon, 1991).

6. Although many individual movements have been led by women, in many others men have served as leaders, especially those that have risen out of the drive for racial justice. See Bullard, note 2.

Works Cited

Abram, David. *The Spell of the Sensuous: Perception and Language in a More-Than-Human World.* New York: Vintage, 1996.

Brice, Jennifer. "Earth as Mother, Earth as Other in Novels by Silko and Hogan." *Critique* 39, no. 2 (1998): 127–138.

Bruchac, Joseph. "To Take Care of Life: An Interview with Linda Hogan." *Survival This Way: Interviews with American Indian Poets.* Ed. Bruchac. Tucson: Sun Tracks and University of Arizona Press, 1987. 119–134.

Barbara J. Cook

Coltelli, Laura. *Winged Words: American Indian Writers Speak.* Lincoln: University of Nebraska Press, 1990.

Dryzek, John S. *The Politics of the Earth: Environmental Discourses.* New York: Oxford University Press, 1997.

Hoefel, Roseanne. "Narrative Choreography Toward a New Cosmogony: The Medicine Way in Linda Hogan's Novel *Solar Storms.*" *Femspec* 2, no. 2 (2000): 33–47.

Hogan, Linda. "Aunt Moon's Young Man." In *Best American Short Stories.* New York: Houghton Mifflin, 1989. 128–147.

———. *The Book of Medicines.* Minneapolis: Coffee House, 1993.

———. *Dwellings: A Spiritual History of the Living World.* New York: W. W. Norton, 1995.

———. "An Interview with Linda Hogan." *Missouri Review* 17, no. 2 (1994): 109–134.

———. *Mean Spirit.* New York: Ivy Books, 1990.

———. *Solar Storms.* New York: Scribner, 1995.

Johnson, Brad. "Western Voices Interview with Linda Hogan." 2 March 1998. <http://members.aol.com/Hogan_interview.htm>.

Krasteva, Yonka Kroumova. "The Politics of the Border in Linda Hogan's *Mean Spirit.*" *Studies in American Indian Literature, Series 2,* vol. 11, no. 4 (1999): 46–60.

Low, Nicholas, and Brendan Gleeson. *Justice, Society, and Nature: An Exploration of Political Ecology.* London: Routledge, 1998.

Murphy, Patrick D. *Farther Afield in the Study of Nature-Oriented Literature.* Charlottesville: University Press of Virginia, 2000.

Owens, Louis. *Other Destinies: Understanding the American Indian Novel.* Norman: University of Oklahoma Press, 1992.

Stein, Rachel. "An Ecology of Mind: A Conversation with Linda Hogan." *ISLE* 6, no. 1 (1999): 113–118.

Tarter, Jim. "Dreams of Earth: Place, Multiethnicity, and Environmental Justice in Linda Hogan's *Solar Storms.*" In *Reading Under the Sign of Nature: New Essays in Ecocriticism.* Ed. John Tallmadge and Henry Harrington. Salt Lake City: University of Utah Press, 2000. 128–147.

STORIED EARTH, STORIED LIVES
Linda Hogan's *Solar Storms* and Rick Bass's *The Sky, the Stars, the Wilderness*

ANN FISHER-WIRTH

IN THE WINTER OF 2001 THE 1,000-MEMBER INTERNATIONAL ORGANIZATION known as ASLE—the Association for the Study of Literature and Environment—presented Linda Hogan with a special award in recognition of her work. Novelist, poet, essayist, autobiographer—for decades she has been a major American writer and one of the most passionate, lyrical, and imaginative U.S. environmental artists. At the time of the award, many ASLE members wrote accompanying statements about the significance of Hogan's work for their own lives and teaching; most of those who wrote—myself included—mentioned her 1995 novel *Solar Storms* above all. In this chapter I first situate *Solar Storms* in the context of contemporary American environmental issues and writing and then specifically link it with Rick Bass's 1997 novella *The Sky, the Stars, the Wilderness*, with which it shares a deep ecological vision, mapped onto and lyrically articulated through different kinds of journeys into wilderness and the search for the protagonists' lost mothers. Then I return to *Solar Storms*, hoping to give some sense of its great beauty and importance.

Ann Fisher-Wirth

"The Owl of Minerva Takes Flight Only at Dusk" (Hegel)

It is bitter but no paradox that in a country characterized by overwhelming—and escalating—environmental depredation, both environmental writing and the academic study of this literature are thriving. Our roads are widening, our trees are falling, our rivers and oceans are poisoned. Several years ago, *Greenpeace Magazine* described the lower Mississippi River near my home as a chemical soup beyond scientific understanding. All across the United States, fertile ecosystems are paved over and perishing. At the same time, however, ordinary citizens have increasingly become aware that there *is* an environmental crisis. They have begun to want to learn about the rapidly diminishing natural world, about the possibilities for meaningful action, and about ways of life that provide alternatives to dominant, environmentally lethal world practices. Likewise, a growing number of American literary scholars have begun to develop an environmental focus in their research and teaching. Their reasons for doing so vary. Many seek what Pierre Bourdieu has called "a scholarship with commitment," a professional practice that would both "transcend the sacred boundary . . . between scholarship and commitment, in order to break out of the academic microcosm" and "enter into sustained and vigorous exchange with the outside world" (44).

Both within and outside the academy, environmental writing has received a great deal of attention in recent years. Bill McKibben, author of *The End of Nature,* goes so far as to call this writing "America's strongest suit in contemporary letters, our most distinctive gift to world literature" (BW01). In this as in many things, the owl of Minerva takes flight only at dusk. For as one ecotheorist recently pointed out, "[O]ur understanding of the environment has come about through the disruption of nature by agriculture and industrialism and the concomitant rise of science. Without environmental crisis . . . there might be no 'environmental imagination'" (Phillips 598).

But what *is* environmental writing? Let me sort out some terms that define overlapping fields but that are not strictly interchangeable. Nature writing is simply writing about the natural world; the phrase implies no particular critical practice or political or ethical orientation. Environmental writing includes some but by no means all nature writing and a substantial body of other literature as well—for instance, certain works of science fiction that take inspiration from the environmental crisis or works about urban rather than rural or wilderness environments. Fiction, nonfiction, or poetry—environmental writing specifically foregrounds environmental issues; regardless of whether it has an activist agenda, it overtly expresses an ecological vision of life. Defining the boundaries more loosely, what Lawrence Buell, author of *The Environmental Imagination,* calls "*environmentally oriented*" literature includes environmental writing but much else as well (7; emphasis added).

Buell offers four criteria for distinguishing such work. First, as opposed to the conventional, anthropocentric presentation of nature as merely a setting or backdrop for human affairs, in environmentally oriented literature the nonhuman environment is depicted "not merely as a framing device but as a presence that begins to suggest that human history is implicated in natural history" (7). A fine example of this occurs in Willa Cather's novel *O Pioneers,* which shows how the protagonist, Alexandra Bergson, shapes and is shaped even more intensely by the harsh, fertile farmland of the Nebraska Divide than by her relationships with other human characters. Second, in environmentally oriented literature "[t]he human interest is not understood to be the only legitimate interest" (7). *Moby-Dick,* for instance, focuses not only on the dual philosophical visions of Ishmael and Ahab or on the mighty themes of human aspiration and tragedy but also on whales. Reading from an environmental perspective makes the cetology chapters—which readers so often dismiss—both fascinating and crucial and reveals Melville's shattering critique of wholesale environmental destruction, whether it be wrought for vengeance or for profit. Third, "Human accountability to the environment is part of the text's ethical orientation" (7–8). For example, *Light in August,* William Faulkner's savage indictment of man's inhumanity to man, sets Lucas Burch's use and abandonment of his pregnant girlfriend Lena Grove against the use and abandonment of northern Mississippi pinewoods by the sawmills for which Lucas works—which for more than a century have clear-cut, trashed the forests, and moved on. And fourth, a result of the first three, "Some sense of the environment as a process rather than as a constant or a given is at least implicit in the text" (8). In environmentally oriented literature the beginnings, at least, or a holistic view of life are present—a view of life that perceives the human and nonhuman worlds to be interdependent and interpenetrant, constantly in the process of mutual transformation, and that perceives the meaning of existence to extend far beyond ourselves.

Although many literary works are not environmentally oriented, any literary work can be read ecocritically. Coined in 1978, the term *ecocriticism* denotes the critical practice that investigates "interconnections between human culture and the material world, between the human and the nonhuman" (Rueckert quoted in Glotfelty 2, note 2). David Mazel has recently argued that although the term is recent, "proto-ecocriticism" has been central throughout American literary history, for an emphasis on nature in the New World enabled writers to define what was specifically American about our literature and therefore to create the fields of American literature and, later, American studies. In the past decades ecocriticism has gathered enormous momentum out of traditional academic disciplines' reluctance to respond to the environmental crisis; the extent to which it should espouse an activist political mandate is hotly debated. As befits the study of intermeshing systems, ecocriticism is also interdisciplinary, limited only by the knowledge of its practitioners. One of its biggest challenges—and a challenge met knowledgeably by both Linda Hogan and Rick Bass—has been to bridge the humanities and the natural sciences; to integrate scientific, spiritual, and artistic systems of meaning.

Rick Bass and Linda Hogan

In a recent essay Michael Branch argues that two of the dominant forms environmental literature takes are the jeremiad and the elegy.[1] The jeremiad, one of the "earliest and most enduring American literary forms," stemming from the Old Testament and depending "upon anger for its generic structure, lyrical force, and social valence" (232), originally served to chastise Puritan congregations for backsliding and to urge them to reform by threatening them with hellfire. Secularized, the form has been prominent throughout American literature. In the last few decades environmental jeremiads—such as Rachel Carson's *Silent Spring* (1962), Edward Abbey's *The Monkey Wrench Gang* (1975), and Terry Tempest William's *Refuge* (1991)—have replaced God's judgment with the "scientifically describable consequences of our ecological errors"; as Branch says, they "chastise our culture for its environmental sins; urge us to thoughtfully adjust our behavior . . . and, ultimately, attempt to reinvigorate our hope that it is not too late to avoid the unhappy consequences of the bleak, ecologically impoverished world which they so powerfully envision" (235).

The pastoral elegy, an equally ancient form, is "centrally concerned with honoring its subject . . . in the face of loss" (Branch 240); both structurally and thematically it enacts the trajectory of grieving. In environmental literature the elegiac impulse is practically ubiquitous, particularly if one includes works such as Peter Matthiessen's *The Tree Where Man Was Born* (1972), Edward Abbey's *Desert Solitaire* (1968), "Marshland Elegy" in Aldo Leopold's *A Sand County Almanac* (1949, 1993), and Cormac McCarthy's *The Crossing* (1994) that attempt to forestall despair by beginning the process of mourning while their subjects are still alive, still present, but doomed and vanishing. One great challenge for environmental writers, in fact, is not to write always too late, always elegiacally, when the forests and rivers are trashed and the body is cold on the table. Rick Bass has commented that "all literature is about loss" and the recognition of loss (in Slovic 133). This is likely true. But environmental literature runs a special risk, for confronting the extinction of species, the destruction of habitats, the threatened dissolution of the great globe itself can simply inculcate a sense of paralysis or despair among both writers and readers who recognize the losses to be unspeakable, overwhelming.

A third, immeasurably valuable impulse in environmental writing mitigates the darkness of the first two. This is the impulse to imagine and express what Wallace Stevens calls "the particulars of rapture" (392). The elegist situates plenitude in the past, mourns a diminished present, and desires to move through grief to consolation. The composer of a jeremiad situates virtue in the past, castigates the audience for a backsliding present, and seeks to realign it with virtue for the future. In contrast, the impulse to express the particulars of rapture is an impulse to be subsumed in the present and, as William Carlos Williams writes, "to refine, to clarify, to intensify that eternal moment in which we alone live" (178). Such a desire need not lead to escapist fictions or sentimental nostalgia; it can intermingle bittersweetly with anger and mourning, affirming the abiding presence of the sacred and envisioning human life in harmony with, learning from, and honoring the natural world. Narratives with this aim exemplify deep ecology. Counter to the Judeo-Christian tradition's anthropocentric belief that the universe was created for human benefit—or, in the greener version, for human stewardship—deep ecology maintains that the meaning of creation is *creation,* all of it; that humans are just one form of life with particular gifts and abilities; and that human fulfillment lies in participating in creation rather than in dominating and expropriating the resources offered by the nonhuman environment. The paradox, then, is that even while the world is emptying out and is sunk in destructiveness and greed, it is also complete and perfect at every moment. Two particularly eloquent manifestations of this vision are Rick Bass's novella *The Sky, the Stars, the Wilderness* and the central section of Linda Hogan's novel *Solar Storms,* to which I now turn.

Since moving to the Yaak Valley in Montana in 1987, Rick Bass has emerged as one of the preeminent U.S. environmental writers. The decision he made at the end of his first Montana book, *Winter* (1991), has held firm: "I won't be leaving this valley" (162). All too soon, however, he began to realize that indiscriminate logging threatened the Yaak, which is one of the last unprotected roadless wilderness areas in the United States, an immeasurably rich ecosystem, and an essential corridor for wildlife—among them caribou, wolves, and grizzlies—traveling between the United States and Canada. With *The Book of Yaak* (1996) he launched a campaign to protect the valley. Since then he has traveled indefatigably, speaking and reading on behalf of the Yaak; spearheaded a nationwide letter-writing campaign to the U.S. Forest Service, the president, and Congress; and continued to foreground the region's environmental crisis in books such as *Fiber, Colter, Brown Dog of the Yaak,* and his first novel, *Where the Sea Used to Be.* Bass writes, "There is no choice. If you love a piece of country, or an issue, and see that subject being harmed, you have to act" (*Brown Dog* 71). He realizes as well, however, that "too much activism can lead to a violence of the soul—a destruction of the inner peace that can otherwise make art, or a life lived, fruitful"—and bitterly laments the ways in which "the hours spent on art—fiction, say, or poetry, or creative nonfiction—or the hours spent reading great literature . . . are whittled down by each meeting, each phone call, each letter, each drive to town; each twist and clench of the furious and frantic heart" (*Brown Dog* 81).

Of the difference between his fiction and his nonfiction, Bass says that whereas with nonfiction "I'm asking for something," fiction "takes pressure off the reader to agree, and then the reader follows farther with the heart." The only problem is that "where I live, the issues are too urgent. For example, the grizzly might be gone in ten years" (Writers' workshop). In 1997, at the peak of his activist involvement, Bass published a book of stories, *The Sky, the Stars, the Wilderness,* one of which is a beautiful novella bearing the same name. Written years after his move to Montana, the story is nevertheless set in the Texas hill country of his childhood out of a longing for "a point where my language—memory—will intersect with the hill country's language: the scent of cedar, the feel of morning mist, the blood of deer, glint of moon, shimmering heat, crackle of ice, mountain lions, scorpions, centipedes, rattlesnakes, and cactus. The cool dark oaks and gold-leaved hickories along the creeks; the language of the hill country seems always to return to water" (Bass in Slovic 127). Setting *The Sky, the Stars, the Wilderness* in his childhood's Texas enables Bass temporarily to eschew the "franticness" of action; of all his works, perhaps it most fully creates a deep ecological vision of life and allows the reader to follow "with the heart."

Bass takes as his epigraph a passage from John Graves's *Self-Portrait with Birds,* in which Graves writes of his regret that he has not "known the land when it was whole and sprawling and rich and fresh," of his passion "to have viewed it entire, the soul and guts of what we had and gone forever now, except in books and such poignant remnants as small swift birds that journey to and from the distant Argentine and call at night in the sky" (Graves in *Sky* 90). True, Graves admits, "without any virtuous hindsight, I would likely have helped in the ravaging as did even most of those who loved [the North American continent] best" (90). *The Sky, the Stars, the Wilderness* creates a protagonist with a similar passion but also with virtuous hindsight; mythically resonant, it is the story of a modern woman whose "tradition-minded people" (Graves) and early losses have taught her what she passionately chooses to preserve.

All literature is about loss, Rick Bass has commented; all literature is therefore elegiac. Environmental writing mourns the loss of the natural world, but in this novella Bass creates an unlost wilderness and displaces loss onto the figure of the mother, who dies when the narrator, Anne, is still a girl and who chooses to be buried—or, as she says, "planted"—at home, where the east-west line and the north-south line cross on the family's 10,000-acre Prade Ranch. "Four hundred feet above the Nueces River," under "the largest oak we'd ever seen, an oak alive when Cabeza de Vaca staggered through" (91), the mother's grave becomes an axis tree, an omphalos centering creation; and the dead mother herself becomes a totemic figure, a force that sanctifies the land for those who loved her. The ranch extends in a charmed circle around her grave, and her presence—"gone but not absent" (105)—fills the family's daily lives with the numinousness of sacred time and space.

Like Wordsworth's Lucy, the mother becomes part of "rocks, and stones, and trees" (Wordsworth 115); as her daughter grows, the mother is "changing . . . she's growing, too. She turns with the earth. She is still learning things" (*Sky* 126). Anne's life story, then, becomes a ceremonial process of commemorating her mother by learning by heart all the "deep wild places" that are just blanks on the maps, going forward "into those wild places, where even Grandfather, on a horse, could not go" (93). She keeps the mother alive and keeps her family whole by worshiping at "the altar of specificity, not abstraction. The altar of the senses" (99). In doing so, she moves ever deeper into the intimate knowledge of place, the connectedness with place, that reveals "growth and death" to be not opposite states of being but "a simultaneous braiding and unraveling" (94). "We'd run until Mother was alive," Anne writes, remembering her nighttime adventures with her little brother Omar. "It was like blowing air on a fire, bringing coals to flame. We'd run until we ignited, until we blossomed, in her presence" (104). By the time Anne is a teenager, she realizes that she has "become a part of the land, every bit as much a part of it as sparrow eggs or thrasher nest, garter snake or oak tree, and that the rest of my life, or anyone's life, would be a gradual learning process, a journey toward fitting into one's home, for those of us lucky enough to still recognize what is home . . . that which we are a part of, rather than estranged from" (114).

Older, she becomes an ornithologist, a mapper, studying sciences in college and "crawling through the cedars" on the ranch, "intent upon knowing every square foot of this place" (124). Like Bass, she comes to understand science as "at best only the peripheral trappings to . . . mystery—a ragged barbed-wire fence through which mystery travels, back and forth, unencumbered by anything so frail as man's knowledge" (123). Over time, her choice to remain so close to the natural world—studying its births, lives, and deaths—issues in a deep ecological vision. "We try and map the boundaries, and to string fence," she says, "we try to set up a border between life and death, between man and nature, and complicity versus innocence. But the truth is, there is no complicity, there is no innocence; and there is no death, there is only life. We're all interrelated: we're all one organism—hawk and rabbit, daughter and mother" (120).

The Sky, the Stars, the Wilderness offers few of the inducements we generally expect from contemporary fiction: few psychological crises, little character conflict, scant drama. Events do occur: Anne's father, a county agent, fights the local Predator Club that mindlessly kills coyotes and endangered eagles; Anne's father wages war for years against a character down in San Antonio known as the Catfish Man, who is "stealing water" from Real County by striking into an artesian well that drains the Edwards Aquifer (132). One learns a fair amount about the Edwards Aquifer, the fault line through Texas called the Balcones Escarpment, and the overly great water usage in Austin and San Antonio—built along the Balcones Escarpment—that drains the hill country's water. The surviving family members go about their daily affairs, and Anne eventually has lovers. The novella's events do not foreground human affairs so much as ecological interconnections between human and nonhuman realms; Bass rewrites plot to incorporate the values of deep ecology. The novella constantly calls into question the "artificial systems wherein we are mighty predators, or mighty *thinkers*, or sagacious, benevolent rulers of the universe—allies with God, even"—for Anne has spent her life, as has her family before her, "outside of those artificial systems" (124; original emphasis). She has "spent [her] life in the brush—and [has] seen what it is we do best, and that is to love and honor one another: to love family, and to love friends, and to love the short days" (124). Therefore, convinced that humans are "only peripheral trappings . . . on the outside of the mystery" (124) and witnessing how the lands outside Prade Ranch change and the species—unprotected—vanish, she decides to stay on the ranch until, finally, "only Mother and I remain" (126). She lives alone, childless, like a nun in her devotion to the "grace" of place (114), watching and listening as "the land, the place—*life* begins to summon its due," content to be "square in the middle of the metamorphosis, constantly living and dying" (189; original emphasis).

"The price of life; the price of inclusion in life! *There are no boundaries*," Anne rhapsodizes at one point in *The Sky, the Stars, the Wilderness* (121; original emphasis). Ironically, however, the only things that enable her to attain this vision are boundaries, for only private property protects this "island of wildness" (125). Ten thousand acres may not be big for Texas, but for most of the world it is a lot of land—and the Prades came by it through a fraught political history, as "homesteading land given to them by the territory of Texas, which had won it from Mexico in the War for Independence—the Mexicans having been awarded it by Spain, who had (with a few cursory words and pencil strokes on a map far away) claimed it from the Indians" (93). *The Sky, the Stars, the Wilderness* is unconcerned with the dark side of this history. Linda Hogan, a Chickasaw author and a major U.S. writer, offers a very different picture in her novel *Solar Storms*. She agrees with Bass that, in his words, modern America has "traded away our mysticism for a few ears of corn, for a crop of maize, or chickens, or cows, or trinkets" (154) and that without "*ceremony* . . . we've lost everything, and are only wandering in the dark, like chickens or lambs waiting for eagles" (162; original emphasis). In fact, some lines from Bass's novella almost uncannily offer a gloss on the central action of Hogan's novel: "We must participate in this world that has birthed us. We must not sit around in rawhide rocking chairs with our heads sunk in grief, while the waters trickle past. We must join the waters" (162). But for Angel, the Native American protagonist of Hogan's novel, and for her aged female relatives who have lost virtually everything *but* their "mysticism," the path to those waters is marked with suffering and dispossession far beyond anything Bass's narrator ever imagines.

A highly acclaimed novelist, poet, and essayist; an expert in wildlife rehabilitation; for many years an English professor at the University of Colorado, Linda Hogan is also a leading voice in the American struggle for environmental justice and writes powerfully of the ways in which environmental destruction also targets minorities. She is descended from people forced out of their homeland along the Trail of Tears and then robbed of their oil-rich land in Oklahoma. She grew up in poverty, the "depressed, neglected" daughter of an alcoholic Marine sergeant, plagued by "silences of both family and history" (*Woman* 43, 56). Surviving the suffering of her "lost years" (53), she discovered adult education and the courage to affirm and explore her heritage. Writing, she says, saved her. But Hogan's recently published memoir, *The Woman Who Watches Over the World*, provides an autobiographical dimension for part of the tragedy behind *Solar Storms* in the story of her adopted daughters. "The story of my daughters began a hundred years ago" (*Woman* 78), she writes, in the history of "a shattered world," the "near obliteration of a people" (77). Marie, the older daughter, whom Hogan adopted at age six,

> was a girl violated and tortured. . . . She had been abused, even as an infant, burned by cigarettes and hot wires, and raped. She was a girl who was once dropped off by her mother and her mother's boyfriend on a dark country road in their attempt to lose her. Somehow she survived. . . . But she never found her way back to herself as a child. . . . She is yet, over twenty years later, still a tangle of threads and war-torn American history that other Americans like to forget. Her story is not yet fully deciphered. (*Woman* 76–77)

Angel's mother, Hannah Wing, obviously modeled on Marie, is a girl so damaged by personal and tribal history that she becomes "a skin that others wore" (77). She is "*the house,*" "*the meeting place,*" "*her life going backward to where time and history and genocide gather and move like a cloud above the spilled oceans of blood*" (*Solar Storms* 101; original emphasis). Unable to love, herself the daughter of an abusive mother, Hannah neglects and tortures her child; and although in the novel's back story female relatives try to rescue the baby Angel, when *Solar Storms* begins Angel has spent years as a foster child—shunted around the system, repeatedly getting in trouble and running away. "My beginning was Hannah's beginning," she says,

> one of broken lives, gone animals, trees felled and kindled. Our beginnings were intricately bound up in the history of the land. I already knew that in the nooks of America, the crannies of marble buildings, my story unfolded. This, I suppose, was the true house of my mother. The real place from which I originated was in the offices of social workers. . . . But it went even farther back than that, to houses of law with their unkept treaties, to the broken connections of people to the world and its many gods. (96)

Her return to her community of female relatives in Adam's Rib, a Cree-Anishinaabe village in northern Minnesota, marks Angel's admission that she has come to the end of her life in "one America" (26). Summoned by her great-grandmother Agnes Iron, whom she has finally located in a court record and who has mailed her a pile of worn one-dollar bills, she approaches her new life full of "fear, fear of everything" and an "anger I inhabited permanently," bearing only the flotsam of loss—"the makeup I used, along with my hair, to hide my [scarred] face, and a picture of an unknown baby, a picture I'd found in a one-dollar photo machine at Woolworth's," for "there were no snapshots of me, nothing to say I'd been born, had kin, been loved" (26–27). No longer will she run from her inheritance. Instead, she tells us, "I would try to salvage what I could find inside me. As young as I was, I felt I had already worn out all the possibilities in my life" (27). For much of the novel Angel longs for her mother, but unlike Anne in Bass's *The Sky, the Stars, the Wilderness,* she must finally admit that her mother is truly lost. When she locates Hannah at last, Hannah is knife wounded, dying, and longing to die—"a woman in the grip of ice," as Angel's great-great-grandmother Dora-Rouge describes her. "It held her in its blue fingers. It froze her heart" (247). Even more painful, Angel discovers not only that Hannah tried to kill her when she was born but also that she caused her terrible scarring. "Your face," a woman tells her, "like a dog, she bit your face" (247). But although Hannah cannot be reclaimed, although there can never be "an unbroken line between [Angel] and the past" (77), she discovers nonetheless that she has many "grandmothers"—Dora-Rouge, Agnes, Bush—women who grieved for Hannah and for her and who now begin to instruct her in tribal ways.

The central action of *Solar Storms,* which intersects with historical events from the 1970s, recounts the four women's canoe journey northward to find Angel's mother, to take Dora-Rouge back to her childhood village to die, and to join the protests opposing a massive James Bay dam project that is destroying tribal villages and caribou migration routes. When the women arrive at Dora-Rouge's ancestral land of the Fat-Eaters, now taken over by "plans for dams and drowned rivers" (224), they find a culture and a people in their death throes:

> The young children drank alcohol and sniffed glue and paint. They staggered about and lay down on the streets. Some of them had children of their own, infants who were left untouched, untended by their child-parents. Sometimes they were given beer when they cried. It was the only medicine left for all that pain. Even the healing plants had been destroyed. Those without alcohol were even worse off, and the people wept without end, and tried to cut and burn their own bodies. . . . The devastation and ruin that had fallen over the land fell over the people, too. Most were too broken to fight the building of the dams, the moving of the water, and that perhaps had been the intention all along. (226)

The devastation that occurs in the James Bay area is simply the most recent chapter in a history of violence and betrayal that, as Hogan writes, has made of Native Americans "fragments and pieces left behind by fur traders, soldiers, priests, and schools" (77) and that is all too familiar in this era of global capitalism. As Angel realizes, those who protest are the ones "who could still believe they might survive as a people" (226). And some do protest: organizers arrive from outside and develop from within the community, petitions circulate, crowds swell, protest lines face off against the bulldozers. But the opposition lacks both an ecological and a sacramental vision; consequently, "our words were powerless beside their figures, their measurements, and ledgers. For the builders it was easy and clear-cut. They saw [the land] only on the flat, two-dimensional world of paper." Therefore the protests are doomed. Although precious to the heart and spirit, community building, consciousness raising, and personal redemption such as Angel finds with her people have little power against the forces of "officials, governments, and business," for which the vision of life held by the protesters—the "sacred treaties held by humans and animals," the "regard for the land that sustained people from the beginning of time" (279)—has no credence or authority.

"Mirrors cost us our lives" (69), Angel's surrogate mother, Bush, tells her. The statement has enormous resonance for *Solar Storms*: it not only comments on Angel's anxieties about her scarred face and overall appearance and on the damaging effects of racist and ethnic bigotry on nonwhite Americans but also seems to reject the whole psychoanalytic—specifically Lacanian—model of identity in which, mirrored, the child learns of, and learns to conceive of itself in terms of, its separation from the mother in favor of a phenomenological model of self-creation. Mirrors reflect one's small, imperfect sameness to oneself; they foster one's narcissistic obsession with image and with the inability ever to close the gap between self and self-and-other. Consequently, they create a closed circle of self-concern. Although bereft of her mother, at Adam's Rib Angel learns to see from the center of her being—without mirrors—and discovers that she is firmly at home in what the poet Robinson Jeffers calls "the mother" (9): the "faces and lovings of gods," the "dense soup of love, creation all around us" (Jeffers 81). As the novel progresses she is increasingly conjured by a different kind of mirroring, a phenomenological knowing of oneself through others' responses: "Our lives, the old people say, are witnessed by the birds, by dragonflies, by trees and spiders. We are seen, our measure taken, not only by the animals and spiders but even by the alive galaxy in deep space" (80). This knowing of oneself knows the universe itself to be the ground of being and the other—not just the self—to be real and important; it is a sacramental source of the environmental imagination.

A long, stern grief pervades *Solar Storms*. Before, after, and all around the canoe journey the four women take throng the losses and wrongdoings that give rise in environmental writing to elegy and jeremiad. The journey itself is far more tenuous and fleeting than the sheltered space of Rick Bass's Prade Ranch. Still, although it is framed by struggle and suffering, by "murder of the soul" (226) and hunger, shame, and violence, it nevertheless opens out into the particulars of rapture. On the lakes and rivers with her grandmothers, Angel enters the true creation state, a "gap in time . . . a place between worlds" (177) that is not on any written mappings. She becomes a plant dreamer, able to find medicines by dreaming the "pathways" of the world's "own invention" (170). She learns "the languages of land, water, animal" and even the "harder languages" of her human companions (193). She learns trust, skill, surrender, and the beauty and power of her grandmothers, whose path on the earth is rich but whose possessions are not material. She gains a sense of the sacred too vast and deep to articulate; if elegy and jeremiad can be spoken, rapture overflows and at the last is silent.

I'll close with Angel's haunting evocation of the plenteous, vanishing world and of what is possible for humans within it. "I was under the spell of wilderness," she tells us,

> close to what no one had ever been able to call by name. Everything merged and united. There were no sharp distinctions left between darkness and light. Water and air became the same thing, as did water and land in the marshy broth of creation. Inside the clear water we passed over, rocks looked only a few inches away. Birds swam across lakes. It was all one thing. The canoes were our bodies, our skin. We passed through green leaves, wild rice, and rushes. In small lakes, dense with lily pads, tiny frogs leaped from leaves into the water as we passed.
>
> Sometimes I felt there were eyes around us, peering through trees and fog. Maybe it was the eyes of land and creatures regarding us, taking our measure.

And listening to the night, I knew there was another horizon, beyond the one we could see. And all of it was storied land, land where deities walked, where people traveled, desiring to be one with infinite space. (177)

Angel ends this passage with an image that reminds me of the conquistadors first sighting the green continent. "We were full and powerful," she tells us, "wearing the face of the world, floating in silence" (177). Dangerously close to the language of imperialist self-aggrandizement, this image of selves as full and powerful is yet completely different, for floating in silence these travelers are at peace with, at home in, existence. And wearing the face of the world, how could they wish to harm it, for where does the human self stop, the nonhuman other begin? In this space of rapture the land is full and good; it has not been lost, it does not need to be changed. Storied earth is not threatened by storied lives. Rather, both intermesh, intertwine, in the waters of infinite space.

Acknowledgment

My deep thanks to my daughter, Jessica Fisher, and my husband, Peter Wirth, for their responses to and suggestions for this chapter.

Note

1. A reviewer of this chapter points out that these are also "favored rhetorical modes in narratives about American Indians, particularly the elegiac lament of the vanishing Indian that Renato Rosaldo has termed 'imperialist nostalgia.'" See Renato Rosaldo, *Culture and Truth: The Remaking of Social Analysis* (Boston: Beacon, 1989).

Works Cited

Bass, Rick. *Brown Dog of the Yaak: Essays on Art and Activism.* Credo Series. Ed. Scott Slovic. Minneapolis: Milkweed Editions, 1999.

———. "On Willow Creek." *Los Angeles Times Magazine* (28 November 1993).

———. *The Sky, the Stars, the Wilderness.* Boston: Houghton Mifflin, 1997.

———. *Winter (Notes from Montana).* Boston: Houghton Mifflin, 1991.

———. Writers' workshop, Lafayette County Public Library, Oxford, Mississippi, 9 June 2001.

Bourdieu, Pierre. "For a Scholarship with Commitment." Trans. Loïc Wacquant. *Profession 2000* (2000): 40–45.

Branch, Michael P. "Jeremiad, Elegy, and the Yaak: Rick Bass and the Aesthetics of Anger and Grief." In *The Literary Art and Activism of Rick Bass.* Ed. O. Alan Weltzien. Salt Lake City: University of Utah Press, 2002. 223–248.

Buell, Lawrence. "The Ecocritical Insurgency." *New Literary History* 30, no. 3 (Summer 1999): 699–713.

———. *The Environmental Imagination: Thoreau, Nature Writing, and the Formation of American Culture.* Cambridge: Harvard University Press, 1995.

Glotfelty, Cheryll. "Introduction." In *The Ecocriticism Reader.* Ed. Glotfelty and Harold Fromm. Athens: University of Georgia Press, 1996. xv–xxxviii.

Hegel, Georg Wilhelm Friedrich. *The Phenomenology of the Spirit.* Oxford: Clarendon, 1977.

Hogan, Linda. *Solar Storms.* New York: Scribner, 1995.

———. *The Woman Who Watches Over the World: A Native Memoir.* New York: W. W. Norton, 2001.

Jeffers, Robinson. *Selected Poems.* New York: Random House, 1965.

Keats, John. "Ode to a Nightingale." In *The Complete Poetry and Selected Prose of Keats.* Intro. Harold E. Briggs. New York: Modern Library, 1951. 205–207.

Mazel, David, ed. "Introduction." In *A Century of Early Ecocriticism.* Athens: University of Georgia Press, 2001. 1–20.

McKibben, Bill. "Editorial." *Washington Post* (22 April 2001): BW01.

Phillips, Dana. "Ecocriticism, Literary Theory, and the Truth of Ecology." *New Literary History* 30, no. 3 (Summer 1999): 577–602.

Slovic, Scott, ed. "Rick Bass: A Portrait." In Rick Bass, *Brown Dog of the Yaak: Essays on Art and Activism.* Minneapolis: Milkweed Editions, 1999. 123–139.

Stevens, Wallace. "Notes Toward a Supreme Fiction." In *The Collected Poems of Wallace Stevens.* New York: Alfred A. Knopf, 1965. 380–408.

Williams, William Carlos. "Spring and All." In *The Collected Poems of William Carlos Williams. Volume I: 1909–1939.* Ed. A. Walton Litz and Christopher MacGowan. New York: New Directions, 1986. 175–236.

Wordsworth, William. "A Slumber Did My Spirit Seal." In *Selected Poems and Prefaces.* Ed. Jack Stillinger. Boston: Houghton Mifflin, 1965. 115.

LINDA HOGAN'S "GEOGRAPHY OF THE SPIRIT"

Division and Transcendence in Selected Texts

BENAY BLEND

"WE NEED NEW STORIES, NEW TERMS AND CONDITIONS THAT ARE RELEVANT to the love of land," writes poet Linda Hogan, "a new narrative that would imagine another way to learn the infinite movement and work in this world" (*Dwellings* 94). For Hogan, the word is a sacred object, part of an oral tradition that links past culture with the present and carries it into future generations. This chapter explores the multidimensional nature of Hogan's writing, the ways she collapses chronological distinctions and mediates between her own and Anglo views. As a participant in two cultural traditions, Hogan draws from each to create new patterns of individual and communal identity. In *West of the Border: The Multicultural Literature of the Western American Frontiers,* Noreen Groover Lape describes the American frontier as a "liminal or transitional" space that is often internal, especially in the case of writers (6). Hogan is such a border person. By navigating social, political, and identity frontiers, she mediates across cultures in her writing.

Although the values of her tribe are transmitted, she says, through the "power of our talking, our words," Hogan also uses story and place to communicate "something else beyond our knowing" (*Woman* 16). In her work, then, culture means the same thing as story, knowledge that transcends words and binds the community together. It also brings to mind the "storied land" (*Solar Storms* 177), and land is the language of home. "To walk on this earth is to walk on a living past," Hogan writes, "on the open pages of history and geology" (*Dwellings* 79).

In this vein Hogan refers to a "geography of the human spirit" (*Dwellings* 40), as evidenced in the title of this chapter. In *Mixed-Blood Messages*, Louis Owens describes the term *Indian* as a "deeply contested space" where "authenticity" (13) depends upon the telling of indigenous perspectives and reappropriating out of those viewpoints another version of history.

Aware that those who control the land have also controlled its story, Hogan's work centers on imaginative tellings of these places (both physical and mental) of cultural contact. Her inspiration arises from this concern—a "journey home" (*Red Clay* 1), she says, that attempts to define the question of her mixed heritage in ways imposed not from the outside but from within. In *Solar Storms*, for example, Hogan uses oral tradition and contemporary events to chart the course of particular characters who are defining themselves within an older and larger history. Recalling Owens's distinction between notions of territory (unoccupied space) and frontier (place of contact), Hogan writes here about a place where differing accounts of history come into contact.

Shifting and reshifting her story's perspectives, she turns the tables of historical experience, exposes stereotypes, and creates a new literature out of border zones. Serving as a mediator between cultures shapes her self-perception. "Home is in blood" (*Red Clay* 1), she writes, and "blood / is a map of the road between us" ("Two Lives" 248). A map that resists the falsely rigid bounds of outwardly imposed culture, it integrates all fragments of her being into what she depicts as whole.

This reconstruction and restoration of identity—dependent upon a rediscovered sense of place in relation to the community and the land—are at the center of *The Book of Medicines, Solar Storms, The Woman Who Watches Over the World,* and *Dwellings,* all texts included in this chapter. In these works Hogan acknowledges her invisibility within the dominant society; as her protagonist expresses in *Solar Storms,* "To the white men who were new here, we were people who had no history, who lived surrounded by what they saw as nothingness" (280). According to Katerie Damm, a mixed-blood poet from Toronto, "'[W]ho we are' has been constructed and defined by others to the extent that at times we too no longer know who we are" (11). To bring about "healing and restoration" of tribal peoples' place within and connection to the universe, Hogan suggests that ceremonies must be revitalized and maintained to mend a "broken connection" (*Dwellings* 40) among tribal peoples, animals, and the land. Telling an "Indian story, calling the lies out of history" (*Woman* 331), Hogan replaces misconceptions with what she considers truth. In her own life and work, the continuance and vitality of ceremony and tradition constitute one way she returns to a "place of balance; [her] place in the community of all things" (*Dwellings* 40). Tribal stories, legends, myths, and songs, then, are at the core of her texts. "Memory," she writes, "is . . . a path toward something, a source" (*Woman* 62). Memory provides a frame of reference for dealing with contemporary problems by looking to the past, Hogan writes. It is also "a source that carries us into the future" *(Woman* 62), she adds, thereby serving as a means for collapsing time.

As the creation of new ideas from older worldviews proceeds, the writer acts out her role as a mediator-initiator. In such areas Hogan's development as a writer meshes tightly with her personal development. By defining and exploring social and cultural problems in this border area, Hogan uses her writing to ensure her own survival and that of her people. This process of active transformation, her self within the larger framework of community, negates the stereotype of Native women as passive victims of oppression. For Hogan, as for many indigenous writers, the process of writing becomes an act of resistance—a way, she discloses, of making herself visible; "you can't take a man's words," she maintains, privileging the sanctity of language. "They are his even as the land / is taken away / where another man / builds his house" (*Red Clay* 32).

Hogan's passage from object of discourse to speaking subject comprises several issues this chapter covers: (1) the difficulty of her journey toward achieving a sense of self-identity and self-esteem, complicated by being caught between two cultures; (2) the coming to terms with her mixed-blood status and viewing it as a positive rather than a negative condition; (3) the primacy of family ties and unity with nature, both seen by Hogan as inherent in self-healing; (4) and finally, appropriating both the language and the literary forms of the colonizer as a means, Hogan says, to "remake the world" (*Woman* 101) with words. Thus the act of writing—for Hogan as for others—is a political act, stemming from her "deepest wanting of justice and survival"; through the construction of her text, Hogan envisions that the "world might be changed by the word and the telling" (Hogan in Harjo 331) of her stories. To be free herself, Hogan also has to "offer up" her "pain and grief and sorrow," for she realizes that "denial and repression" are the "greatest hindrances" ("Two Lives" 241) to growth. To write, Hogan concludes, not only "put[s her] life in order" ("Two Lives" 241), it also gives voice to those who do not have agency to speak—for the job of storytellers, she adds, is to open our eyes, to "witness, and [to] keep accounts" ("Two Lives" 241). Having "compassion," in her words, for the "many ways [she has] been lost by an American education" (*Woman* 108), Hogan concedes that to claim visibility and authenticity in the world, she must conform to a socially imposed identity. Nevertheless, despite her long history of personal and tribal dislocation, she has learned to embrace her multiple identities and places of origin. In this way she achieves a healing that permits her to survive.

For Native Americans, as Louis Owens notes, self-identity is a "deeply contested space" (lvi). In it legitimacy must arise from defying essentialist interpretations of indigenous peoples. Thus Hogan's work involves remembering geographic, cultural, and discursive spaces, or in her view, the map that exists inside tribal thoughts and traditional knowledge. In *Solar Storms,* for example, Hogan's protagonist, Angel, who Hogan says was modeled on herself, rejects an essentialized identity imposed by others' definition of "Indian." By claiming the power to reimagine herself within a fluid, always shifting space, Angel finds herself "becom[ing] full, or . . . growing towards it," thus moving away from a colonized conception of containment toward a place where "everything start[s] to change" and she is "no longer empty space" (106). Here she transcends geographic location, which, according to Owens, is the very essence of so-called Indian territory. Such a frontier, Owens says, inverts the "closed" logic of the historian Frederick Jackson Turner (27). Accordingly, Angel notes that "change was the one thing not accounted for" (*Solar Storms* 123) by the makers of maps, those who preferred boundaries marked and defined by the Euro-American imagination. If closed frontiers enable the power of the dominant group, as Owens claims, then open frontiers—such as Hogan's—are murky, discordant, subversive, and enduring. Because "that land refused to be shaped by the makers of maps" (123), Hogan's character notes, it exerts its own will, much like Native people who resist colonization by refusing to be contained, clearly mapped, or controlled by the dominant culture.

As a Native American who publishes for a wider audience, Hogan inhabits a place "between," a space she locates "at the very root" of her existence (*Woman* 34). She stresses that this blended artistic world reflects her lived experience, having grown up intermeshed with two cultures and perspectives. Possessing more than one set of hands ("In [her] left pocket a Chickasaw hand" and in her "right pocket / a white hand" [*Seeing* 4]), Hogan views her mixed ancestry as an asset, for it allows her to speak from multiple perspectives. Such "mediational" texts, according to James Ruppert, "harmonize the contradictions, creating unity and legitimating both spheres of discourse" (17). For Hogan, integrating both traditions in her texts meshes with her coming to terms with her own identity.

As Hogan aspires to translate the oral into the written and Native American perspectives into terms recognizable to Western readers, she tacks between two cultural frameworks. For her, being mixed-blood necessarily affects her writing, not simply how she writes but that she chooses to do so at all. Although

Hogan develops a compelling critique of Euro-American society, she also insists on using the tools of that community to further her own goals. Like the author's mixed identity, her writings are literary hybrids, works drawn from various cultural traditions. As the frontier she describes is a zone of cultural contact, so her literature is a confluence that encourages deep cross-cultural questions. For example, aware that autobiography is not a traditional Native American form, Hogan appropriates it to reach a broader audience and to further the collective identity of her tribe. Acknowledging that "self-telling" is "not common for Native women," she claims "young people on reservations want to know how [she] survived her life" (*Woman* 14). By telling from an insider's point of view, she confronts long-standing misconceptions of history with the realities of her life story; "I think of my work as part of the history of our tribe," writes Hogan, "and as part of the history of colonization everywhere" ("Two Lives" 231). In so doing Hogan probes, blurs, and displaces stereotyping of Native women of mixed ancestry and replaces rigid definitions by asserting her own space.

This chapter addresses the question, What is it to be a Native American woman writer in America, a mixture of old traditions but also an individual who translates those ideas to her own and other cultures? Hogan's work reflects her search for her true identity. It traces her quest for self-acceptance as a woman of Chickasaw-white pioneer ancestry. This journey, and the writing of it, have to include both sides of her background; "about these hands, I'd like to say / I am a tree, grafted branches, bearing two kinds of fruit" (*Seeing* 4). But she knows that as a mixed blood she will never be allowed to forget her position as an outsider, an alien living in mainstream America; "it's not that way. The truth is / we are crowded together / and knock against each other at night" (*Seeing* 4). Standing midstream, Hogan feels her dual perspective can bridge the gap between indigenous and white societies. Yet she asserts that her life has "never fully existed in the other, mainstream America" (*Woman* 2), one she feels will never understand Native values: "girl, I say, / it is dangerous to be a woman of two countries," not belonging in either (*Seeing* 5).

At such times Hogan's stance assumes difference over commonality, reflecting the viewpoint of Craig Womack, who rejects what he calls an "assimilationist ideology," which is one that denies, he claims, an "uncorrupted" (5) Indian actuality not influenced by European contact. Keenly aware of her positioning as a writer of mixed descent, however, Hogan more often strives to ride the boundaries of both cultures, thus tearing down the walls she sees as deleterious to her culture. And so the best she can ask for, perhaps, is "amnesty" (*Seeing* 4) to write stories that witness her own and tribal history. Although she is the "child of humans, / who has witnessed their destruction inside [her]self," words are proof, she says, that "there is healing" (*Book of Medicines* 63) through writing her life back into a permeable space that is self-defined. By harmonizing all aspects of her identity and resisting the falsely rigid bounds of the larger culture, Hogan assimilates the fragments of her existence—the stories, the cultures—and becomes an integrated human being.

A central theme of Hogan's work is exploration of cultural hybridity, or, in Gloria Anzaldúa's terms, "the borderlands," a literal and figurative terrain that by its very nature encourages the integration of ancient and modern cultural beliefs. According to Owens, there are differences that inform contemporary Native American writing, as each author speaks from individual experience. But there are also common bonds, among them the "informing role of the past within the present" (22)—a role that for Hogan signifies as a "high form of truth" (*Dwellings* 51). Through cultural stories, she explains, tribal people return to the creation, a place of "crossed beginnings" (*Book of Medicines* 28) where the natural world finds its voice. In this way Hogan weaves one generation into the fabric of life of the next, "circ[ling] around and com[ing] back to look at . . . human myths and stories" (*Dwellings* 93) in a continuous cyclic sense of time.

By ancestral connections Hogan means she never looks upon the land without seeing it as storied. Marked with "ancestors in and around her / the mothers of trees and deer and harvests" ("Two Lives" 246), natural surroundings in Hogan's writing refuse to be contained as territory. Instead, "frontier space" (Owens 26), in the sense that Owens uses it to define a border region characterized by "self-imaginings, continual fluidity, and rebirth" (28), provides a context for literature that rides both sides of the border. "Our stories and myths remain," Hogan maintains, "because skin isn't where a person ends. We live not only inside a body but within a story as well, and our story resides in the land" (*Woman* 204). Opening the borders between the material world and the spiritual, Hogan pursues a reality found beneath the surfaces of places where she lives and travels, thereby focusing on the present but in a way that allows her tribal past to show through.

In *Borderlands/La Frontera,* Gloria Anzaldúa's theory of the New Mestiza provides a paradigm for the way Hogan also defines her narrative form as negotiation between two cultures. A borderland between past and present and between genders as well as genres offers Hogan a creative space in which she seeks, she says, "understanding of the two views of the world, one as seen by native peoples and the other as seen by those who are new and young on this continent" (*Dwellings* 11). Although boundary crossing is sometimes fraught with dangers, Owens notes that Native American narratives often highlight what he calls a "frontier," a "shimmering always changing zone of multifaceted contact within which every utterance is challenged and interrogated, and referents [are] put into question" (2). An unstable place where, in Hogan's words, "boundaries are all lies," this frontier contrasts Native views to those who re-

Linda Hogan's "Geography of the Spirit"

quire "walls," Hogan says, "to keep the rich and poor apart / . . . ris[ing] up like teeth out of the land / snapping" (*Seeing* 67). Borderlands, then, in her terms, become an "other" space; in contrast to rigid territory, it is infinitely permeable from both sides.

This imagery of borders, constantly crossed and continuously present, implies an effort to affirm an essential but universal unity. "My human history within a larger one" (*Woman* 59), she calls it, that is specifically tribal and finds its way into other women's writing. "The real alchemy of our being here is the finest of transformations," she maintains, revealing her sense of a constantly transforming universe; "we do not know it," she continues, "except to say that we are atoms that use other patterns and arrangements of form" (*Dwellings* 95). Just as Hogan's "I" is framed through a process of critiquing and celebrating her tribal history, so her work highlights the necessity of community in the formation of mixed-blood identity, no matter how difficult her search for community might be. Personal history, Hogan believes, relates not only to tribal stories but to "all [her] relations" (*Dwellings* 40)—histories of "land, time and space, water and exploitation" (*Woman* 49), everything around her, including both the animate and inanimate worlds. Speaking for but, more important, also with all creatures, Hogan longs to cross an "illegal border," she says, so she can communicate in the "black alphabet" of a horse. An animal that has also been "owned and owned again" (*Seeing* 39), it signifies here a common bond across species borders with another who has also known oppression. Self-in-relation, then, rather than the bildungsroman model of self-in-isolation that characterizes Western writing, drives Hogan's work. As a mixed-blood woman, she lacks a grounding in a particular place and time: "From my family I have learned the secrets of never having a home" (*Red Clay* 21). What centers her are words that are her own, language that stems from a fusion of individual identity with that of the larger natural world and tribal consciousness.

According to Hogan, her life has never been part of the "other, mainstream America" but rather is part of that world that "reveres the land, that is attached to where we dwell" (*Woman* 14). "I've concluded over the years that the two ways, Native and European, are almost impossible to intertwine," she explains, "that they are parallel worlds taking place at the same time, bridges only sometimes made, allowing for a meeting place of lives" (27). At such times her alienation from the dominant culture runs deep; "I only know that the heart and mind are created by culture," she confides, and as one who has survived oppression, Hogan finds it difficult to "explain to those who don't know it" (27)— especially when those others are responsible for her repression.

More optimistically, Hogan feels at other times that a consciousness of the value of life is inherent in all people. Moreover, her warning that Indian people must not be the only caretakers of the land implies a willingness to cross borders to ensure healing of the earth and perhaps its people, too. To this end, Hogan strives in her texts to reconcile her existence between two worlds so her words can reach out to those she believes want healing. In this way, she claims, "bridges" are made at least sometimes, allowing for a "meeting place" (*Woman* 27) between worlds.

Her texts thus illustrate the plurality of spaces in which Native American women writers have learned successfully to negotiate and dwell, spaces that have allowed them a relationship to the land that continues tradition as well as introduces change. As in other classic works describing the journey home, Hogan achieves a sense of identity by returning to Oklahoma, the homeland of her heart. As Owens notes, for those who are mixed bloods, the "hybridized, polyglot, transcultural" (27) home is often an internal one. Echoing this idea, Hogan writes that "home is in blood," and she is still on the "journey of calling [her]self home" (*Red Clay* 1) even after returning from Oklahoma. Speaking of her people, Hogan concedes that "they are always leaving" (31), for she knows her sense of multiple identities arises from displacements in her history and family background. Being of Chickasaw-Anglo ancestry, however, Hogan also maintains that out of her return came "a deep knowing and telling how [she] was formed of these two powers called ancestors and clay" (1). Here she defines landscape as encompassing both the interior and exterior worlds; both are crucial to her self-understanding and identity.

Crossing borders, bridging borders, or simply recognizing the limits of borders is integral to Hogan's work. She has experienced all the negative aspects of being a contemporary mixed-blood woman. As a light-skinned person, Hogan says, she is viewed as a "person of betweens . . . a person of divided identities" ("Two Lives" 243). Aware that her skin color might gain her privilege, Hogan knows from watching others how exclusion works in a racist culture, especially if one's skin is darker than that of others. In her writing, dispossession encompasses both the personal and the tribal, the linguistic and the aesthetic. "As a young woman I was lost" (*Dwellings* 54), writes Hogan, addicted as she was to alcohol and other forms of self-destruction. Hogan links these patterns of internal violence to cultural violence and domination. Both have resulted in oppression of and poor self-image for Native peoples, which in turn have led to estrangement from self and community. Her work describes this transformation in angry terms but also in ways that relate repression to the natural world, suggesting that repression of Native voices—especially those of women—is inherently associated with destruction of the earth. "Human colonizing and conquering others have a propensity for this," explains Hogan, "for burning behind them what they cannot possess or control, as if their conflicts are not with themselves and their own way of being, but with the land itself" (44). Although the land has been colonized, it eventually prevails, for a strong sense of connectedness with landscape characterizes Hogan's writing—becoming the "answer," she concludes, to her "broken heart" (*Woman* 54).

Hogan's mixed-blood status has clearly been a burden, yet she has survived because of her relationship to the land, transcending the division between mind and body, between humans and nature, inherent in Western thinking. She has also arrived at a point where she finds strength by negotiating conflicting ambiguities and contradictions. Living always in-between, she comes to see that exclusion might work to her advantage by allowing her "a place created by words" (*Woman* 58), a space in which she forges new alignments across various restrictive borders of race, class, and gender. Looking to the words of Audre Lorde, "The Master's tools will not dismantle his house" (quoted in "Two Lives" 244), Hogan asserts that her own work has focused on "new tools, the dismantling, the rebuilding." Writing is her "primary crowbar," she concludes, a way of creating a space outside of but not "depowered" by mainstream culture (244). Hogan's sentiment is echoed by Paula Gunn Allen, who writes, "having never lived in the master's house, we can all the more enthusiastically build a far more suitable dwelling of our own" (*Off the Reservation* 175). Hogan's shame from being rejected by both cultures initially turned into self-hatred and reached serious, destructive proportions in adulthood. Yet her story, albeit woven with alcoholism and suffering, is one of survival and subsequent viewing of liminality as consistent with a pragmatic utopian vision.

In *Solar Storms,* Hogan's novel about five generations of Native American women in the harsh landscape of the Boundary Waters between Canada and Minnesota, art echoes life. In her story, conquest, enforced change, and assimilation become a means for transformation even as they all function as engines of self-devastation and destruction of the tribes. Just as Hogan prevailed because of her closeness to the land and other tribal values, so her Native protagonist is transformed. From white-imaged genocidal victim she evolves into the more traditional Native woman who establishes a secure identity by immersing herself in the ritual life of the community. At the heart of *Solar Storms* is the vision quest of Angel Iron, a young woman who—returning home in 1972 at the height of the Red Power movement—comes to feel that spiritually and politically she is "something back in place" (29). According to Kathleen M. Donovan, power for mixed-blood women lies in coming to terms with multiple and often shifting identities (8). For Angel, this means her journey home involves reconciliation not only of her mixed heritage but also with her mother. An abusive woman, "born of knives, the skinned-alive beaver . . . and the chewed off legs of wolves" (345), Hannah Wing turned that violence first inward, then—as a projection of self-hatred—on her daughter. "My mother had been taken in by some horrible, terrible force," explains Angel. "It inhabited her flesh, bone, and spirit" (22).

If, as Hogan says in *Dwellings,* "to see whole is to see all the parts of the puzzle" (97), then only when Angel asserts control over her identity is she able to undo some of the damaging effects of colonization. Angel no longer wants what she now knows will not happen: "an unbroken line between [herself] and the past . . . not to be fragments and pieces left behind by fur traders, soldiers, priests and schools" (*Solar Storms* 77). By integrating all aspects of her being, Angel resists the falsely rigid boundaries fabricated by a culture in which she cannot be whole. "In time," she concludes, "all things would break and would become whole again" (329). In this way Hogan not only honors her protagonist's mixed and relational identities but takes her back to what Owens might call a "frontier world of possibility and change" (34). Here Angel appropriates and inverts the European notion of marked, fixed, and terminal territory, turning it into a place where endings evolve into new beginnings. A seamless, cyclic construct, it resembles her self that she describes as "together anew, [albeit] a shifted pattern" (*Solar Storms* 235). In this way she comes to terms with her sense of otherness created by gender, race, class, place, and spirituality.

After Angel reconnects with her great-grandmother and great-great-grandmother, she leaves with them on a canoe trip to join an indigenous resistance movement against the construction of a hydroelectric power plant. As an Indian woman, Angel's knowledge, values, and belief system are derived from closeness to the land. Serving as a plant dreamer, one responsible for finding healing plants, Angel develops new insights into human relations, as well as a rich understanding of plants and animals. "New senses came to me," she says. "Equal to the other animals, hearing as they heard, moving as they moved, seeing as they saw" (172), Angel breaks down borders between the world of humans and that of nature. In fact, the landscape in *Solar Storms* dominates human activity. "Its wildness, its stubborn passion to remain outside [the government surveyors'] sense of order" (123), asserts Angel, ensures that nature will be a primary balance in her universe; and any human attempt to change that relationship brings repercussions. The Europeans had "trapped themselves inside their own destruction" of the land, Angel says, and their "legacy" was "the removal of spirituality" (180) from those things the Indians thought were alive. Although the land has been colonized, she implies that it will inevitably prevail.

Indigenous cultures have long survived, as Hogan makes clear in *Solar Storms,* because of their relationship to land. As Angel comes to realize, her "heart and the beat of the land, the land [she] should have come from, were becoming the same thing" (236). Like her, Angel says, it was "native land" (224), a transcultural space that has always been vulnerable and in endless flux. But "it had survived" (224), she continues, because within the mutability of both land and its inhabitants lie vitality and the ability to change. Regardless of what awaits their future, in *Solar Storms* Hogan presents an ideological struggle in which the Indians attempt to live within a fluid, ever-changing "place of shifting boundaries" (118). In contrast, the Euro-American world, with its "limited" (315), authoritative way of life, attempts to "reverse the [natural] world" and thus deny possibilities of rebirth (289). Although Angel knows that "in time, all things would break and would become whole again," the Euro-Americans lived in a world that honored only endings, not creation, and so would force her people into containable territory where the only Indians were vanishing or of the past (325). But in her richly imagined Indian world, which Angel knows has "no map to show [her] where to step, no guide to tell [her] how to see" (346), Hogan suggests that cultures are capable of "still returning" (325).

By appropriation and transformation of territory, the author creates a space in which the "world [is] made up of pathways of its own invention" (70). In the end, then, Angel is not the tragic mixed blood or the victim of self-destruction, nor is her tribe culturally impotent. "I've shaped my own life, after all" (346), she says; and moreover, successfully resisting, "stand[ing] in [the] way" of "making new geographies," means "nature . . . would open" for her people "a future we couldn't know yet" (314).

In *Solar Storms* Hogan acknowledges the uniqueness of tribal views. Her writings, she affirms, stretch to reflect the "different histories of ways of thinking and being in the world" (*Dwellings* 12). In this way Hogan creates a space between opposing worlds: the Native American and the mainstream, the secular and the religious, a kind of reconciliation between opposing elements that she says she wants to learn. "There is a still place, a gap between worlds," a space she refers to here and looks to, one she claims arises from the "tribal knowings" (20) of many years. Residing in a space not recognized by dominant culture, Hogan's is a borderland grounded in but not restricted to geographic space. Just as Anzaldúa's revisionary discourse encourages her to look inward while claiming a new, multifaceted spirituality, so Hogan's writings are "a doorway," she says, "into the mythical world" (19)—one that negotiates between "dimensions both sacred and present" (12). In *Solar Storms,* then, she appropriates her own territory, offering a space for transcending and reconstructing history.

Not only is Hogan a prolific writer, but in works like *Solar Storms* she distinguishes herself as a political activist and an environmental theorist. Believing that as an Indian woman she has a special responsibility for "caretaking of the future" (*Dwellings* 11) of her own and other species, Hogan writes out of a lifelong concern for the living world and its inhabitants. In *The Sweet Breathing of Plants* she explains that "knowing [the green world] intimately has been a way of knowing who we are, and passing on that knowledge has been a way of ensuring not only our own survival but the survival of our species" (xiii). This holistic representation of human connectedness also makes whole the "broken off pieces of [her]self" (*Dwellings* 40); only by honoring the interdependence of all life-forms, she says, can one fully respect and put together the fragments of oneself.

Reflecting her ability to transcend the boundaries between herself and others and between humans and their environment, Hogan's environmental ethic grows out of a ritual or ceremonial understanding of human life. In *Song of the Turtle* Paula Gunn Allen suggests that "liminality is [a] chronic state" for tribal people, and "transformation is our daily enterprise" (11). For Hogan, the ceremony itself implies the state of being on a threshold, between past and present, human and other worlds—all crossings that bring "intimate kinship" (*Dwellings* 41) across various kinds of borders: "In the coldest weather / I recall / that I am in every creature / And they are in me" (*Savings* 6). "We remember that all things are connected. Remembering this is the purpose of the ceremony," Hogan writes, and as such it is "part of a healing and restoration" (*Dwellings* 40) for those who feel disassociated from the natural world. In Native American traditions, Hogan adds, healers are often known as interpreters because they are best suited to cross portals into other worlds and pass on that wisdom to those on the other side (*Dwellings* 41). Writers, too, she says, are such "cartographers," artists who "introduce us to foreign worlds" (195).

On this journey she realizes that spiritual rejuvenation is only one ingredient of justice for Native peoples. If tribal communities are to end their victimization, she maintains, they must become attuned to an "inner map" (*Dwellings* 40), a path toward a return to truly Native values and a remembering "inside people" (80) of the land. But Hogan is also aware that colonization has brought about the loss of Native peoples' land base, language, children, and stories. Her works call, therefore, for political as well as personal transformation. In *Solar Storms,* for example, Angel Iron sees resistance as necessary for survival. A necessity not only for human continuation but also for the earth, political action, Hogan concludes, becomes a requirement for all who truly believe it is a "duty to be custodians of the planet" (Hogan in Coltelli 79).

Given the prominence of women in Native American society, it follows that literary texts by a mixed-blood Chickasaw woman feature strong female characters who know, as does Hogan, that to speak at whatever the cost is to become empowered. Because she feels women have an "ancient bond" (*Sweet Breathing* xiv) with nature, both are aligned as primary players in her texts. Hogan's focus on relationships between women suggests that gender is allied not only with the natural world but also with oral tradition and a sense of place. In her poem "Calling Myself Home," she writes that "this land is the house / We have always lived in" (*Red Clay* 7); for Hogan, place becomes an agent of cultural affirmation and transformation. But for that process to be complete, she

Linda Hogan's "Geography of the Spirit"

calls on her female relations—"women," she says, "whose bones [hold] up the earth" (7). In this way Hogan not only preserves certain aspects of her culture but also transforms it to show that the past and present, as well as women and nature, are vital parts of a continuous cycle of endings and—more important to her—also of beginnings. "We have taken on the story of endings," Hogan warns, and "assumed the story of extinction" (*Dwellings* 84). Through the construction of her texts, Hogan looks back on her life with a renewed vision and a stronger connection to her powerful female ancestors who make possible a story of new beginnings.

Works Cited

Allen, Paula Gunn. *Off the Reservation: Reflections on Border-Busting, Border-Crossing, Loose Canons.* Boston: Beacon, 1998.

———, ed. *Song of the Turtle: American Indian Fiction 1974–1994.* New York: Ballantine, 1996.

Anzaldúa, Gloria. *Borderlands/La Frontera.* San Francisco: Aunt Lute Books, 1987.

Coltelli, Laura. *Winged Words: American Indian Writers Speak.* Lincoln: University of Nebraska Press, 1990.

Damm, Katerie. "Says Who: Colonialism, Identity, and Defining Indigenous Literature." In *Looking at the Words of Our People: First Nations Analysis of Literature.* Ed. Jeannette Armstrong. Penticton, B.C.: Theytus Books, 1993. 10–25.

Donovan, Kathleen M. *Feminist Readings of Native American Literature: Coming to Voice.* Tucson: University of Arizona Press, 1998.

Harjo, Joy, ed. *Reinventing the Enemy's Language: Contemporary Native Women's Writings of North America.* New York: W. W. Norton, 1998.

Hogan, Linda. *The Book of Medicines.* Minneapolis: Coffee House, 1993.

———. *Dwellings: A Spiritual History of the Living World.* Greenfield Center, N.Y.: Greenfield Review Press, 1991.

———. *Red Clay: Poems and Stories.* Greenfield Center, N.Y.: Greenfield Review Press, 1993.

———. *Savings.* Minneapolis: Coffee House, 1988.

———. *Seeing Through the Sun.* Amherst: University of Massachusetts Press, 1985.

———. *Solar Storms.* New York: Scribner, 1995.

———. "The Two Lives." In *I Tell You Now: Autobiographical Essays by Native American Writers.* Ed. Brian Swann and Arnold Krupat. Lincoln: University of Nebraska Press, 1987. 231–251.

———. *The Woman Who Watches Over the World: A Native Memoir.* New York: W. W. Norton, 2001.

Hogan, Linda, and Brenda Peterson, eds. *The Sweet Breathing of Plants: Women Writing on the Green World.* New York: North Point, 2001.

Lape, Noreen Groover. *West of the Border: The Multicultural Literature of the Western American Frontiers.* Athens: Ohio University Press, 2000.

Owens, Louis. *Mixed-Blood Messages: Literature, Family, Place.* Norman: University of Oklahoma Press, 1998.

Ruppert, James. "Mediation in Contemporary Native American Writing." In *Native American Perspectives on Literature and History.* Ed. Alan R. Velie. Norman: University of Oklahoma Press, 1995. 7–25.

Womack, Craig S. *Red on Red: Native American Literary Separatism.* Minneapolis: University of Minnesota Press, 1999.

RHETORICS OF TRUTH TELLING IN LINDA HOGAN'S *SAVINGS*

Jennifer Love

Scholars of ecocriticism and American Indian literatures have explored the ways Linda Hogan foregrounds a communicative relationship between humans and nonhuman species—plants, animals, and nonanimate nature. Melani Bleck, for example, in her essay "Linda Hogan's Tribal Imperative: Collapsing Space Through 'Living' Tribal Traditions and Nature," shows how Native understandings of interspecies connection help shape Hogan's view of language. Bleck writes that "Hogan questions the power structure behind a worldview that allows for the privileging of one language through the perceived inadequacies . . . of an 'other' " (38). Human characters in Hogan's prose, Bleck finds, "benefit from their exposure to nature's languages" (38). These characters often learn to listen to the voices of streams, wind, and animals, unsettling the power differentials inherent in Western views of language that—unlike most Native traditions—privilege human speech and writing above other forms of communication.

Hogan articulates this philosophy of listening to and learning from the languages of nonhuman nature in her essay "A Different Yield" from her book *Dwellings*. The rustling of corn plants, the communicative power of wind, the

Jennifer Love

abilities of horses and other animals to respond to minute nuances in human behavior—all are evoked in the essay. For Hogan these voices are able to recall, teach, prophesy. She describes the linguistic properties of growing corn and its sustaining environment—leaves, wind, soil, field-dwelling creatures—as potentially accessible to humans: "At night, in the cornfields, when there is no more mask of daylight, you hear the plants talking among themselves. The wind passes through. It's all there, the languages, the voices of wind, dove, corn, stones" (62). The languages of nonhuman nature are for Hogan animate and persuasive, with "voices and intentions of their own" (Tarter 132). Although she suggests that American Indian traditions in particular enable recognition of these voices, Hogan regards nature's languages as accessible by non-Natives as well; she writes of biologist Barbara McClintock, a Euro-American who in her genetic research was able "to listen to what corn had to say, to translate what the plants spoke into a human tongue" (*Dwellings* 48). This ability to hear and communicate nature's sounds is for Hogan one way to heal the Western-inscribed alienation between humans and nonhuman nature. In a time of ongoing destruction by humans—of wilderness, of the animal and plant species these areas sustain, and of other humans—"our lives," Hogan believes, "depend on this listening" (52).

Hogan stresses that humans' ability to communicate not only with nonhuman nature but with other members of our species develops from our relations (both evolutionary and intuitive) with nonhuman life:

> [T]here are communications that take place on a level that goes deeper than our somewhat limited human spoken languages. We read one another via gesture, stance, facial expression, scent. And sometimes this communication is more honest, more comprehensible, than the words we utter.
>
> These inner forms of communication are perhaps the strongest core of ourselves. (*Dwellings* 57)

In this passage Hogan underscores a connection between human and nonhuman species in our ability to "read" one another through nonspoken communication—as many (nonhuman) animals do. Hogan suggests that the resources for this common language with other life-forms are both around us—part of the natural world of trees, streams, and deer—and within us. In his discussion of Hogan's 1995 novel *Solar Storms,* Jim Tarter clarifies this connection: "Hogan is discussing not so much a universal human nature as a common animal or plant nature that humans possess" (134). Thus Hogan explores our capacities to listen to and learn from nonhuman species, as well as to communicate in nonverbal ways with other humans. It is for the sake of these intersecting relationships that she urges us to be attentive to the nonverbal, nonwritten languages in our lives.

Yet Hogan's writing does not always generate confidence in humans' ability to listen to and learn from nature's languages. Representations of heedless destruction of animals and ecosystems, often as a result of limited abilities to hear and communicate with these presences, are bound up in her written activism. Hogan's 1993 collection of poems, *The Book of Medicines,* an ecofeminist exploration of animal-human interactions, depicts the verbal violence that often accompanies humans' forays into animal-inhabited terrain. The fishermen in the poem "Harvesters of Night and Water," for example, who roughly attempt to haul an octopus into their boat, are described on three different occasions in the poem as "screaming" at one another and at the octopus—unable to listen to the subtler language of this little-known sea creature:

> The tentacles fold over themselves
> and inch down,
> with the men screaming,
> jabbing at it. (23)

Although the octopus is represented as silent, perhaps silenced (the fishermen seem to drown out any sounds it might make), the female narrator expresses a desire to communicate the complexities of its life to the fishermen:

> I want to tell them what I know,
> that this life collects coins
> like they do
> and builds walls on the floor of the sea. (23)

In this poem, then, the language of nonhuman nature—the octopus's ability to communicate with those who pay attention to its life beneath the sea—is represented as unheard or unheeded by the (male) humans who interact with it. The fishermen cannot recognize the verbal and nonverbal connections between themselves and the nonhuman, sea-dwelling creature they are struggling to claim and kill.

An essay in *Dwellings,* "What Holds the Water," also represents this incompatibility of nonhuman and human languages. Hogan's narrator describes a dominant, legalistic Western language that, unlike many tribal languages and rituals, fails to be attentive to the languages of nonhuman nature: "Ours is a language of commerce and trade, of laws that can be bent in order that treaties might be broken, land wounded beyond healing. It is a language that is limited, emotionally and spiritually. . . . The ears of the language do not often hear the songs of the white egrets, the rain falling into stone bowls" (45–46). Hogan's emphasis here is on humans' need—and ability—to create forms of language that enable us to listen to the earth's languages: "So we make our own songs to contain these things, make ceremonies and poems, searching for a new way to speak" (46). Hogan sees humans as already dependent in some ways on languages that are responsive to our nonhuman natural surroundings: "[W]e want

Jennifer Love

a new way to live in the world, to say that wilderness and water, blue herons and orange newts are invaluable . . . in the workings of the natural world that rules us whether we acknowledge it or not" (46). Yet Hogan's narrator also indicates the ways human language often limits our expression—how the "songs . . . ceremonies and poems" we create are often marginalized as forms of expression, forgotten or neglected in our compulsion toward "commerce and trade."

Hogan clearly sees a need for humans'—both Native and non-Native—increased attentiveness to the voices of nature. Poems such as "Harvesters of Night and Water" and essays such as "What Holds the Water, What Holds the Light" depict humans as unable to communicate with the natural world because we wrongly see ourselves as detached from it. In this chapter I explore this idea of troubled or failed communication between plants/animals and humans as represented in Hogan's 1988 volume of poetry, *Savings*. Many of the poems in *Savings* evoke the tribal, ecologically sensitive idea of a primal language shared by plants, animals, and humans. Although they represent a yearning for commonality, the poems also question humans' (both Native and non-Native) ability to learn and speak such a language. Rather than represent a common language, many of the poems in *Savings* depict the trauma of nonintersecting communication, with humans—victims of Western, ecologically insensitive ideology—censoring their own voices, inhibited by rules and "fear about what neighbors think" (17). At the same time, nonhuman creatures and other natural phenomena—geraniums, chickens, stars, stones, horses, trout—are represented as more direct or "honest" in their self-presentation than the humans who live around and among them.

In looking at the ways the poems in *Savings* resist rather than inscribe the ideal of a common language, I wish to complicate a familiar view of Hogan's work as eroding the Western-entrenched hierarchy between nature and culture. I believe that in much of her work Hogan does resist this hierarchy; her larger project as a writer is supported by a cautious optimism about humans' capacities to be attentive to nonhuman nature.[1] Yet in *Savings*, rather than transform this dichotomy, Hogan in many ways allows it to persist. In doing so she invokes the Western, individualist assumption of "total human alienation from the rest of nature" (Murphy 63)—alerting her readers to its disturbing potency. Too, Hogan restructures a nature-human dualism so that nonhuman nature is often credited as more sensitive and forthright than evasive, self-absorbed humanity. This reversing-yet-sustaining of the nature-culture divide, I suggest, is deliberate and effective—showing the binary's perhaps insurmountable persistence and critiquing overly optimistic assumptions of escaping its power.

In many of the poems in *Savings*, Hogan foregrounds the ideal of honesty or truthfulness—rhetorical traits she generally assigns to nonhuman subjects. For readers and scholars trained in poststructuralist and feminist theory (and

Truth Telling in Linda Hogan's *Savings*

other postmodern practices that resist universalizing and biological determinism), Hogan's use of these and related words, such as truth and lying, may seem disturbingly essentialist. Yet as I argue, Hogan's appropriation of these words is an effective rhetorical-political gesture, supported by American Indian theories of orality and by ecofeminist rhetorical theories. In the *Savings* poems, representations of directness and sincerity and of humans' inability to emulate or respond efficaciously to the truth-telling languages of nonhuman nature can be read as lessons about the necessity and difficulty of listening to, speaking with, and learning from the natural world.

The poems in *Savings* emphasize the difficulties of human-nonhuman communication by foregrounding particular points of view. Human presences in the poems include the self-reflexive narrator, an invoked audience with which she identifies (the "we" of the poems), and an addressed audience from whom she tends to distance herself—often referred to as "you" and sometimes, but not always, coded white and male. The rhetorical struggle between these speakers and nonhuman nature is represented in the poem "The Truth of the Matter" (in a section of the book also titled "The Truth of the Matter"). The poem evokes the shifts between morning and night, the circadian rhythms influencing all beings. Humans and nonhuman animals are shown as responding in similar ways to the fall of darkness, the turning of the earth:

> Thank heaven,
> the light is off in day's house
> and everything can be itself.
> The boar fears hunger.
> The crab shelters herself with armor,
> and we remove our clothes
> and lie down afraid
> of our own true colors. (47)

For Hogan, there is continuity among the boar's fear, the crab's need for its shell protection, and humans' nervousness in revealing our "own true colors" as we prepare for sleep. Our nighttime unconsciousness allows us to communicate with nonhuman nature:

> At last,
> emptiness admits it wants to steal your breath
> but didn't I know it all along,
> hearing those stars chatting
> with their brothers, the stones,
> and telling the truth. (47)

But despite humans' ability to hear the sounds of stars and stones at night, the comparison between sleeping humans and nocturnal nature soon shifts to a critique. With the arrival of morning, in Hogan's view, humans lose their ability to listen to nature's languages:

> Such honest dreamers we are
> at night,
> such honest tongues we wag,
> but what liars in the morning
> with our faces back on,
> even the sky,
> and we are liars at breakfast
> and crossing ourselves
> and our fingers
> behind our backs. (47)

Hogan suggests that humans' ability to hear and speak the languages of nonhuman nature is temporary—dependent on the darkness and solitude nighttime provides. Representing humans' daytime inability to speak and listen to nature's languages, Hogan also draws a distinction between the "truthful" language we speak at night—with the natural phenomena we then recognize as part of us—and our deceptive behavior during the day: "what liars in the morning . . . we are liars at breakfast / and crossing . . . our fingers / behind our backs / at five o'clock / and after dinner" (47). The poem's final image—"when the dark puts her first card / down on the table"—suggests the surety and directness of nightfall in contrast to the evasiveness of humans, with our crossed fingers and disingenuous conversation (47).

Hogan's use of the tropes of honesty and truth, her attribution of these traits to animals, plants, and nonliving natural phenomena, develops from a culturally diverse web of teachings. In the next section I provide a brief background on the idea of truth in Western rhetorical traditions—traditions that influence but do not dominate Hogan's use of these terms. I will show how this classical idea of truth is refigured in recent postmodernist scholarship on autobiography (a genre that can be seen as encompassing Hogan's poems, with their first-person narrators and self-reflective stance). Then I will discuss briefly the trope of honesty in American Indian traditions of oral storytelling and in ecofeminist rhetorical theory. Both of these theoretical frameworks can help readers revisit Hogan's representations of nature's honesty. Both frameworks also help clarify Hogan's association of the language of truth with plants, minerals, and nonhuman animals.

"Truth" in Western Rhetoric and Autobiography—Hogan's Interventions

The trope of truth has a long history in Western rhetorical and philosophical discourse. Many of Plato's writings are concerned with accessing a "higher" wisdom referred to as truth.[2] Other classical (Greek and Roman) rhetoricians insist upon the importance of a public rhetor being not only well-informed and credible but also honest and sincere.[3] Such traits are problematized by feminist rereadings of rhetorical histories, which recognize that what humans perceive as truth is contingent, socially constructed, and shifting. One example is Susan Jarratt's *Rereading the Sophists,* which revises the traditional view of the Sophists of the fifth century B.C.E. as spinners of false logic. For Jarratt, these rhetors prefigured contemporary postmodern and feminist theories in their belief in historical contingency and in language as constructing human perceptions of truth (xviii).

Current feminist research in autobiography takes up this critique of truth as well. As theorist Leigh Gilmore writes, autobiography has traditionally been seen as a project emerging from the Western Enlightenment in which a single, authoritative (often male) individual produces truth (125–126). In Gilmore's feminist readings the idea of authority or "truthfulness" is problematically raced and gendered—often associated with canonical autobiographies such as Franklin's *Autobiography* and Augustine's *Confessions.* First-person writing that strays from this Western humanist ideal—in which a speaker presents himself or herself as autonomous, sincere, and self-authorized—may be marginalized because of its failure to represent dominant narratives and belief systems (Gilmore 126).

Linda Hogan's writing, much of which can be considered autobiographical or semiautobiographical,[4] is relevant to discussions of truth in first-person narrative. In one sense Hogan seems to allow the problematic associations of "truth" (and synonyms such as honesty) to remain unexamined in her work, including *Savings.* Yet although she aligns truth with sincerity and upholds it as ideal, she problematizes the site at which—and the speakers by whom—this truth is spoken. Hogan's celebration of honesty and truth telling foregrounds traditionally marginalized speakers of autobiography—in Hogan's case, nonhuman animals, plants, and other natural phenomena. Although Hogan does not deconstruct the dominant associations of "truth," she nonetheless appropriates the term, reassigning it from the possession of white male speakers to the nonhuman subjects of the earth. Thus Hogan turns the traditional Western conceptualization of a self-authorized speaker on its end, showing that often it is beings ignored or repudiated in dominant Western ideology (assumed unable to access realms of truth)—crows, trees, fish, wind—that speak with perspicacity and substance.

Hogan's emphasis on the ideals of truth and directness is theoretically grounded, too, within American Indian traditions of storytelling and orality. Hogan's discussion of an interspecies communication that is "more honest, more comprehensible, than the words we utter" (*Dwellings* 57) invokes her Chickasaw heritage of spoken telling, a traditionally spontaneous mode of utterance very different from the prescripted speeches and written stories of dominant Western traditions. Hogan's emphasis on honesty and directness resembles other Native women writers' descriptions of tribal storytelling. Laguna Pueblo author Leslie Marmon Silko, for example, in her essay "Language and Literature from a Pueblo Indian Perspective," invokes this rhetoric of nondeliberation: "Where I come from, the words most highly valued are those spoken from the heart, unpremeditated and unrehearsed" (*Yellow Woman* 48).[5] Both these Native women writers support a discourse of directness—linking spontaneity and truthfulness and locating this direct language within traditions of oral storytelling.[6]

Hogan's emphasis on truth and honesty is supported as well within an ecofeminist framework—a discipline that, it can be argued, Hogan has greatly helped build. Noël Sturgeon writes that ecofeminism articulates "the theory that the ideologies that authorize injustices based on gender, race, and class are related to the ideologies that sanction the exploitation and degradation of the environment" (23). Hogan communicates a similar message in her essay "First People." She draws on her Native heritage to emphasize the interconnected plight of tribal peoples and of plants and nonhuman animals in the face of ecological destruction: "Those of us who came from this land can see before our eyes and in our own bodies that what has happened to this land and the animals is the same thing as what has happened to us" (18).

The ecofeminist theorist Starhawk explains that the roots of this dual oppression lie in a dominant culture that regards human instincts as chaotic, "in need of repression and control"—just as nature is seen as "in need of order imposed by human beings" (7). Starhawk's argument that many humans resist their biological impulses and desires, seeking to repress and channel them, resembles Hogan's emphasis on directness and spontaneity and her association of these qualities with the noninhibited (nonhuman) natural world. For Starhawk, "self-hater" rhetors, speakers who have internalized societal messages of dominance and oppression, "constantly censor and monitor their desires and impulses in order to conform to the patriarchal world. . . . Afraid to tell others who they are, self-haters keep their fears and their identities hidden inside" (Starhawk in Foss, Foss, and Griffin 171–172). Starhawk's discussion of self-censoring, self-hating rhetors' "disengagement from the world" (Foss, Foss, and Griffin 175) informs Linda Hogan's celebration of the directness of the nonhuman natural world and her critique of discourses of withholding and evasion.

Savings: Strategically Invoking and Altering a Nature-Culture Dichotomy

Whereas Hogan constructs honesty and directness as ideals, she also (as I have shown) represents these characteristics as the province of nonhuman beings. Presenting forthright, outspoken verbal behavior as the province of flowers, fish, and other nonhumans, Hogan invokes the Western separation between nature and culture. This hierarchy typically presents humans, especially white males, as more enlightened than plants and animals (a group that often implicitly includes women[7]). Donelle N. Dreese notes how ecofeminism seeks to transform this and other hierarchies: "Culture/nature, mind/body, black/white, man/woman, intellect/emotion are all examples of structures which lie at the root of subordination . . . the ecofeminist agenda involves healing these artificial separations and challenging existing power structures" (14). Like many Hogan scholars,[8] Dreese sees Hogan's work actively transforming these and other Western cultural hierarchies. What makes the poems in *Savings* rhetorically unusual is that the persisting separation between nonhuman and human nature is often not only attested to but also re-presented as part of Hogan's activism. Rather than evade the Western dictum of spoken/written language as more powerful than the languages of nonhumans, in *Savings* Hogan reverses the dichotomy—suggesting that animal and plant languages are more expressive and sustainable. To restate the original binary in new terms may seem risky to many feminist readers (as it does to me)—liable to entrench the old hierarchy by sticking within its limits. Yet I believe Hogan's strategy, although unsettling, is also instructive. By reenacting the nature-human dichotomy in *Savings,* Hogan calls attention to its ongoing presence, creating a powerful argument about language-rhetoric and humans' place within the ecological community.[9]

Hogan's poem "The Other Voices" is an example of the way human speakers in *Savings,* unlike their nonhuman earthmates, suffer from chronic evasion, an inhibiting lack of directness or honesty. The poem begins,

> There are things we do not tell
> when we tell about weather
> and being fine.
> Our other voices take sanctuary
> while police with their shepherds
> stand guard
> at the borders of breath
> lest our stories escape
> this holy building of ourselves. (45)

Here Hogan's narrator does not simply separate human and nonhuman nature. The poem's title and emphasis on humans' instinctive voices taking "sanctuary" suggest that these voices are a part of us, although often unacknowledged by or inaccessible to us. Yet as Hogan suggests, we create large barriers—"holy building[s]" guarded by "police" ready at any moment to silence our stories—to contain our instincts to speak more candidly than we often do. The idea of a common language between nonhumans and humans, explored elsewhere in Hogan's work, is given a nod here; but the commonalities are rigidly monitored, unacknowledged by too many humans.

Jennifer Love

In the next stanza the narrator evokes greater disparities between nonhuman animals and humans—creatures separated by their different communicative habits and training:

> How did we come to be
> So unlike the chickens
> clucking their hearts out
> openly in the rain,
> the horses just being horses
> on the hillside,
> and coyotes howling
> their real life at the moon? (45)

The chickens, horses, and coyotes speak their languages from their "hearts . . . openly"; they communicate "their real life," not the small talk of weather or the reserved responses we often make when asked how we are doing. The poem ends optimistically, suggesting that the narrator can hear the voices of the nonhuman natural world even if she cannot always attain or be healed by them: "[T]he other voices speak / and they are mine / and they are not mine / and I hear them / and I don't" (46). Yet the speaker's permanent pain, described in the third stanza, suggests a serious correlation between evasive language and physical illness:

> We don't tell our inner truth
> and no one believes it anyway.
> No wonder I am lying
> in the sagging bed,
> this body with the bad ankle
> and fifteen scars showing,
> and in the heart, my god,
> the horrors of living. (46)

Hogan's narrator suggests that humans suffer physical illness and psychological trauma at least in part as a result of our verbal inhibitions. Hogan does not suggest that humans' tendency to censor their speaking is shaped by isolated or individual forces. The "police" who "stand guard / at the borders of breath" may be understood as a culturally sanctioned ideology of evasion concerning matters of health and well-being. Thus, although the speakers who fall ill may, like Hogan, be of tribal origin, the larger conditions shaping and forcing their limited language are represented as Western ideologies.[10]

Hogan articulates this web of influences in "First People":

> It is not now the case that all of us who are tribal people are living in a traditional way. We, too, have suffered the loss of our relationships with

animals and plants by force and conquest, and we have become dependent on the same forces that have caused such devastation, but still we can look to the roots of Native tradition for the intelligence that once sustained our lives and hope to understand it again. (18)

Although some speakers or invoked audiences in these poems recognize their rhetorical shortcomings, Hogan sees humans as a species suffering from, and perhaps complicit in, a dominant culture that denies them access or ability to respond to nonhumans with their more forthright deliveries.

In her poem "Geraniums," Hogan continues this rhetorical project. Her narrator celebrates the red geraniums she sees blooming determinedly in a nearby house:

> Life is burning
> in everything, in red flowers
> abandoned in an empty house,
> the leaves nearly gone,
> curtains and tenants gone,
> but the flowers red and fiery
> are there and singing,
> let us out. (*Savings* 17)

For Hogan's narrator the flowers are "burning" with life, "fiery," "there and singing"—traits that suggest their lack of inhibition and constraint. As speakers, these flowers don't just murmur. Despite their abandonment by human caregivers, they sing.

The poem continues,

> Even dying they have fire.
> Imprisoned, they open,
> so like our own lives blooming,
> exploding, wanting out,
> wanting love,
> water,
> wanting. (17)

The geraniums bloom out unhesitating, although they lack water and nourishment. Emphasizing their tenacity, Hogan's narrator draws a connection between the geraniums and herself/other readers of the poem. All are "wanting out, / wanting love." Despite the suggestion of what the flowers and humans share (both are needy and demanding, struggling for life and freedom from constraint), Hogan shows them separated by an insurmountable barrier. The final line of the stanza has a double meaning: humans both desire things—physical sustenance, continued life—and lack crucial awareness in interactions with the natural world. Hogan makes this explicit in the last stanza of the poem:

Jennifer Love

> And you, with your weapons and badges
> and your fear about what neighbors think
> and working overtime
> as if the boss will reward you,
> you can't bloom that way
> so open the door,
> break the glass. There's fire
> in those flowers. Set off the alarm.
> What's a simple crime of property
> when life, breath, and all
> is at stake? (17)

The "you" of this stanza, seemingly a male figure (perhaps a police officer, given the "weapons and badges"), is addressed suddenly and sternly. With his absorption in paraphernalia, self-defense, and professional advancement, he "can't bloom" the way the geraniums do. To open the door or break the glass would emulate the flowers' ability to communicate without self-consciousness or fear of consequence. But the poem ends with an unanswered (rhetorical) question: "What's a simple crime of property" compared to our need to shout our needs, to speak of our dying, our survival? The word *breath* sustains the poem's rhetorical dimension. Without breath, humans lack both orality and life. If we cannot speak out, articulating our needs in language as stirring as that of the geraniums, we remain constricted by our efforts to conform and alienated from the natural world—a world we nonetheless both inhabit and yearn for.

In her essay "The Terrestrial and Aquatic Intelligence of Linda Hogan," Dreese writes that Hogan's "activist texts . . . demand the relationship between . . . humanity and non-human nature . . . be reconsidered and transformed" (20). The poems in *Savings* urge us to rethink this relationship by presenting it not as healthy or healable but as rhetorically troubled and in need of reassessment. *Savings* depicts a communication gap between nonhumans and humans; it assigns to nonhuman nature a spontaneity supported by tribal and ecofeminist theories. In doing so, the volume both invokes and unsettles Western philosophies of truth telling and interspecies relationship. The narrator of *Savings* seeks to realize her connections with nonhuman nature, yet the poems continually reaffirm the differences between humans and nonhumans—differences exaggerated by Western teachings.

Where is the remedy for this struggle? Hogan avoids easy answers in her poems, fiction, and essays. An interview with Phebe Davidson, published in 1998, suggests Hogan's ambivalence regarding the idea that human and nonhuman species have basic capacities for mutual understanding. When asked "about the idea that each of us carries, inside, the knowledge of those other species with whom we share ancestors," Hogan responds cautiously: "I don't know. If we did we would behave very differently in the world, if we carried that inside ourselves, if we knew other species" (93).

For Hogan, what keeps us from understanding other living beings is mainstream Euro-American education, with its tendency to neglect the habits, needs, and accomplishments of animal and plant species: "Our educations have been completely negligent. . . . Students don't learn in school about the natural world or about the incredible achievements of other species. I sometimes think that when we imagine we know something, that it's mostly conjecture, and that it actually diminishes the world and the animals around us when we imagine that we know what they're about" (Davidson 94). By implication, Hogan is calling for rhetorical, ecologically sensitive action: rather than imagining we know what plants and nonhuman animals experience, we must learn to listen to and communicate with them—despite the persistence of the Cartesian duality. In a time when oil drilling in the Arctic Wildlife Refuge hovers on the brink of reality and thousands of plant and animal species are threatened or endangered (in my home state of Oregon, hundreds of species—from Steller's sea lions to Wallowa primrose to tailed frogs—are at risk), these lessons are crucial. Humans destroy plant and animal habitats and lives when we close our ears to the languages they offer. And we limit our ability to articulate our experiences when we turn from the sounds of our ailing bodies, a clucking chicken, a brilliant geranium, "the songs of the white egrets, the rain falling into stone bowls" (*Dwellings* 45–46).

Hogan's *Savings*—although it does not valorize a common language among plants, nonhuman animals, and humans—suggests that nonhuman beings with their often unheard voices communicate in ways humans can, with difficulty, learn to take part in and listen to. Hogan's writing as a whole, it has been said, asks us "to reconstruct our notion of language" (Tarter 145). The poems in *Savings*, with their unexpected rhetorical messages, help make this reconstruction possible.

Acknowledgment

My thanks to Barbara Cook and to the reviewers at the University Press of Colorado for their suggestions and encouragement as I was revising this chapter.

Notes

1. In an interview with Phebe Davidson, for example, Hogan is asked, "How do you sustain [a] hopeful vision in a world that appears, in many ways, to have gone insane?" Hogan replies, "I don't know, but I always have faith. I think that things may yet be all right. And for all of the damage, the world still is pretty resilient. I do find that these are very difficult times. I don't hold to total optimism. It's just a balance so that a person doesn't fall into despair that renders them helpless, joyless, apathetic" (86).

Jennifer Love

2. A famous example is Plato's *Phaedrus,* which explores the distinction between "persuasion-to-belief" (so-called bad rhetoric) and "persuasion-to-knowledge" (good rhetoric). As Plato's dialogue suggests, a good rhetor must seek truth so he can persuade his listener(s) of a knowledge he knows to be true (Bizzell and Herzberg 59).

3. Two examples are Cicero, who in his *Of Oratory* questions the idea that "eloquence can exist . . . apart from philosophy" (226), and Quintilian, who in *Institutes of Oratory* emphasizes the need for teachers of future orators (and orators themselves) to be "good men": sincere, unostentatious, and committed to teaching students methods that eschew the devious motives of "flattering and pleasing" (319, 321).

4. Most of the poems in *Savings* feature a narrative presence—a recurring "I" or "me"—that shares this and other features in common with most memoirs, as well as the first-person narrator of Hogan's essays. The essays in *Dwellings,* for example, are narrated by a speaker often identifiable with Hogan herself (see note 10).

5. In her essay "Landscape, History, and the Pueblo Imagination," Silko also discusses the ways Pueblo Indian traditions constructed communal rather than absolute truth: "For [the ancient Pueblo people] this truth lived somewhere within the web of differing versions, disputes over minor points, outright contradictions tangling with old feuds and village rivalries" (88).

6. Similarly, Laguna Pueblo–Sioux author Paula Gunn Allen, although she does not refer specifically to a truth-spontaneity symbiosis, explores the ways dominant understandings of truth are refigured in many Native ritual traditions. "[W]ithin the workings of ritual, the impossible becomes the very probable, the imaginary becomes the factual, the primitive becomes the sophisticated, and the false becomes the actuality. Within the ritual universe the entire matter of true/false is turned on its head" (8).

7. Ecofeminism generally posits a nature-culture separation to involve the debasing of women, especially women of color, alongside a devaluing of nature. In other words, many ecofeminists (including myself) see women and the nonhuman natural world as linked and oppressed in dominant Western discourses. For the purposes of this chapter—because the poems in *Savings* generally locate humans of both sexes in their critique of Western culture—I am minimizing references to a women-nature conjoining. But I do see Hogan making frequent use of this connection in her work.

8. See, for example, Bleck, Tarter.

9. The idea of a deliberate reusing of a dominant or oppressive rhetoric as a decolonizing strategy is explored by many well-known feminist and cultural theorists. Henry Louis Gates Jr., for example, discusses the "repetition . . . with a signal difference" notable in many African American communities (51). Luce Irigaray, writing from a feminist psychoanalytic perspective, describes how a speaker who mimes a dominant language tries "to recover the place of her exploitation by discourse, without allowing herself to be simply reduced to it." The miming subject attempts to make "'visible,' by an effect of playful repetition, what was supposed to remain invisible" (124). This idea is also taken up by Judith Butler in her book *Bodies That Matter,* where it takes on explicitly rhetorical significance. Butler notes that the speaker who mimes or refigures an official discourse "takes on a language that effectively cannot belong to her, only to call into question the exclusionary rules of proprietariness that govern the use of that discourse" (37–38). Native scholars explore discourses of refiguration as well. Malea Powell, a scholar of Ameri-

can Indian literatures focusing on nineteenth-century Indian intellectuals such as Sarah Winnemucca Hopkins, examines how the autobiographical writing of Winnemucca and others, such as Charles Eastman, both uses and critiques Eurocentric discourses—creating what Powell calls "rhetorics of survivance." In a recent essay Powell shows how Winnemucca, in her *Life Among the Piutes,* "uses the very imperial discourse that would doubt her subjectivity in order to create herself as a subject, not a victim" (415). These theorists assert the importance of rearticulation as a transformative strategy. Powell, Butler, and others guide my examination of Hogan's implied narrator as a speaker who takes on a colonizing language—the language of culture-nature separation—and in doing so, questions its "exclusionary rules."

10. The stanza I have quoted beginning "We don't tell our inner truth / and no one believes it anyway" has strong autobiographical associations. Hogan has testified in interviews, as well as in her memoir *The Woman Who Watches Over the World* (2001), that she suffers from a chronic muscle illness, fibromyalgia—a disease that affects many Native peoples. I do not suggest that Hogan is representing herself or other tribal people as literal victims of their modes of communication. Rather, Hogan suggests that dominant culture authorizes such constrained speech, indirectly enabling the chronic illness and pain Hogan and others suffer from.

Works Cited

Allen, Paula Gunn. *Grandmothers of the Light: A Medicine Woman's Sourcebook.* Boston: Beacon, 1991.

Bizzell, Patricia, and Bruce Herzberg. *The Rhetorical Tradition: Readings from Classical Times to the Present.* Boston: Bedford Books of St. Martin's Press, 1990.

Bleck, Melani. "Linda Hogan's Tribal Imperative: Collapsing Space Through 'Living' Tribal Traditions and Nature." *Studies in American Indian Literatures Series 2,* vol. 11, no. 4 (1999): 23–45.

Butler, Judith. *Bodies That Matter: On the Discursive Limits of "Sex."* New York: Routledge, 1993.

Cicero, Marcus Tullius. "From *Of Oratory.*" In *The Rhetorical Tradition: Readings from Classical Times to the Present.* Ed. Patricia Bizzell and Bruce Herzberg. Boston: Bedford Books of St. Martin's Press, 1990. 200–250.

Davidson, Phebe. *Conversations with the World: American Women Poets and Their Work.* Pasadena: Trilogy, 1998.

Dreese, Donelle N. "The Terrestrial and Aquatic Intelligence of Linda Hogan." *Studies in American Indian Literatures Series 2,* vol. 11, no. 4 (1999): 6–22.

Foss, Karen A., Sonja K. Foss, and Cindy L. Griffin. *Feminist Rhetorical Theories.* Thousand Oaks: Sage, 1999.

Gates, Henry Louis, Jr. *The Signifying Monkey: A Theory of Afro-American Literary Criticism.* New York: Oxford University Press, 1988.

Gilmore, Leigh. *Autobiographics: A Feminist Theory of Women's Self-Representation.* Ithaca: Cornell University Press, 1994.

Hogan, Linda. *The Book of Medicines.* Minneapolis: Coffee House, 1993.

———. *Dwellings: A Spiritual History of the Living World.* New York: W. W. Norton, 1995.

Jennifer Love

———. "First People." In *Intimate Nature: The Bond Between Women and Animals*. Ed. Linda Hogan, Deena Metzger, and Brenda Peterson. New York: Ballantine, 1998. 6–19.

———. *Savings*. Minneapolis: Coffee House, 1988.

Irigaray, Luce. "The Power of Discourse and the Subordination of the Feminine." In *The Irigaray Reader*. Ed. Margaret Whitford. Oxford: Basil Blackwell, 1991. 118–132.

Jarratt, Susan C. *Rereading the Sophists: Classical Rhetoric Refigured*. Carbondale: Southern Illinois University Press, 1991.

Murphy, Patrick D. "Voicing Another Nature." In *A Dialogue of Voices: Feminist Literary Theory and Bakhtin*. Ed. Karen Hohne and Helen Wussow. Minneapolis: University of Minnesota Press, 1994. 59–82.

Powell, Malea. "Rhetorics of Survivance: How American Indians *Use* Writing." *College Composition and Communication* 53, no. 3 (2002): 396–434.

Quintilian, Marcus Fabius. *From Institutes of Oratory*. In *The Rhetorical Tradition: Readings from Classical Times to the Present*. Ed. Patricia Bizzell and Bruce Herzberg. Boston: Bedford Books of St. Martin's Press, 1990. 297–363.

Silko, Leslie Marmon. "Landscape, History, and the Pueblo Imagination." In *On Nature: Nature, Landscape, and Natural History*. Ed. Daniel Halpern. San Francisco: North Point, 1987. 83–94.

———. "Language and Literature from a Pueblo Indian Perspective." In *Yellow Woman and a Beauty of the Spirit: Essays on Native American Life Today*. New York: Touchstone, 1996. 48–59.

Starhawk. *Dreaming the Dark: Magic, Sex, and Politics*. Boston: Beacon, 1982.

Sturgeon, Noël. *Ecofeminist Natures: Race, Gender, Feminist Theory, and Political Action*. New York: Routledge, 1997.

Tarter, Jim. "Dreams of Earth: Place, Multiethnicity, and Environmental Justice in Linda Hogan's *Solar Storms*." In *Reading Under the Sign of Nature: New Essays in Ecocriticism*. Ed. John Tallmadge and Henry Harrington. Salt Lake City: University of Utah Press, 2000. 128–147.

CIRCLES WITHIN CIRCLES
Linda Hogan's Rhetoric of Indigenism

Ernest Stromberg

Chickasaw author Linda Hogan has been one of the most prolific writers in the ongoing Native American literary renaissance. The critical acclaim and awards her poetry, novels, and essays have earned place her among the elite Native American writers. Indeed, one could argue for her status as one of the major U.S. contemporary writers. Considered specifically as an American Indian novelist, however, a curious difference emerges when we compare her novels with those of a number of her contemporaries. Whereas most Native novelists have written about and from their specific tribal heritage, Hogan has yet to write a novel explicitly about the Chickasaw. Instead, her focus has ranged to the south with the fictional Florida tribe, the Taiga, in *Power* and to the north with the Cree and other First Nations people in *Solar Storms*. Indeed the closest she has come to writing a novel about the Chickasaw is with her focus on the Osage in *Mean Spirit*.

Hogan's decision to write about tribal communities other than the Chickasaw may strike some readers as insignificant. After all, isn't it the writer's right, even his or her duty, to go beyond such parochial limits? Is not the exploration of perspectives beyond one's own at the very heart of the imaginative enterprise? In the most idealistic sense, the answer to both questions might be an unqualified yes. In terms of Native American literature, however, such questions can only be addressed within the context of the history of representations of "Indians." The problem of representation has long been at issue for North America's indigenous peoples. From Christopher Columbus's journal entries through the "Indian Arts and Crafts Act" of 1990, literary, discursive, and artistic definitions of "Indians" have had a profound effect upon the lived experiences of actual Native peoples.

Representations, whether in images or words, are ways of knowing; and what we know or think we know about an object or people informs how we treat it or them. For example, the bizarre descriptions of cannibalism and promiscuity among the natives of what is present-day Brazil in Amerigo Vespucci's *Mundus Novus* were instrumental in shaping Spanish policies of forcible conversion to Christianity and enslavement. It made little difference that his texts reflected his own licentious projections more than any observed behavior; the rhetorical effects were devastating. Throughout U.S. history, literary and artistic representations have influenced the various policies designed to solve the "Indian problem." From Cooper's last Mohican to Edward S. Curtis's "The Vanishing Race—Navaho," representations of "Indians" have reinforced the belief that Native Americans were or are doomed to extinction in the name of progress and evolution. Even today, federal definitions (representations) still determine which groups and individuals are entitled to the official status of "Indian," with all the attendant rights and responsibilities.

Within the realm of literary studies, this history of the relationship between representations and policies provokes important critical questions about who is representing whom and to what end. As Robert Berkhofer asserts in his seminal study *The White Man's Indian,* the idea of "the *Indian* was a White invention and still remains largely a white image" (3). The idea of the Indian served to reduce hundreds of complex individual cultures into a single category. Indeed, "For most Whites . . . the Indian of imagination and ideology has been as real, perhaps more real, than the Native American of actual existence" (71). For the past 500 years the majority of literary representations of Indians have been composed by non-Indians. Although these representations have varied in form, remarkably consistent across this literary history has been the fundamental assumption that America's indigenous peoples were of a primitive, less evolved, if perhaps noble caste.

Yet over the years numerous Natives have written their own representations, from Guaman Poma in seventeenth-century Peru through D'Arcy McNickle in the first half of the twentieth century. Many of these writers have assumed oppositional positions to challenge and counter the representations offered by

Europeans and Euro-Americans. Only since the early 1970s, however, has the writing of Native Americans approached full flowering in terms of publication. From N. Scott Momaday's Pulitzer Prize in 1969, to Louise Erdrich's National Book Critics Circle Award in 1984, through Sherman Alexie's regular appearance on the best-seller list, Native American writers are both getting published and getting read. Linda Hogan numbers among the brighter blossoms of this flowering.

With this increased publication and readership, however, have come questions about the price and purpose of this success. Are the works popular because, out of a rhetorical concern with audience, they avoid challenging the assumptions of non-Indian readers? More to the point, at least for a number of Native critics, what is the relationship between the literary productions and ongoing struggles by specific Indian communities to assert their political sovereignty and insist upon their treaty rights? If literature is bound up with ideology, what can be said about the tribal politics of these works? In other words, what is the rhetorical force and trajectory of these works of fiction?

No critics of Native American literature have raised this question more forcefully than Elizabeth Cook-Lynn and Craig Womack. Both have articulated critical positions that insist upon the relationship between literary productions and the struggle for Native rights. In his *Red on Red: Native American Literary Separatism,* Womack asserts, "Native literary aesthetics must be politicized and . . . autonomy, self-determination, and sovereignty [must] serve as useful literary concepts" (11). In her collection of essays *Why I Can't Read Wallace Stegner,* Cook-Lynn makes a related point when she asks provocatively "whether successful American Indian writers . . . may . . . have moved away from nationalistic concerns in order to gain the interest of mainstream readers" (80). Given the function of narrative to shape our understanding of the world and the history of representations of Indians, these points and questions seem well worth pursuing.

In addition to their emphasis on the ideology of Native literature, both Cook-Lynn and Womack argue for the sovereignty of specific tribal literary traditions. Cook-Lynn, for example, in a series of otherwise laudatory comments on Leslie Marmon Silko's *Almanac of the Dead,* criticizes the novel for "not tak[ing] into account the specific tribal/nation status of the original occupants of this continent" (93). What Cook-Lynn criticizes is the effacement of specific tribal–Indian nation definitions and concerns beneath the stroke of a "pan-Indian journey toward retribution" (93). In a similar vein, in *Red on Red* Womack argues against writing that represents an "Indian genericism . . . that obscures concrete tribal and land relationships" (235). Like Cook-Lynn, Womack insists upon the importance of recognizing and representing individual Indian nations' unique cultures and political statuses.

Cook-Lynn and Womack share a serious concern about the relationship between Native literary expressions and Native political sovereignty. Womack conveys this idea powerfully when he asserts:

> Native literature, and Native literary criticism, written by Native authors, is part of sovereignty: Indian people exercising the right to present images of themselves and to discuss those images. Tribes recognizing their own extant literatures, writing new ones, and asserting the right to explicate them constitute a move toward nationhood. . . . The ongoing expression of a tribal voice, through imagination, language, and literature, contributes to keeping sovereignty alive in the citizens of a nation and gives sovereignty a meaning that is defined within the tribe rather than by external sources. (14)

We may understand Womack's position in light of the rhetorical function of non-Indian representations of Indians to define Native American sovereignty and identity. From blood quantum to the federal recognition process, the imagination and language of "external sources" have set the legal and political terms for Native American sovereignty.

The implications of Womack's and Cook-Lynn's arguments, however, raise potentially troubling questions when applied to the study and criticism of contemporary literature written by Native Americans. In Cook-Lynn's essay "The American Indian Fiction Writers: Cosmopolitanism, Nationalism, the Third World, and First Nation Sovereignty," she cites critic William Bevis's comment that Native writers "don't even trespass upon each other's tribes" (*Why I Can't Read Wallace Stegner* 88). Yet a quick examination of the writing by Native authors shows that this is not always the case. Obviously, Linda Hogan's novels provide three clear examples of such literary "trespass." In all her novels she arguably violates the limits of literary sovereignty described by Womack. That is, Hogan, as a non-Osage and a non-Canadian First Nations' writer, arguably writes as another "external source" creating images of these people.

Hogan is hardly the only or even the first Native writer to focus on communities outside her own specific heritage. N. Scott Momaday, of Kiowa and Cherokee heritage, tells a Pueblo story in *House Made of Dawn*. More recently, Blackfeet–Gros Ventre writer James Welch tells a Lakota story in *The Heartsong of Charging Elk*. Clearly, some Native writers do "trespass" upon each other's tribes. Is this a problem? In the terms of Cook-Lynn and Womack, do these novels by "outsiders," albeit Native American outsiders, violate the respective subject people's literary sovereignty?

Obviously, the answer to this question resides outside the purview of this chapter or the work of any critic, for that matter. The members of a given community will determine if their sovereignty has been violated. Rather, I would like to use Hogan's work, especially *Mean Spirit*, as a test case for the limits of the critical positions offered by Cook-Lynn and Womack. At the same time, I will examine the extent to which Hogan's novel advances their nationalist and separatist agendas. Finally, in the context of Native sovereignty, I would like to tease out the assumptions that seem to underlie Hogan's acts of literary trespass.

In her 1990 novel *Mean Spirit,* Hogan provides a revisionary history of the Osage oil boom in Oklahoma during the 1920s. As the *Voices from the Gaps* website describes the novel, "Though a work of fiction, *Mean Spirit* functions as an ethnohistory as it re-tells the story of 'the great frenzy' from an Osage perspective" ("Linda Hogan"). Within the recent history of Western literary aesthetics, Hogan's decision to write a novel from an Osage perspective although she is not an Osage might be considered an example of artistic license. Indeed, as mentioned earlier, within the Western tradition one could argue that it is the highest calling of the literary imagination to place oneself in the shoes of another and to imaginatively represent the other's view.

Yet the representational act is never simply an innocent aesthetic act. Issues of power and politics are always intertwined with the literary act. And within the United States the power and politics of publishing have a lot to say about whose representations of whom get published. For example, consider Beatrice Medicine's comments regarding Ruth Beebe Hill's novel *Hanta Yo*: "Native people living in the contemporary world are usually the last to know and have something to say about what is being published concerning us" (Medicine in Cook-Lynn 67). This lack of awareness is perhaps less the case today than it was in the early 1980s when Medicine wrote this observation, as the controversy over Ian Frazier's *On the Rez* suggests. Although the widely published criticisms of Frazier's book by Sherman Alexie indicate a degree of change, *On the Rez* nonetheless provides another example of a non-Indian's book about Indians gaining as much or more popular attention than similar works authored by Native writers.

With the numerous denunciations of *Hanta Yo* and the debates over *On the Rez* in mind, where do we locate Linda Hogan's acts of literary trespass? Both Womack and Cook-Lynn argue that works of fiction by and about Native Americans are inescapably enmeshed in the politics of tribal sovereignty. Taken to its logical conclusion, Womack's argument implies only a member of the Osage nation can truly write from an Osage perspective without violating the tribe's sovereignty. Has Hogan violated that sovereignty? Or does her status as a Chickasaw grant her immunity? More seriously and to the point, is her work qualitatively different from a *Hanta Yo*? Addressing this question is where things get interesting. For although Womack makes a compelling case about ultimate perspective, surely any author can successfully incorporate perspectives that are Osage in origin. At the conclusion of *Mean Spirit,* Hogan offers acknowledgments for the information she includes in the novel; she includes Osage scholar Carol Hunter and Diane Fraher, also Osage. She also mentions a number of

Osage writers from whom she obtained information, among them John Joseph Matthews and Carter Revard (376–377).

Hogan has clearly gone to great lengths to authenticate events and give voice to perspectives that might be considered distinctly Osage. In this sense she attempts to make her novel a rhetorical vehicle for Osage voices and views. Yet this does not make *Mean Spirit* an Osage novel in terms of the way Cook-Lynn and Womack define the limits of cultural sovereignty. For Womack especially, an Osage literary work would derive from Osage traditions and an Osage landscape. He asserts, "Literature plays a vital role in [sovereignty] . . . since it is part of what constitutes the idea of nationhood; people formulate a notion of themselves as an imagined community through stories" (60). And my sense is that Hogan would agree. In other words, I do not think Hogan would claim to have written an "Osage novel." The function of her novel is not to assist the Osage in the ongoing process of creating a sense of themselves.

Nevertheless, in the terms established by Womack and Cook-Lynn, Hogan may be seen as violating Osage literary sovereignty. I have invoked the legal metaphor humorously; however, it is less amusing in light of the comments from the *Washington Post Book World* that grace the cover of my paperback edition of *Mean Spirit*: "Mean Spirit is about the cultural disintegration of the Osage Indian tribe as the white world intrudes." Although I think the reviewer's comments reflect a serious misreading, I can imagine that some members of the Osage nation might be troubled by pronouncements of their cultural disintegration.

Clearly, in writing a novel about the history of an extant people, Hogan walks a precarious line. The reviewer for the *Washington Post* suggests that Hogan's representation of the Osage in *Mean Spirit* conforms to the pattern established by earlier writers such as Cooper or photographers such as Curtis: Indians are vanishing or in this case disintegrating. Interestingly, in all three of her novels Hogan seems to anticipate an expectation of the vanishing Indian motif. The last words of *Mean Spirit* are "and they were alive" (375). *Solar Storms* ends with the assertion, "Something beautiful lives inside us. You will see. Just believe it. You will see" (351). And her most recent novel, *Power*, concludes in a similar fashion: "I dance and as the wind stirs in the trees, someone sings the song that says the world will go on living" (235). All three novels, although not shying away from the horrors that have been and continue to be committed against the respective Native peoples, assert their continued survival. According to Gerald Vizenor, "Simulation of the tragic has been sustained by the literature of dominance. . . . [T]he stories that turn the tribes tragic are not their own stories" (15–16). Hogan's refusal to close on a tragic note and her emphasis on survival provide rhetorical resistance to the "literature of dominance" and the meta-narrative of vanishing Indians. In this sense Hogan's work serves a different rhetorical function than the majority of novels written about Indians by non-Indians.

Linda Hogan's Rhetoric of Indigenism

Although the endings of her novels indicate a significant departure from those representations that suggest an end to Indians, the question remains of what we are to make of her decision to write about the Osage, Cree, or Taiga. To engage this question, let us begin with the first of the three novels, *Mean Spirit*. The fictional community of *Mean Spirit* is clearly composed of Osage primary characters, yet initially this is not made explicit. The first time the word *Osage* is mentioned, it comes in reference to someone named "Osage Star-Looking." Shortly thereafter, mention is made of John Stink, "an old Osage hermit." Yet neither of these characters figures prominently in the novel's central narrative. Indeed, Osage Star-Looking does not figure in the novel at all beyond this reference. Although the novel centers on the Osage, the specific cultural identity of the main characters is left rather uncertain through much of the novel. Rather than use the word *Osage*, Hogan refers to the characters as "Indians": "Belle Graycloud . . . was a light-skinned Indian" (4), "Moses Graycloud . . . was a good Indian man" (6), and Grace Blanket is "a Hill Indian" (5). We learn that the "Hill Indians were a peaceful group who had gone away from the changing world" (5). But we do not learn of which tribe: Osage, Chickasaw, Choctaw, Creek? Their specific cultural identity remains ambiguous. Later Michael Horse describes the congregation at church as "Indians . . . they were from one of the tribes around Watona" (12). No tribal names are mentioned. This is the case throughout much of the novel; the term *Indian* is used rather than specific tribal designations. This is unusual, as most American Indian people retain a clear sense of themselves as members of specific tribes prior to identification as Indians. As Jace Weaver asserts, "Despite a growing pan-Indian discourse, a Native person's primary self-identification remains that of his or her own tribe" (xiii).

I mention this ambiguity not to chastise Hogan for ignoring issues of cultural specificity. Instead, I see it as an example of her careful negotiation of the circle she is within and the circle she is not within. I use circles as symbols to represent the overlapping relationship between pan-Indian and tribal-specific definitions of identity. Hogan, as a Chickasaw writing about Osage experiences, is outside the Osage circle; she is not part of that specific community. She does, however, belong to the larger pan-Indian circle forged in part by U.S. policies that treat all Indians the same, such as relocation programs, allotment, and boarding school assimilationist pedagogies. These circles—the tribal-specific and the pan-Indian—overlap yet remain distinct. As an American Indian woman, Hogan belongs to a history shared by the Osage and other Native Americans living within U.S. borders. Thus when writing about the Osage or any other Native community, Hogan is something of both an insider and an outsider. She clearly does not have the complete vantage point of an Osage, but she has a perspective in many ways unavailable to most non-Indians.

Ernest Stromberg

Hogan's limited use—almost avoidance, in fact—of the term *Osage* suggests an implied acknowledgment of Womack's argument that specific tribes have the right to craft their own representations. This leads to something of a balancing act, by which I refer to the challenge of creating a cast of Osage-identified characters who are complex and detailed without "misrepresenting" the Osage. (Of course, from a poststructuralist position, one could argue that all we have are misrepresentations.) Are the characters identifiably Osage, or is the novel an example of what Womack calls an "Indian genericism"? Arguably, Hogan's repeated use of the term *Indian* rather than specific tribal names can be seen as an example of what Berkhofer refers to as "giving a . . . reality to the original White image of the Indian as a separate but single collectivity" (195) or of Womack's "Indian genericism."

For both Berkhofer and Womack, the collective "Indian" is a diminished term. For Berkhofer, it implies a collective identity imposed upon all Indian people. In this model tribal specificity becomes homogenized in a white-manufactured pan-Indian melting pot. And there is something to this claim. The boarding school settings that brought children from a variety of tribes under a standardized curriculum were designed to melt away tribal identities. Yet history is also filled with Indian-framed alliances. In this sense we might think of the term *pan-Indian* as an oppositional term, signifying a unified front of indigenous people joining to oppose the incursions of European colonists. Prominent examples of this version of pan-Indian identity include "Pontiac's confederation of Ottawas and other peoples" (Stiffarm and Lane 32) and the Shawnee Tecumseh's alliance. On a spiritual level, the Ghost Dance is a pan-Indian movement. In more recent times political organizations such as the Society of American Indians, the National Indian Youth Council, and the American Indian Movement have gathered under a collective pan-Indian identity.

This oppositional and Indian-determined sense of a collective identity pervades *Mean Spirit*. Indeed, the setting of the novel in Oklahoma calls attention to the history of Indian removals in the early nineteenth century that relocated Cherokee, Creek, Choctaw, and Chickasaw peoples from the Southeast to "Indian territory"—much of present-day Oklahoma. Within the novel we follow some of the characters through a peyote ceremony and witness Osage participating in a sweat lodge ceremony conducted by a Lakota medicine person. The novel reveals a recognition of common ground, not simply an imposed collective identity.

How, then, might we categorize Hogan's novels? The issues raised by Cook-Lynn and Womack have led critic Arnold Krupat, in an effort to distinguish recent directions in the theorizing of Native American literature, to identify three major critical perspectives: "Nationalism, Indigenism, and Cosmopolitanism." According to Krupat, "From an indigenist perspective, it is not the nation, but the 'earth' that is the source of values on which a critical perspective must be based. Thus, in Linda Hogan's novel *Power,* Omishto . . . remembers a time when 'The whole earth loved the human people'" (220). This indigenist ethos infuses all of Hogan's work. Krupat draws from a number of Native sources to define indigenism as a worldview that privileges a spiritual relationship with the land and nonhuman nature (220). Cook-Lynn defines the indigenous view of the world as one in which the "origins of the people are . . . rooted in a specific geography (place), [and] that mythology (soul) and geography (land) are inseparable" (88).

From *Mean Spirit, Solar Storms,* and *Power* through her essays and many of her poems, Hogan clearly believes this worldview is held by Native Americans across tribal lines. In her book *The Woman Who Watches Over the World,* Hogan expresses her own sense of indigenism: "There is something that we Indian people share at the deepest levels of ourselves and it is a living present thing . . . in a voice always at the ear, an old song, the land we come from" (27–28). Hogan places this indigenist perspective in opposition to Western European views: "I've concluded over the years that the two ways, Native and European, are almost impossible to intertwine" (27). In *Mean Spirits* one character hears "the sound of earth speaking . . . the deep and dreaming voice of the land" (188). And in *Solar Storms* the narrator wonders, "How could it be . . . that all people who came from their own earth, who lived there for tens of thousands of years, could talk with spirits, could hear land speak, and animals? . . . Could they all have been wrong? I didn't think so" (189). Clearly, part of Hogan's rationale for writing about tribes outside her specific heritage is a firm belief in an indigenist worldview that transcends tribal borders. Traditions from a wide variety of sources suggest that a reverence for the land and the importance of maintaining the right relationship with the land are indeed significant components of what might be called an indigenous worldview. Thus as an indigenist woman with an understanding of this spiritual outlook, she can write of the Osage, Cree, and Indians of Florida in a way that reflects at least a partial sense of their worldviews.

From this perspective, Hogan's decision to understate the Osage identity of *Mean Spirit*'s characters and to repeatedly use the term *Indians* is a way for her to advance an indigenist position. To put it another way, the characters are Osage, but part of what makes them Osage is that they are indigenous—that is, they have an earth-based spiritual outlook shared by most tribes, including the Chickasaw. From an indigenist perspective, then, there is no contradiction in representing perspectives that are simultaneously Osage and Indian. The novel further promotes the idea of specific beliefs transcending tribal lines during a scene depicting a sweat lodge ceremony. Before the ceremony, Lakota FBI agent Stace Red Hawk learns of Michael Horse's role as the firekeeper. He thinks to himself, "[He] understood. They had firekeepers, too, in South Dakota"

(216). Hogan illustrates a specific cross-tribal practice as a way of supporting an indigenist perspective. The novel, with the depiction of the peyote ceremony, illustrates how Native Americans have developed pan-tribal ceremonies that cohere around a shared sense of indigenousness. Indeed the sweat ceremony depicted in the novel is not an Osage ceremony and is conducted by a Lakota medicine person, Lionel Tall.

Although the existence of shared beliefs and perspectives provides Hogan with material to write confidently about diverse tribal cultures, things get sticky when the novel depicts practices or ceremonies that might be considered specific to an individual tribe. On the subject of writing about tribal-specific ceremonies, Paula Gunn Allen has questioned the appropriateness of Leslie Marmon Silko's use of a traditional Keres narrative in *Ceremony*: "[T]he story is a clan story and is not told outside the clan" (Allen in Cook-Lynn 92). The novelist who would write about another culture faces the dilemmas of knowing traditions from that culture to imbue the novel with authenticity and also of knowing which traditions it is permissible to share outside the tribal circle. In *Mean Spirit* Hogan opts to write mainly about pan-tribal ceremonies, the peyote and sweat lodge ceremonies, for example. She may tread close to the line, however, in the novel's depictions of bat medicine. The novel describes the bat medicine bundle held by Joe Billy, son of Sam Billy, "a practitioner of bat medicine, one of the strongest traditions of healing" (136). As the novel progresses, we learn more about bat medicine. Yet the discussions of the bats and their sacred functions beg two questions. Do bats and bat medicine hold the position in Osage tradition the novel claims? And if they do, is this information meant to be shared with non-Osage? As a non-Osage I am not privy to the answers to these questions, and if I were, it might not be my place to answer them.

So are *Mean Spirit* and, by implication, Hogan's other novels examples of Womack's "Indian genericism"? The answer is complex. On the one hand, yes. For as Osage poet and scholar Carter Revard emphatically asserts, *Mean Spirit* "is a good novel but not an Osage novel." In the same sense, *Solar Storms* is not a Cree novel and *Power* is not a Taiga novel. It could thus be argued that Hogan fails to meet Womack's call for Native writers "to pass on the traditions of their respective tribal nations" (15). Womack then asks, "If Indian writers write only about tribes other than their own . . . what happens to the next generation in their own communities back home"? (15). If we agree with Revard that *Mean Spirit* is not an Osage novel, we might well ask what kind of novel it is.

One answer would be that it and Hogan's other novels are pan-Indian or indigenous novels. Yet is this really a failing? Are they examples of "Indian genericism"? If so, consider that Hogan shares this criticism with no less than D'Arcy McNickle with his novel *Wind from an Enemy Sky* and Leslie Marmon Silko with both *Almanac of the Dead* and *Gardens in the Dunes*. Given the history of multitribal alliances, pan-Indian traditions, and assimilationist policies, it should come as no surprise that Hogan and other Native writers would not write only about their specific tribal background.

Perhaps a more pressing question is, what is accomplished in making these choices? In *Mean Spirit* Hogan writes about actual historical events that primarily involved a specific tribal nation. In doing this she avoids the kind of criticism Cook-Lynn directs at Silko's *Almanac of the Dead*. *Mean Spirit* does take into account specific treaty issues as they pertained to the Osage in the 1920s. In one scene Hogan effectively brings attention to the hypocrisy of the competency rulings used to prevent Osage people from collecting royalties on the oil drilled on Osage land. *Mean Spirit* explicitly engages the political issues facing the Osage as a specific tribe; it is not another example of the "mythic self-absorption" Cook-Lynn finds fault with in the work of some Native writers. *Mean Spirit* engages politics in the nationalist vein both Cook-Lynn and Womack advocate. Similar claims can be made about *Solar Storms*, a novel that describes the Canadian government's hydroelectric project's dams that flood First Nations' lands. Hogan's novels, then, provide a rhetorical function as they both challenge our understanding of history and directly confront ongoing policies detrimental to Native peoples.

The balancing act Hogan performs in *Mean Spirit*, *Solar Storms*, and *Power* may be understood as an example of what Peggy Ackerberg calls Hogan's "boundary breaking imperative" (Ackerberg in Bleck 29). According to Melani Bleck, "Hogan's novels seek to demonstrate that, although Western society remains bound by its inability to look past . . . spatial barriers . . . tribal relations remain free . . . and unbound because of tribal ties to nature" (30). That is perhaps Hogan's "trespass" on other tribes' turf with her writing to show that the spiritual values uniting the tribes transcend the specific cultural differences that might divide them. Indeed in *Mean Spirit*, not only do we have Osage people participating in peyote ceremonies and Lakota sweats, but a white Catholic priest converts to paganism, and Joe Billy's white wife becomes a bat dreamer. In essence, the imagined borders of race and religion crumble and are shown to be fluid and impermanent.

Perhaps more important, *Mean Spirit*, *Solar Storms*, and *Power* exemplify what scholar Jace Weaver calls communitism: community + activism. "Literature is communitist to the extent that it has a proactive commitment to Native community, including what I term the 'wider community' of creation itself" (xiii). In using her talents as a writer to expose a buried chapter in Osage and U.S. relations, to reveal to a larger audience the ongoing assaults against Canadian First Nations' people, and to articulate a holistic indigenous spiritual outlook, Hogan demonstrates a proactive commitment both to the specific tribes she writes about and to pan-Indian concerns and values. Hogan articulates her understanding of this commitment in her essay "All My Relations": "[T]his is the purpose of the ceremony. It is part of a healing and restoration. It is the mending of a broken connection between us and the rest. . . . 'All my relations' . . . those words create a relationship with other people, with animals, with the land" (*Dwellings* 40). In her novels' indigenist stance, Hogan attempts to do just that: to use "words [to] create a relationship with other people, with animals, with the land."

Works Cited

Berkhofer, Robert. *The White Man's Indian: Images of the American Indian from Columbus to the Present.* New York: Vintage, 1978.

Bleck, Melani. "Linda Hogan's Tribal Imperative: Collapsing Space Through 'Living' Tribal Traditions and Nature." *Studies in American Indian Literatures, Series 2*, vol. 11, no. 4 (1999): 23–45.

Cook-Lynn, Elizabeth. *Why I Can't Read Wallace Stegner and Other Essays.* Madison: University of Wisconsin Press, 1996.

Hogan, Linda. *Dwellings: A Spiritual History of the Living World.* New York: W. W. Norton, 1995.

———. *Mean Spirit.* New York: Ivy Books, 1990.

———. *Power.* New York: W. W. Norton, 1998.

———. *Solar Storms.* New York: Scribner, 1995.

———. *The Woman Who Watches Over the World: A Native Memoir.* New York: W. W. Norton, 2001.

Krupat, Arnold. "Nationalism, Indigenism, Cosmopolitanism: Three Critical Positions on Native American Literatures." In *Mirror Writing: (Re-)Constructions of Native American Identity.* Ed. Thomas Claviez and Maria Moss. Berlin: Galda and Wilch Verlag, 2000. 214–235.

"Linda Hogan." *Voices from the Gaps: Women Writers of Color.* 31 January 2002. <http://voices.cla.umn.edu/authors/LindaHogan.html>.

Revard, Carter. "Re: Query: Native Writers from Oklahoma." E-mail to Association for the Study of American Indian Literature. 15 December 2001.

Stiffarm, Lenore A., and Phil Lane Jr. "The Demography of Native North America: A Question of American Indian Survival." In *The State of Native America: Genocide, Colonization, and Resistance.* Ed. M. Annette Jaimes. Boston: South End, 1992. 120–149.

Vizenor, Gerald. *Manifest Manners: Postindian Warriors of Survivance.* Hanover, N.H.: Wesleyan University Press, 1994.

Weaver, Jace. *That the People Might Live: Native American Literatures and Native American Community.* New York: Oxford University Press, 1997.

Womack, Craig S. *Red on Red: Native American Literary Separatism.* Minneapolis: University of Minnesota Press, 1999.

VISIONING IDENTITY
Ways of Seeing in Linda Hogan's "Aunt Moon's Young Man"

BARBARA J. COOK

> Lower your head
> through the many eyes
> that burn into flesh
> and beyond.
> —Linda Hogan, "Nativity"
>
> A mirror is such a circle
> of revelations.
> —Linda Hogan, "Glass"

MIRRORS, CRYSTAL, GLASS—ALL ARE REFLECTIVE SURFACES that join with references to an individual's eyes and ways of seeing to permeate Chickasaw writer Linda Hogan's body of work. These images become metaphors reflecting constant observation of self and others, or in feminist terms, gazing. In feminist theory the term *the gaze* usually refers to patriarchal voyeurism, control, and objectification of the other—the female.[1] Hogan reverses this concept of the term in her short story "Aunt Moon's Young Man" by exploring the ways women attempt to control each other within a community where the women act as spectators and voyeurs. She uses the feminist concept of the gaze as a touchstone but challenges its negativity to encompass ways of seeing as a means of coming to terms with identity. Within this story Hogan depicts looking, reflections, gazing, and seeing as both a negative force—attempted control—and a positive force—observation as a key to one's development—creating a "circle of revelations" for her young protagonist ("Glass" 15–16). Hogan uses a variety of motifs based on ways of seeing and looking to tell the story of Sis, a young mixed-blood girl within a mixed tribal community, as Sis comes to understand her own identity and the identities of those close to her. When Sis leaves the community, maybe forever, she takes visual signifiers of her ancestors' traditions with her in the form of an eagle feather and her Aunt Moon's herbs—symbols that represent a commitment to age-old tribal traditions.

As she prepares to leave both physically and emotionally, Sis observes the interaction of her tribal community when a young man, Isaac, comes to town and begins a love affair with an older woman, Bess. Bess is already marginalized by the community because she clings to the old ways—she continues to prepare the old traditional herbal medicines; respects and acknowledges the interrelatedness of all living things (humans, animals, plants, and even celestial bodies); wears braids, silver bracelets, shell necklaces, and colorful shawls; and lives independently, performing the work of a man. Refusing to assimilate white customs and ideals, Bess seems to live and move with a magical self-assurance that makes her different from the other women of the town. When she takes a younger lover, those women isolate her even more, and only when Isaac appears to have abandoned Bess do they attempt to support her by purchasing her medicinal herbs once again. As Sis prepares to seek an education in another town, Isaac returns to Bess. Rather than abandoning her, he has been in jail for selling medicinal herbs—an illustration of the dominant culture's refusal to understand traditional cultural knowledge. As Sis watches their tender reunion, she recognizes that the boundaries imposed by the rules of her world—such as restrictive expectations about ways to live, dress, and act—could drain her energy and happiness if she allowed them to. In contrast to the tensions created by Anglo-American influences on tribal communities, her Aunt Moon (Bess Evening) and Isaac—representing for her the primordial past—seem to be the only adults she knows who are content and full of life.

Aunt Moon rejects the passivity of the women surrounding her. She laughs out loud and lives as she wishes. As a transgressive woman existing outside the limits of the tribal community, Aunt Moon goes beyond the boundaries imposed by the women of the community and lives on the margins of that marginal society—a world where she is identified as different or "other" to a group already ethnically "other." Within this liminal world she attempts to maintain or re-create the old traditions of the culture, but because she lives outside the feminine discipline of that community she is ostracized. Ironically, she becomes "the other" because she is more "Indian"—full-blooded, although a mixture of tribes—than the rest of the town's women. The women of the community attempt to police Bess's actions and seemingly their own through their actions and gazes. Thus "Aunt Moon's Young Man" becomes the story of the interaction within a community as well as the story of Sis and Bess. Although the story focuses on Sis, all of the characters are significant because Hogan is interested not just in an individual but in the process of negotiating identity within community. Hogan says, "[M]y writing comes from and goes back to the community. . . . I am interested in the deepest questions, those of spirit, of shelter, of growth and movement toward peace and liberation, inner and outer" (115).

In "Aunt Moon's Young Man" Hogan's challenge of the feminist concept of the gaze delves into issues of community and spirit, growth, and an individual's movement toward inner and outer peace and liberation. Rather than explore the lives of mixed bloods in a white world, she juxtaposes the full-blooded characters (Isaac and Aunt Moon) against the rest of the tribal community of mixed Indian and white blood. This conflict is established through looking or gazing. The narrator, Sis, first sees Aunt Moon's young man, Isaac, and notices that he stands "in that semi-slumped, half-straight manner of full-blood Indians" (118). She acknowledges that she has always thought of pure bloods as better than her own "Heinz 57" blood. He represents the strength of the traditional ways with his strong yet gentle hands. He knows the narratives from the past and tells Sis the fairgrounds are "where the three tribes used to hold sings" (131). When he sings one of the old songs, it stirs a memory of a song she has heard only in her dreams. Hogan contrasts the strength of Isaac with the town's mixed-blood men, broken by war and the lure of white man's gold: "He was alive in his whole body while the other men walked with great effort and stiffness, even those who did little work and were still young" (123).

Even though Aunt Moon is of mixed Chickasaw and Navajo heritage, she, too, represents the old ways. She gathers and dries medicinal herbs like her parents, and she reads the planets; Sis tells us that "sometimes when I was with her, I knew the older Indian world was still here and I'd feel it in my skin and hear the night sounds speak to me, hear the voice of water tell stories about people who lived here before, and the deep songs came out from the hills" (130). As if the remembrance and practice of the old ways created a whole and healed person, we are told that Aunt Moon is special and has life in her. She is contrasted with the women of the town who are large and nervous, grown sullen with taking care of men broken by war. Bess (Aunt Moon) says of the women, "They have eaten their anger and grown large" (120). As Hogan explores the contrasts between the mixed-blood people of the town and pure-blooded Isaac and Bess, she also explores the conflict between the ways of looking at life—assimilation and tradition—these two types represent.

With this external conflict Hogan seems to be addressing the internal conflict of identity. For many American Indians, according to author and critic Louis Owens, "the problem of identity comprehends centuries of colonial and postcolonial displacement, often brutally enforced peripherality, cultural denigration . . . and systematic oppression by the monocentric 'westering' impulse in America" (4). In other words, American Indians have lost their sense of place and identity as white Americans followed their Manifest Destiny, settled the West, and callously took Indian lands and attempted to eradicate their culture by insisting upon conformity to the white man's language, culture, and lifestyle.

American Indian fiction often attempts to recover or rearticulate an identity, "a process dependent upon a rediscovered sense of place as well as community" (Owens 5). Native American writers, especially those of mixed blood, as Owens argues, use fiction to deconstruct "the verbal artifacts of Indian—mixed blood—identity"; and for some, their writings "represent a process of reconstruction, of self-discovery and cultural recovery" (5). Russian critic Mikhail Bakhtin (although not writing specifically about Native American works) contends that in the dialogic process, context is crucial to understanding. In this process of discussing and examining Native American literature, it is crucial that readers understand to some extent the world depicted. As Native American authors reconstruct their identity, both they and their non-Indian readers face the challenge of understanding the two worlds Native Americans live in. As Bakhtin points out, all discourse is already "charged with [alien] value and enveloped in an obscuring mist" (276–277). Native American writers are faced with the additional dilemma of a discourse that presents points of view from two very different cultural perspectives—one imposed by white American culture and one reaching back to a past American Indian culture. Hogan writes that the stories of Indian people "do not begin with us as individuals" (*Woman* 78). For her their stories begin at least 100 years ago. Whereas Bess represents a past culture, the women of the town represent the influence of the dominant white culture. But both stories begin in the past.

For most non-Native readers Native American literature is an entry to a world they have long been fascinated with—from the "noble savage" of the 1800s to the romantic Indian of the New Age movement. As Hogan deconstructs and reconstructs her characters, she—like many other American Indian writers—is "redefining American Indian identity" (Owens 7). Hogan plays with this identity by contrasting traditional images of Bess and Isaac with motifs from the dominant white culture—images and motifs observed by Sis. One example in this story is the contrast between the traditional "braid" of Aunt Moon's hairstyle (a style common to both Chickasaw and Navajo traditions) and the rollers Sis's mother uses in an obvious effort to copy a hairstyle from the world of white women.

Sis sees Aunt Moon as the personification of the freedom of a traditional Indian woman. She lives on the borders of the community but does not seem bothered by it. Sis admires the way "she move[s], slowly, taking up as much space as she want[s] and doing it with ease" ("Aunt Moon" 119). Hogan's depiction of Aunt Moon can be better understood if we see Aunt Moon as living in

Visioning Identity

defiance of the dominant society's discipline directed against the body that Michel Foucault describes. Foucault theorizes that this discipline "invades the body and seeks to regulate its very forces and operations, the economy and efficiency of its movements" (Foucault in Bartky 61). Foucault believes this discipline is initially enforced by the power of the dominant society, but eventually the discipline is self-imposed. According to feminist theorist Sandra Lee Bartky, this self-surveillance is a form of obedience to patriarchy, and we see the women in the story trying to impose their standards (adopted from those of the dominant society) on the "other" (Bess) within their own marginal community. This sets up a conflict among the women of the town as Bess becomes a site of resistance to the rules women of the community are expected to obey. She doesn't go to church, she throws "back her head and laugh[s] out loud," she does a man's work, and she lives "in sin" with a younger man ("Aunt Moon" 127). In light of the matriarchal structure of some Indian cultures, including Navajo and Chickasaw, it is significant that this site of resistance to the community of mixed-blood women is represented by full-blooded Bess. She continues her Native tradition of feminine control and resists ideals derived from the patriarchal culture outside the tribal community.

Also suggestive of this theory of self-imposed discipline is the way Hogan uses the gaze and actions of the women in the community as they seek to police Aunt Moon's actions and their own as well. The female roles of the community seem self-imposed rather than imposed by a patriarchy; that is, they are imposed by matriarchal custom. The community of women is, however, imposing patriarchal ideas from the dominant culture even though the women themselves are marginalized. This, too, falls in line with Foucault's theory that subordinate groups allow themselves to be subordinated or give in to the loss of power. Native American folklorist and writer Rayna Green explains how this patriarchal model of subordination and the resulting loss of women's power came about in U.S. tribal communities in the introduction to her anthology *That's What She Said*:

> Native women from many tribes show a natural appreciation of feminist concerns since they either come from tribes that were matriarchal and matrifocal in nature—and therefore find themselves dispossessed by the encroachment of European patriarchal forms—or come from tribes where female spheres of power remain denigrated in favor of male power. (10)

Green believes that although politics are usually subtle in female Native American authors' works, there is recognition that the root of Indian women's problems appears attributable "to the callousness and sexism of Indian men and white society equally" (10). She proposes that the writers "often reveal a poignant desire to return to older social and ceremonial forms, [to] intertwine men and women in mutual, complementary roles as religious leaders, healers, political figures, and educators" (10). As a rhetorical strategy this provides a foundation from which Native American women are able to construct identity. Although acknowledging the liminal location of Indians in modern society, this identity is grounded in traditional ways of being.

The tribal cultures represented in this story, Navajo and Hogan's Chickasaw tribe, are historically matriarchal in nature; however, only one event specifically addresses the balance of power between the men and women of the tribal community—that occurs when Sis is forbidden to visit Aunt Moon's house while Isaac is living there. Her mother indicates that the matter is not open for discussion, and Sis realizes that "it was my father who made the decision. My mother had probably argued my point and lost to him again, and lost some of her life as well" (132). So it would seem that even though the men were "broken by the war" and appeared not to be in control, in reality the mixed-blood women were in a subordinate position—a position dictated by the Anglo-American colonizers' values rather than their own tribal heritage.

Hogan's exploration of power and place through the trope of the gaze as a pathway to finding identity is the central issue in this story. She uses looking in a variety of ways—there are mirrors, broken and small; clear glass and windows; and many descriptions of "eyes." We first see Bess Evening's house through the window glass as it appears as a model sitting on Sis's mother's shoulder. Later, Sis and her mother gaze at Isaac while pretending to watch the sky. As they look at Bess's house sitting up on the hill, they remark that she can see everything from up there and everything can see her—a trope reminiscent of Foucault's discussion of *panoptica*. Sis discovers that her mother can read her mind by reading her face—"the inner workings of the mind were clear in her face, like words in a book" (120).

Later, at a community dance Isaac is reflected in Bess's eyes, and like a hypnotist his large black eyes pull Bess to him. All of the women are looking at and nervously flirting with him, blushing and talking too loud. The local men are unaware of the newly arrived distraction, and Sis notes that her father and the other men have their usual "faraway, unfocused gaze" (124). As Isaac and Bess dance together, the others leave a large empty space around them—a form of isolation in the midst of a community, a way of setting them apart wherein they become the focus of the gaze.

Following the dance, the women of the town turn against Bess; she is carrying on with a stranger young enough to be her son. They forget they had been staring at him with longing themselves, and thus "one of the oldest dances of women took place, for women in those days turned against each other easily, never thinking they might have other enemies" (126). Hogan is clearly depicting more than stereotypical female jealousy here. For the women of the community Bess is living in sin, and they are sure Isaac is full of demons. Although they ostracize Bess even during her pregnancy and refuse to buy her medicines, as soon as they hear Isaac has disappeared they focus their attention on her and rush to support her, since she has apparently suffered the consequences of her independent ways.

It is interesting that Hogan uses the act of looking to reveal more than the plot of the story, since in Native American culture individuals commonly limit direct eye contact. Perhaps this is reflective of the mixed-blood culture she is writing about and a bow to the dominant society—patriarchal and white. In *Ways of Seeing* John Berger and his coauthors say, "[S]eeing comes before words" and "seeing establishes our place in the surrounding world" (7). What we believe or know, our experience, affects the way we see people and objects. The women of the town gaze longingly at Isaac as a promise of escape from their unpleasant situations, and both Isaac and Bess—representing the traditions of their ancestors—depict personal freedom the mixed-blood women, with "hearts like withered raisins" (137), do not have access to. Sis, as a young woman coming of age, tutored in life's opportunities by Bess, and encouraged by her mother to seek education outside the closed community, sees with a clarity usually available only to the very young or the very old. She recognizes that we must create our own identity or it is forced on us.

Berger also points out that "the eye of the other combines with our own eye to make it fully credible that we are part of the visible world" (9). Hogan combines the eye from within and the eye of the imagination in her story. Contrasting them with the vitality of Aunt Moon, she calls the other women in the town "cold in the eye" (120). When describing a psychically wounded war veteran she says, "His eyes were broken windows" (12). We know immediately what she means—he is a shattered soul. We are also told that Bess has second sight, surely a magical power, alluding to psychic ability.

It is perhaps Aunt Moon's description of the soul as "a small woman inside the eye who leaves at night to wander new places" that brings an even stronger Indian worldview into the story, a view comfortable with blending and intertwining time and space (127). This spiritual reference is repeated when Bess is described as breaking all the rules, resulting in ostracism by the women—"the small woman inside her eye was full and lonely at the same time" (127). Another time, Sis's mother is fed up with the foolish women, and Sis notes that she looks "like the woman inside her eye had just wandered off" (133). When Isaac leaves, Sis hears that "the young man inside Aunt Moon's eye was gone" (135). She later sees Isaac and Bess together when he returns, and she "could tell there were many men and women living inside their eyes that moment" (137). Their union draws strength from their ancestors and implies a union representing the strength and continuance of the old ways. Drawing on the inner strength of her own soul, Sis says as she leaves town and moves into her future, "And I had a small, beautiful woman in my eye" (138).

Hogan ends her story with Sis's triumph over inner as well as outer obstacles. Hogan refers to this viewpoint in an interview with Patricia Clark Smith: "That's what peace and equality must mean to us all—that we can have joy in living and no more cold war of the inner self" (155). The inner self is seen in the eyes of the characters. In another interview, this one with Bo Schöler, Hogan says: "It's a lifelong job to peel the layers back and see what's really underneath our trained conditioning and emotional responses. . . . It is about the inner journey, about others before us who have gone that way, and civilizations" (111).

A mirror plays a part in peeling back those layers as Sis, after she wipes away the memory of her first kiss, looks into the bathroom mirror and sees nothing, "just shelves of medicine bottles and aspirin" ("Aunt Moon" 137). She has forgotten that the mirror was broken mysteriously one night during an argument. The family had been using a "small framed mirror in the living room" (123). Berger suggests that a mirror is often used in art and literature as a symbol of women's vanity when in reality it allows one to join others in gazing at self (50–51). I suggest that Hogan uses the mirror to represent the possibility of a self that grows smaller or disappears—a loss of identity, perhaps a moving away from cultural traditions. First the family has to use the smaller mirror, and then when Sis forgets about the broken mirror, there is no reflection; she disappears. "Glass," a poem in Hogan's *The Book of Medicines,* reinforces this reading of Hogan's use of mirrors:

> When I was a child
> I would stand between mirrors
> and see myself grow small,
> infinite
> and far away. (65)

Hogan uses the image of Sis and her disappearing image in the family mirror, and "Glass" allows another insight into possible meanings of Hogan's use of mirrors in her work and supports the interpretation of a self that sometimes grows smaller as a result of interaction with the "self" in a mirror. This reflective surface adds multiple dimensions to her protagonist's search for identity and allows for more than one possible future.

Another step in Sis's awakening to possibilities of negotiating her individual identity between two worlds is her observation of the gentleness of the love Isaac expresses for Bess. Just as more than one possibility exists for her as an individual, choices are available in relationships between women and in those between men and women. Her learning is enabled by what she sees, and as Sis gazes at Isaac and Bess when they are dancing, she observes that "they held each other gently like two breakable vases" (125). When Isaac touches Bess on the arm so softly Sis isn't sure Bess felt it, she reflects that she has never seen a man touch a woman that softly. Several times she notices the gentleness with which he holds Bess and pulls her toward him. She sees their gentle love shortly after she lets Jim Tens kiss her goodbye and contrasts his "cold" kiss with that warm, gentle love. Once again Hogan is endowing Isaac and Bess with an almost mythic purity—a purity that represents the sacredness of ancestral stories and unions from the beginnings of Indian culture.

Hogan incorporates a preoccupation with origins, marginality, and otherness in her work. In "Aunt Moon's Young Man" Hogan gives the reader a character steeped in tribal traditions who represents the other to a community already on the margins of the dominant society. Native writers often seem to move in the crosscurrents between oral tradition and the Western literary tradition. The return to traces, the fragments and debris of memory and history seen in Native literatures, presents a postmodern construction and, according to postmodernist critic Brian McHale, "produces new insights, new or richer connections, coherence of a different degree or kind, ultimately *more discourse*" (McHale in Vizenor 4; original emphasis). Although the postmodernist view has opened the tribal literatures to more formal literary criticism and thus discourse, I believe it is the individual writer's process of self-discovery and cultural recovery at the center of many contemporary narratives that draws most readers to their work. There is value in looking at Sis's individual quest as readers attempt to understand the construction of their own identity. Native American writers reach back to their tribal oral traditions of storytelling, myth, and song; blend them with contemporary issues and signifiers; and in the process recover an identity—a sense of place and community. In speaking of her mixed blood Hogan has said, "[I]t allows for a great amount of freedom. If you live on the boundaries between cultures, you are both of those cultures and neither of those cultures, and you can move with great mobility in any direction you want" ("'A Heart Made out of Crickets'" 114).

As Native American writers move between these cultures in their works, they move toward a unification of the past and future with the present and toward "a coherent personal identity entirely dependent upon a coherent cultural identity" (Owens 20). In shaping a cultural identity in her work, Hogan draws on reflective metaphors. From Grace Blanket's "rooms of cut glass" that create a "cool, shimmering opulence" in her "icy palace of crystal" (*Mean Spirit* 48) and her daughter's marriage, fragile "like glass" (195) in *Mean Spirits,* to the fragments of Angel's pocket mirror, which she finally abandons as she begins to read people's "eyes to see what kind of souls they had" (85) in *Solar Storms,* she uses these surfaces not just to fragment but to construct a thoughtful identity.

Barbara J. Cook

According to Owens, in contrast to the postmodernist celebration of fragmentation and chaos of experience,

> [L]iterature by Native American authors tends to seek transcendence of such ephemerality and the recovery of eternal and immutable elements represented by a spiritual tradition that escapes historical fixation, that places humanity within a carefully cyclically ordered cosmos and gives humankind irreducible responsibility for the maintenance of that delicate balance. (20)

Such grand goals are hard to achieve within the limits of a short story; however, Linda Hogan comes close to accomplishing them in "Aunt Moon's Young Man." As I have discussed, the relationship between Bess and Isaac illustrates and confirms the personal fulfillment available through adherence to their ancestors' traditions. They live in the old way—they prepare herbal medicines, sing the old songs, and read the planets. We have seen that when supported by the power of these traditions, Bess is not controlled by the gaze of the women of the community. Sis observes the community with great clarity and is empowered by Bess as she is taught the ways of her ancestors. Ultimately, pushed by her mother to leave the restrictive community and seek the knowledge offered by the dominant white society, Sis carries the strength of those traditional ways within her, but she also takes signifiers of those traditions (herbs and an eagle feather) as visual reminders of their strength.

By using physical symbols of her tribal traditions, Hogan completes the thread of ways of seeing. Sis, rather than depending on inner memory alone, will be reminded of the traditions personified by Bess when she looks at the herbs and feather. These signifiers function as a kind of visual cultural synecdoche as she moves even further into the dominant white culture, seeking her own individual pathway.

Note

1. British film scholar Laura Mulvey's groundbreaking essay analyzing the male gaze in film, "Visual Pleasure and Narrative Cinema," has been anthologized and reprinted extensively. Originally written in 1973, it appeared in *Screen* in 1975. Mulvey later reflected on this essay in a piece entitled "Afterthoughts on Visual Pleasure and Narrative Cinema," published in *Frameworks* in 1981. Writing from the Lacanian perspective used by French feminists such as Hélène Cixous and Luce Irigaray, Mulvey's essay inspired not only an entire school of film theory but an approach to literature in which narrative point of view, the seeing eye of the text and its reader, is substituted for the gaze of the camera and the spectator.

Works Cited

Bakhtin, Mikhail. *The Dialogic Imagination: Four Essays by M. M. Bakhtin.* Ed. Michael Holquist. Trans. Caryl Emerson and Michael Holquist. Austin: University of Texas Press, 1981.

Bartky, Sandra Lee. "Foucault, Femininity, and the Modernization of Patriarchal Power." In *Feminism and Foucault: Reflections on Resistance*. Ed. Irene Diamond and Lee Quinby. Boston: Northeastern University Press, 1988. 61–86.

Berger, John, Sven Blomberg, Chris Fox, Michael Dibb, and Richard Hollis. *Ways of Seeing*. London: British Broadcasting Corporation and Penguin Books, 1972.

Green, Rayna, ed. *That's What She Said: Contemporary Poetry and Fiction by Native American Women*. Bloomington: Indiana University Press, 1984.

Hogan, Linda. "Aunt Moon's Young Man." In *Best American Short Stories*. New York: Houghton Mifflin, 1989. 128–147.

———. "Glass." In *The Book of Medicines*. Minneapolis: Coffee House, 1993. 65–66.

———. "'A Heart Made out of Crickets': An Interview with Linda Hogan." By Bo Schöler. *Journal of Ethnic Studies* 16 (Spring 1988): 107–117.

———. "Linda Hogan." By Patricia Clark Smith. In *This Is About Vision: Interviews with Southwestern Writers*. Ed. William Balassi, John F. Crawford, and Annie O. Eysturoy. Albuquerque: University of New Mexico Press, 1990. 141–155.

———. *Mean Spirit*. New York: Ivy Books, 1990.

———. "Nativity." In *That's What She Said: Contemporary Poetry and Fiction by Native American Women*. Bloomington: Indiana University Press, 1984. 161.

———. *Solar Storms*. New York: Scribner, 1995.

———. *The Woman Who Watches Over the World: A Native Memoir*. New York: W. W. Norton, 2001.

Owens, Louis. *Other Destinies: Understanding the American Indian Novel*. Norman: University of Oklahoma Press, 1994.

Vizenor, Gerald, ed. *Narrative Chance: Postmodern Discourse on Native American Indian Literatures*. Norman: University of Oklahoma Press, 1993.

"THE INSIDE OF LIES AND HISTORY"
Linda Hogan's Poetry of Conscience

Ernest Smith

> When I discovered poetry I fell in love with it. I thought it was the most incredible thing in the world. It was not only a language, it was an emotion. It was something that moved me, and that I believed could affect change.
> —Linda Hogan, "Interview" 114

Linda Hogan's poetry is a work of seeking and of affirmation. Hogan's poems drive toward deep, ancient, yet forgotten bonds with the earth, animals, and other human beings. Her voice is communal yet individual, political yet lyrical, epic yet personal. Spanning twenty years of work in a variety of genres, her five volumes of verse condense recurring themes from her fiction and nonfiction and establish her as a major figure within the rich traditions of Native American poetry, contemporary women's poetry, and the postmodern lyric mode. In this chapter I consider all of Hogan's poetry as a spiritual journey toward personal and political awareness, one that involves moving through and beyond one's own physical body as a means of understanding our mysterious but essential connections with the earth. This process allows consciousness to become conscience, allows awareness to become a form of action, and questions the viability of boundaries between the self and any other part of the living world.

Much of Hogan's poetry involves a surrendering of the physical body to the rhythms of nature, a waiting and listening for signals of new life springing from elements of the natural world that have survived man's intrusion. "Window in

Stone," from *Seeing Through the Sun* (1985), explores a continuity among human life, the animal world, and the force of a river harnessed for human use yet unaffected as a primal source. In the poem's opening stanza Hogan presents the image of a child sleeping with her head on the speaker's chest, whose own ear is "turned" toward the sound of a nearby river. The stanza concludes: "She hears a remedy of lost sound / she believed was hers" (43). Although the pronoun refers to the child, syntactically it is also possible to read the "she" as alternatively or simultaneously referencing the speaker or even the river. The significance here is that the act of recovering something "lost"—an act consistently constituting a process of "remedy" in Hogan's work—depends on an unspoken relationship among child, adult (not specifically named as mother), and river. The sound carried by the river's current, the song of unceasing movement through time, indeed belongs to the child, offering a nurturing that flows through the ear to the very heartbeat of the adult, awake. Furthermore, for the sleeping child the relationship with the natural world is not learned but felt, intuitively and instinctively.

The second stanza illuminates this relationship with the image of the child moving among a group of pregnant horses, "new life" in turn moving inside them as they gently part to make way for the girl. Hogan both intensifies the focus and furthers the range of the poem's connections in the next stanza, introducing the figures of men working at the dam on the river. But she begins with a two-word sentence, moving attention away from the girl and horses back to "The river." The line is gently insistent, reminding us of the force binding the poem's elements together—perhaps suggesting the life fluids inside the pregnant horses—and then the speaker deepens the associations:

> My heart is a window
> like the one men working the dam
> gaze into
> watching, listening to the inside works. (43)

The first stanza presented the speaker's ear turned to the rush of the river, her heartbeat not named but possibly suggested by the child's head resting on the chest. But now the heart is also "watching, listening" for how things work—how, using the technology of the dam as metaphor, "the measure of some cog / turn[s] water to light" (43). Here is transformation, knowledge, yet mystery in both the gaze of the workers and the "window" of the speaker's observations. Although humans so often move toward ignoring essential ties with nature at other moments in Hogan's poetry, that threat is not suggested here. Rather, in this moment the initiation of hydroelectric power is but one of the many beginnings the poem seeks to observe. As the opening of the final stanza asserts, "There is a beginning for all things, / a quickened pulse we listen for" (43).

In its final stanza "Window in Stone" becomes more fluid and abstract, introducing the imagery of stone but stone that contains a hidden, mysterious light, even (or especially) as it is carved by the contours of the river. Light, and the drive toward light, is the most recurring, central element in all of Hogan's poetry. Here light builds shadow even as it sparkles, calling questions to us, asking for our attention "the way a river asks / to carve faces of lost girls" (43). These lines essentially bring the poem full circle, reversing the figure of the girl listening for the lost sound of the river in the beginning stanza. Now it is the river seeking to define and shape the lost girl, to bring the girl into the "sleeping dark landscape" that holds water, horses, cloud, and rock in balance.

The subsuming of the human body into nature and the concurrent force of land, history, and time present within the human body constitute a crucial dialectic for Hogan. It is established as a central theme within a sequence of short lyrics that opens her inaugural volume, the chapbook *Calling Myself Home* (1978). Reflecting the matrilineal element of Native American culture, the wisdom and rootedness of the animal world are often reflected in women, most notably older women or grandmothers. An important Chickasaw belief is that at one time animals and humans spoke one language, and *Calling Myself Home* begins with four poems that use the turtle as an emblem of the human capacity to draw wisdom from animals and the earth. But first the turtle must be ritualistically summoned, called to as the river calls to the human ear in "Window in Stone." Hence the opening line of the first poem, "turtle": "I'm dreaming the old turtle back" (3). The turtle emerges from a world of water and silt that contains the essential life force of our planet. What is contained within his element and in turn within him is seen through the light in his eyes, a light with the potential to awaken the slumbering world. The turtle's shell, its plate of armor and sustenance, is what he offers to human life as a connection with history and an emblem of endurance.

Turtles and turtle shells play significant ceremonial and spiritual roles in traditions of southeastern tribes such as the Chickasaw. In the Chickasaw Pishofa (Picofa) ceremony, the turtle, as well as other animals, might be called upon in the dances led by the aliktce, or healer. Shells serve in different contexts as rattles, vessels, or shields. The poem goes on to say that we should wear the turtle shell on our own backs, "like old women who can see the years / back through his eyes" (3). Speaking to women, the end of the poem suggests that donning the shell of the turtle will allow an awakening, an awareness of what is contained within, akin to the turtle.

Much of Hogan's poetry attempts to reestablish connection with the spirit of these old, wise women who have witnessed much change but remain in touch with tradition. Asserting that we are "like the turtle / born of an old people" (3), the three poems following "turtle" in *Calling Myself Home* reach for reconnection across dry land. The poems are grouped under a section heading "The Dry Pond," and in the fourth—the title poem "calling myself home"—Hogan presents herself walking a road of dried water, studying the artifacts deposited there.

> There is a dry river
> between them and us.
> Its banks divide up our land.
> Its bed was the road
> I walked to return. (6)

The poem goes on to show how even Native people need to reassert their ancient and necessary bonds with the earth, bonds that, although they may have lain dormant, are as available as ever if one remembers that it is the bones of these very women that "are holding up the earth." With this awareness, never lost by the old women, people take their place in the landscape alongside other living features of the natural world, as in the poem "hackberry trees." Both people and trees "have been in this place so long" that the insects do not distinguish between them, moving alike over human skin and the earth (4).

The third poem of the cluster, "red clay," again uses the turtle to probe the basic but mysterious fact of how the earth is a sustaining force literally present within the human body. Weaving back and forth between the image of a turtle buried in the earth for winter and an unnamed "you" working at a potter's wheel, the poem offers the notion of the earth—the "red clay" being shaped at the wheel that is also the turtle's domain of sleep—entering the body and remaining: "We are here, the red earth / passes like light into us / and stays" (5). The turtle is likewise sustained by the earth, his shell growing larger as he sleeps. This is part of the unceasing movement of time, a slow but insistent rhythm evoked by the moon moving across "iced black water," the turning of the vessel at the wheel, the turning of the earth. In addition to the turtle's specific role in aspects of Chickasaw culture, it is important in several other tribal traditions as a messenger between humans and other spirit beings. Hopi legends tell of ancestors who will return as turtles, and in other tribal cultures the turtle may be a warrior, an earth maker or diver, or a wisdom source. The four poems invoking the turtle seem to suggest a pan-Indian range of powerful associations.

All of the poems I have discussed so far involve human connections or reconnections with both the natural world and vital elements of the self, two entities not quite one and the same but inextricably interwoven in Hogan's vision. Her awareness of history is always ecological and global, even in her quieter lyrics involving intimate and sacred moments of communion with the earth or maternal ancestors. In his foreword to Hogan's 1983 volume *Eclipse*,

Kenneth Lincoln writes that her work "looks to reconciliations for the survival of family, community, and the natural world. Her personal visions of Indian continuance come inseparable from contemporary politics and the scars of history" (v). Hogan herself discusses the theme of healing in the 1993 collection *The Book of Medicines,* citing scars as "evidence of healing" ("Interview" 133). The poems in *Eclipse* sound Hogan's most elegiac note in her consistent confrontation with history and loss in an effort to heal.

"Missing the Animals" reminds us of how we are driving animals from the planet and of the empty, haunting space they leave behind as they fall through space. The tone is almost apocalyptic, the poem ending with the image of gunshots fired "down the edge of the world" at the animals (13). But the gunshots miss the animals for they have already left, many having "escaped" without being killed. So all that is left to kill is death itself, space filled by only the sound of our own breath, and a dying, beached whale for people to carve their initials into. This poem, near the end of the first section of the volume, is particularly poignant in its warning, given the way *Eclipse* opens with two strong lyrics evoking the connection between human and animal life.

"Landscape of Animals" and "In Silence" offer the possibility of observing the way "the world grows" amid silence. The short poem "In Silence" is remarkable for the exactness of its imagery, recalling, as do other Hogan poems of impressive descriptive power, the best work of Elizabeth Bishop. As with "Window in Stone" and other poems, listening and observing the animals' natural presence are essential to learn one's own place amid the order of things. The deer—"delicate mountains of bone" (13)—call to the human listener in "Landscape of Animals" through an air stretching across traditional boundaries of time and space. The speaker detects the shape of her curled body, perhaps a phoetal image, in the "dark horses of sand" (13). In the final two stanzas of the poem, Hogan tests the "soft edges" that allow all distinctions among the different types of animals and between those animals and human life to merge. She offers an astonishing image of her own body as permeable, an element of air the birds can fly through and even inhabit. In the poem's final lines the voices of the birds are indistinguishable from other sounds as the speaker, in being absorbed into the landscape, seems to literally become it.

Following these opening poems, *Eclipse* begins increasingly to present images of the wounded earth and the wounded human spirits that inhabit it. Although on the whole a poem of affirmation, "Ruins" suggests that our contemporary culture may lack the wherewithal to endure as prior Native communities were able to endure:

> I am an intruder
> and won't outlast these pictures of hands

> and painted people
> dancing on the high walls. (8)

"Oil" depicts the exploitation of the land for profit, and "Idaho Falls, 1961" concerns a reactor accident that, a note to the poem tells us, was "termed a small atomic steam explosion," although it killed three people (23). The poem begins in ominous darkness, with children, as in "Window in Stone," "resting their heads / against the breast's rhythm," awaiting a light to illuminate their streets and rooms (23). This light comes from a distant, unseen, but powerful source, as the poem demonstrates in a sudden shift to imagery of a young man being blasted through space as he "opens a switch on power." The remainder of the poem presents a rush of simultaneous events, symbolically connected but oblivious to one another. As the workers are killed instantaneously by the power that brings light to the nearby farms, day dawns on a woman going to the barn for the early morning milking. Hogan presents the animals, exuding their own "warm light," as perhaps instinctively aware of the troubled air emanating from the accident. Birds are quick to leave the power lines where they normally alight, and as the woman milks the cow, her ear, the poem subtly suggests, may also pick up what the animals seem to sense. By the final stanza, the image of day breaking has taken on a range of meanings.

> Earth has made another revolution.
> New worlds burn
> in dark places. (23)

The poem seems to want to emphasize the way lives overlap—whether they be lives lost at the expense of modern convenience, lives that go on in a daily ritual of natural rhythms like those of people living on farms, or animal lives finding a way to coexist with man's modern intrusions. This is a simultaneity to remain aware of, a delicate balance fraught with potential peril. Our modern way of life is dangerous not just to animals but also to ourselves.

Part of the power of "Idaho Falls, 1961" and other such Hogan poems is their ability to present provocative imagery without being didactic. The poem at no point seeks to tell the reader that the reactor accident is a small piece of a larger pattern of man's destruction of the earth, but a chronological reading of all of Hogan's volumes establishes this destruction as a growing concern, even as she emphasizes humans' capacity to heal both themselves and the earth. One of the patterns of imagery running through several poems in *Eclipse* is that of the aftereffects of the atomic bombs dropped on Hiroshima and Nagasaki. These images are brief, intermittent, but inescapable, often interjecting themselves into the present moment—as in the sequence "Daughters, I Love You," where Hogan sees the children of Hiroshima reflected in her daughter's eyes. At other moments the images of nuclear annihilation are woven into poems that at the same time suggest questions about the nature of endurance and renewal. "Half-Life," for example, meditates on various meanings evoked by the poem's title, beginning with the lines,

> Things of the past remain,
> the dancing horse
> inside a cave,
> light filling dark walls. (15)

Art on the walls of caves is a living emblem, but the material evidence of Native cultures is vulnerable, the poem goes on to attest. What can perhaps endure even beyond atomic devastation are legend and spirit. Evidence of this belief is present in the image of a Japanese monk whose legend made people believe in the power of sheep to be "makers of rain," even as those sheep "disappeared before your eyes" as Nagasaki burned. But such destruction leaves its own shadows on walls, the shadows of the lost, "the body's wine / not spilled / but rising like plutonium" (15). Memory's capacity to hold images of what we lose or destroy is powerful, the remainder of the poem suggests. But implicit in this evocation of power is the question of whether memory can be adequate in the face of what is literally destroyed. Again Hogan returns to animals as a way of framing the question, using images of animals made of paper lace, constituted in part by their absence, light shining through what has been cut away. The poem becomes seductively dreamlike in its evocativeness, suggesting that the animals are simply waiting to return from their sleeping state. But "Half-Life" seems another quiet warning, prayerlike in tone, an invitation for reflection on our willingness to negate life.

As *Eclipse* progresses, loss and absence become increasingly coupled with endurance and renewal as central themes. In "Land of Exile" the speaker feels the earth withdrawing from her but takes comfort in the knowledge that what recedes will eventually reappear in a new form.

> Someday the water will return
> as snow,
> the ground will come back in new trees. (50)

In time, the speaker says, she, too, will return as snow, silently listening to people "speaking another language" (50). An ongoing question in Hogan's poetry regards our ability to access that language, a deep concern for what happens within the empty space of absence. In many poems man's various methods of destruction threaten to wipe the earth of presences that will not return. But the majority of Hogan's poems maintain an implicit hope, a learned awareness that there are absences to be endured with a faith in life's capacity to regenerate itself. Waiting becomes a central activity, patience a way of knowing. Loss and renewal are powerful and difficult truths, as organic as the rhythm of breath. This lesson comes through a conscious effort to remain in touch with the spirit of Native existence and to learn by observing the natural world. We see this rhythm in poems such as "A Place for the Eagle," where "stories of loss" become transformed in the eyes of animals—eyes that reflect both human life and "rising dialogues of dust and air / where all things fuse and burn / inhabiting earth" (35).

In "Who Will Speak?" human life is presented as but a small portion of "earth's curve," but within that realm comes the awareness of a responsibility to other living forms. The poem opens with the image of all the animals, fish, and birds emerging from land, water, and sky in a silent demonstration of humankind's place in the natural order. As if in response to this moment, with human life thrown into sharp, instructive relief, the second stanza highlights the speaker's keen sense of the movement of time. Time is a force that "carv[es]" changes in the earth, shaping the landscape in ways that leave "only the empty space, / a longing that passes" (42). This is one of the moments in Hogan's poetry when consciousness becomes conscience, awareness becomes action. Time's corrosive power leads to the poem's central question: Who will speak for the animals? In answering that it is man who must speak, man who must ensure the animals' survival as he "speaks of tomorrow," the poem offers Hogan's most powerful affirmation of the means for harmonious coexistence with animal life. Man's mouth and tongue belong to the earth, come from it; and in speaking for the animals the voice performs an act of "creation," a giving of "golden light" to the world. If anything in Hogan's poetry approaches an *ars poetica*, it may be in this poem, where the power of language becomes a tool for survival—not just human survival but that of the living, natural world as we know it. In a 1988 interview, Hogan, speaking of her poetry, said, "In my whole life I have been a spokesperson for the animals. In my own sense of things I feel that our whole life depends on other creatures on the planet, and I love them, pay them respect, and try to help them" ("'A Heart Made out of Crickets'" 113).

In the first half of *The Book of Medicines* (1993), the poems grouped under the heading "Hunger" extend the role of human language as an instrument of ecological conscience and power. The metaphor of hunger works on multiple levels in these poems. Man's hunger to exploit the earth is motivated by both economic greed and an elemental, unconscious hunger to reconnect with the life-giving forces of the natural world. The earth itself, even as it fulfills its own hunger to consume human life, also shares this hunger to reconnect. Like the human voice in "Who Will Speak?" it is the voice of the poet that is in touch with these dual needs, a voice that recognizes the hunger implicit in earth's organic cycle as well as its own desire to merge with the animals, to go beyond the physical limitations of the human body. In the poem titled "Hunger," hunger is personified as a disembodied consciousness of what we have failed to achieve: "Hunger knows we have not yet reached / the black and raging depths of anything" (17). At the same time, the poet recognizes,

> And it is a kind of hunger
> that brings us to love,
> to rocking currents of a secret wave
> and the body that wants to live beyond itself. (18)

In this poem "destitute men" pull dolphins from the sea for their own ends, to have "their way / with them" as they would with women, unaware of a deeper hunger that pulls them to "be held in / the thin, clear milk of the gods" (18).

"Harvesters of Night and Water" also focuses on the struggle between fishermen, fighting to complete the catch of an octopus by pulling it aboard their boat, and the octopus itself, fighting to return to its natural element. As the poet observes the scene, she is again keenly aware of the competing needs. The fishermen seek to use the octopus for fish bait, bait that can be "taken / from the cut insides of halibut / and used again" (23). The octopus needs its dark, cold domain of water, a mysterious depth that man "will never know" (23). The ocean is a realm of abundance and healing, and the poet is able to envision the inside of this world, the octopus "naked" and "beautiful" as it manages to elude the fishermen and slide down the side of the boat "like an angel / with other wings" (24). The tentacles are compared to the arms of mothers, "desperate for life" (24).

This silent desperation to remain in balance with our natural environment is a need understood and shared by generations of mothers in Hogan's work, a knowledge that the cycle of life depends on a larger circle of nurturing than just the mother-daughter dynamic. The poem then moves from this image of reaching arms to that of the speaker's child, unaware of death, innocent in her youthful affection for fish. At the same time, the language suggests that the child's attraction to the natural world has deeper sources, linking her to the poet's vision.

> Hungry, we are hungry for the whole world.
> We are like the small fish in the sea,
> the ones who swim into the mouths of larger ones
> to take what's there. (24)

The acknowledgment of this hunger is the moment of open vulnerability so crucial to Hogan's vision. The recurring image of opening the body to the natural world entails a surrender of autonomy, an entrance into a cycle of violence, death, and renewal. In the final stanza of "Harvesters of Night and Water," the speaker pares down her language and asserts, "I want the world to be kinder. / I am a woman. / I am afraid" (24). As the poet speaks for the earth, for animals and the elements, her voice becomes open to the possibilities of carnage and estrangement. At the same time, however, this voice is now in touch with a deeper language, a rhythm that binds generations.

More than any other volume by Hogan, *The Book of Medicines* places the voice of the poet alongside, and at times even inside, animals that carry specific symbolic power within Native cultures. "Bear" presents a man haunted by the act of shooting a bear, and the spirit of the bear speaks to the poet and ultimately to the man who killed it as well. In the opening of the poem the bear presents itself in the form of a "dark continent," suggesting the pervasive presence of its power even in death, "beyond comfort." It comes to the poet's door at night with messages of the hard seasons ahead and with images of its death at the hands of man. The poet recalls that the bear's sorrow song of death merged with the cries of the hunter and continues to haunt man's nights: "It follows him" (26). After shooting the bear the man tracked his "red song" into the forest, where the bear lay "covering its face from sky / where humans believe god lives / larger than death" (25). As the bear's death song follows the man, becoming a part of the very landscape surrounding him, he eventually wants to mirror the actions of the bear in turning away from the worldview that places an abstract god above man and man above animals. He comes to question "what he lives by," recognizing that in seeking safety from the bear he has confronted another entity to fear—that of ourselves. The bear is a significant choice in this poem, as Bear is a central character or figure in the narratives of so many tribal traditions.

In the next poem, "Mountain Lion," the poet again explores the estrangement and fear between man and animals from the animals' point of view. The eyes of the mountain lion and the speaker meet in a realm of shared knowledge but one divided by a space inhabited by the "spirits of hunters." Within this space the speaker is able to move back and forth between the human and animal perspectives, recognizing that for the lion "I was the wild thing / she had learned to fear" (27). The poet in essence becomes the lion as she analogizes the look in the lion's eyes with that in her own when she turns away from people for whom "two worlds cannot live / inside a single vision" (27). The relationship between the mountain lion and the woman in this poem anticipates a central motif in Hogan's 1998 novel, *Power.*

Other poems in *The Book of Medicines* also lament the difficulty of attaining this vision of coexistence, a vision that in the past drew wisdom and awareness from observing and listening to the voices and spirits of the animals. "Return: Buffalo" deals with man's betrayal of the buffalo, an animal whose spirit—even in its physical absence—would appear and speak to the old women "like a prophet / coming out from the hills / with a vision / too unholy to tell" (21). In

"The Fallen" the poet's encounter with a wolf caught in a steel trap launches a meditation on the wolf's symbolic role in Indian cultures.

> In our astronomy
> the Great Wolf
> lived in sky.
> It was the mother of all women
> and howled her daughter's names
> into the winds of night. (42)

But "the new people" looked on the wolf as something to be feared and eradicated when it came too close to human life. The poem emphasizes that once the balance between human life and the natural world is lost, it becomes impossible to restore. New mythologies, whether "science" or "story," treat the wolf as a devil rather than a mother, ignoring the capacity of the wolf's song to heal. These poems of the "Hunger" sequence speaking for the animals are warning notes highlighting fissures in the modern consciousness, vital and essential connections in danger of being lost forever.

Another type of Hogan poem celebrates a connectedness that can reestablish bonds with nature and with elements of heritage important to both individual and community. In these poems we listen to a woman in touch with the wisdom of older women and their enduring spirits. The second half of *The Book of Medicines* groups poems under the heading "Medicines," salves to treat the disrepair spelled out in many of the "Hunger" poems; and one of these healing balms is "The Grandmother Songs." In this poem the grandmothers are communal, the "tribal gods" conscious of the power of "song," the "pathway where people met / and animals crossed" (57). These are also the women who gave voice to labor, terror, history itself, all part of what the poem calls "the shawl of family blood / that was their song of kinship" (57). Among the many lessons these elders pass to the poet is the knowledge of death, what the girl in "Harvesters of Night and Water" was on the way to knowing. But death is an opening, or so "The Grandmother Songs" strongly suggests, again returning to the image of the open, permeable body. The dying body opens itself to the presence of the grandmothers, who pass "wearing sunlight / and thin rain" (58). As the poem ends, the song of the grandmothers becomes the song of the river returning to the sea, replenishing the earth along the way. This is one of many moments in Hogan's poetry where the voice of women asserts and affirms what allows the earth to endure. It is a voice that has listened to learn its song, and it is alternately urgent and reflective. In poems focusing on the land, the voice of the elder women is contained in the quiet wisdom of their witnessing eyes; in poems centered on Native and communal heritage, such as "The Grandmother Songs," the voice is clearly audible, a legacy to be absorbed.

The elder women also remind younger women, often represented by the figure of poet-speaker as a younger girl or woman, of elements of the self it is vital not to lose. *Savings* (1988) suggests by its title that the act of preservation is integral to remaining connected to the wisdom of ancestors. The poem "It Must Be" begins in the voice of an old woman whose seemingly many ills are being assessed by intrusive "pathologists," "administrators," and "doctors." In concluding that "it must be" a disease, troubled joints, or a failing heart the woman suffers from, they fail to recognize or understand what the failing body and remembering heart contain—personal and communal memories such as lost love and relatives, as well as the legacy of generations of old women who sustain this particular woman.

> They make me carry on
> under my jeans and sweater,
> traditions and complaints about the sad
> state of the nation. (14)

These are women who have the resources to make do with the materials at hand, to bite through leather, tree bark, or "lies / about the world" (15). If need be, they will pocket garlic to "protect us from the government" (15).

As the poem progresses, Hogan shifts the perspective of the speaker from that of the old woman to that of a younger woman torn between the legacy of the Native elders and the ways of the modern world. This is a familiar character and moment in Hogan's work, represented in the struggles of young women such as Omishto, the protagonist and narrator of the novel *Power*. In "It Must Be" the voice of a younger speaker is momentarily tempted to renounce the elders, to "silence the old woman inside / who tells the truth / and how it must be" (15). But ultimately, as in *Power* when the young girl decides to leave her mother's home to go "home" to the nearby tribal community, the speaker in the poem chooses to open herself to the voice of the "old women" who share simple gifts among themselves. Even, or perhaps especially, the old woman labeled "crazy" has vital lessons to teach in her delight at "baring herself to the world" (16). In the face of aggressive intrusion from an unsympathetic world, including a history of violent genocide, the elder women endure. Their capacity for regeneration is as powerful as that of the land.

The theme of the divided and conflicted self, inhabiting two worlds not commensurate, runs through each of Hogan's volumes of poetry. In *Seeing Through the Sun*, "The Truth Is" speaks directly to this self, one with "a Chickasaw hand" and "a white hand" resting in its pockets (4). Although the poet would like to see the hands as a metaphor of acquired, comfortable coexistence, like a single tree with grafted branches producing two kinds of fruit, she frankly admits to a different reality:

> It's not that way. The truth is
> we are crowded together
> and knock against each other at night.
> We want amnesty. (4)

From here the poem moves into a dialogue with the two sides of the self, one telling the other to ignore this internal conflict, to forget about "who loved who / and who killed who" (4). This sort of political conscience is "dangerous," contends one part of the self, better left sleeping and undisturbed, the sort of "amnesty" desired by one part of the speaker. But the other side is compelled to remember who killed whom, an awareness that keeps "knocking on the door / in the middle of the night" (5). Indeed this awareness contributes to the poet sleeping alone in a "twin bed," even though she is able to offer love willingly to others. "The Truth Is" concludes with what seems an almost whimsical tone, the dialogue dissolving into instructions to think about more mundane matters such as shoes. But in the mundane images that conceal the poem's internal conflict, the pockets and shoes, the poem's language suggests that it is essentially exploring masks—like the imagined metaphor of the fruit tree with grafted branches, "the true masks of the soul." The key to the poem and other poems exploring the same theme is to examine the nature of the masks, to look behind them and examine what motivates their construction, their wearing. This is Hogan's process of examining what another poem from *Savings*, "The Inside of Things," calls "the inside of lies and history" (35).

"The Lost Girls," which concludes the "Savings" cluster, does not treat the divided self or inheritances from the spirit of old women but rather reflects fondly on the poet's stages of womanhood, the "inner women" of a life who so quickly flee or change as one grows. The poem presents a sequence of snapshots of the self, first a "dark child" who "without shame" refused to become too interested in school. Next, a "curving girl" who loved to dance is recalled as one "I loved to love with" (31). The poem develops the argument that these aspects of self are not stages to be moved through and left behind but vital components of the whole personality. Like the elder women, their spirits must not just be preserved but listened and attended to, fed by ongoing interaction. To lose touch with the inner women is to have "wronged ourselves." So the poem concludes with a vision of union between the more mature speaker and the younger girl who remains a part of her, a union akin to a courtship, a dance of celebration, an act of "loving all the girls and women / I have always been" (32).

A poem like "The Lost Girls" embodies a central theme in all of Hogan's work, the drive to what she has termed "the center inside yourself" ("Interview" 127). The eyes of animals and the eyes of old women can lead to this destination, a place of vulnerability yet continuity. The opening of the self to the land, to history, is crucial to this process, and in a poem like "Disappearances" (*Eclipse*) it is part of what allows the world to "continue" in the face of loss, the "disappearances" of children in war. Eyes that have witnessed history—whether the eyes of Japanese mothers in the wake of nuclear annihilation or those of an old Indian woman whose voice remains silent—endure, "with the certain knowledge / that it is a good thing to be alive" (21). These are the eyes that maintain the light, "lumine," that is such a vital source in Hogan's poetry. Light embodies different forms of power, at times potentially destructive, as in "Idaho Falls, 1961" and the images of Hiroshima. Light is also the powerful candle of mourning in a poem like "The Women Are Grieving" (*Eclipse*). It evokes both loss and regeneration and so often illuminates the path toward recognizing the ancient connections between human beings and stronger, older forces—perhaps buried but still accessible. Kenneth Lincoln notes the role of light as a central image in *Eclipse,* and his reading remains pertinent to all of Hogan's poetry: "In the re-emerging Native American consciousness of today, this light is both personal and pan-tribal; it illuminates, fires, and even burns the poet's body to speak of collective Native concerns—tribal families free of suffering, violence, ignorance, and poverty" (v).

The poet's body becomes a metaphor for the broken and healed earth. In "Evolution in Light and Water" (*Seeing Through the Sun* 24) the body flies over this earth, even though it would be much easier to fall, to "let thoughts drown" in the rivers below. But in feeling the pull of gravity, in tracing the veins of "red tributaries" that line the earth, the body is able to at once survey and speak for the land, to sink into its rivers, becoming the element of "[d]ark amphibians." The body becomes the "radiant vault" of the living, the life-and-death force of tradition and history. The spiritual journey in Hogan's poetry is one that takes us back to origins, organic rhythms, the clay from which we sprang.

Works Cited

Hogan, Linda. *The Book of Medicines*. Minneapolis: Coffee House, 1993.

———. *Calling Myself Home*. Greenfield Center, N.Y.: Greenfield Review Press, 1978.

———. *Eclipse*. Los Angeles: American Indian Studies Center, 1983.

———. " 'A Heart Made out of Crickets': An Interview with Linda Hogan." By Bo Schöler. *Journal of Ethnic Studies* 16 (1988): 107–117.

———. "An Interview with Linda Hogan." *Missouri Review* 17, no. 2 (1994): 109–134.

———. *Savings*. Minneapolis: Coffee House, 1988.

———. *Seeing Through the Sun*. Amherst: University of Massachusetts Press, 1985.

Lincoln, Kenneth. "Foreword." In Linda Hogan, *Eclipse*. Los Angeles: American Indian Studies Center, 1983. v–vii.

STANDING NAKED BEFORE THE STORM
Linda Hogan's *Power*
and the Critique of Apocalyptic Narrative

MICHAEL HARDIN

I GREW UP IN THE 1970S AND 1980S IN A FUNDAMENTALIST PENTECOSTAL HOME. As such, the Apocalypse was always a real and imminent event.[1] At church, any event on the calendar was qualified with "should Jesus tarry," a disclaimer that the event would be canceled in case of the Rapture. Both of my grandfathers would cite the creation of the Jewish state in 1948 as proof that Christ would return sometime between 1981 and 1988, depending on whether the Tribulation was an event the Christians would have to experience or not. Thus I never imagined seeing the year 2000. I was not particularly concerned about a future I did not expect to see, yet I was simultaneously terrified of the potential prospect of damnation. This terror, however, does not seem confined to conservative Christians; the crossover appeal of such religious apocalyptic narratives can be seen in the popularity of Hal Lindsey's *The Late Great Planet Earth* (1970) and the current craze, Tim F. LaHaye and Jerry B. Jenkins's *Left Behind* series (1996).

During the early 1990s it was the diminishing ozone layer and global warming that elicited fear. And in 1999 it was the Y2K bug that would return humanity

Michael Hardin

to the Middle Ages. Now, although I no longer dread biblical or cybernetic apocalypse, I am acutely aware of how Americans, raised in an essentially Judeo-Christian environment, inevitably frame and interpret events in apocalyptic terms. It is as if the language of cataclysm is required for us to notice something. Scientists, environmentalists, and politicians have all adopted this vernacular. The problem with apocalyptic narrative, however, is that it is a product of binary thinking and only functions within a victim-oppressor structure: the oppressor makes use of apocalyptic narrative as divine justification for conquest and oppression of "Evil"; victimized groups make use of the narrative when no mortal hope exists, as an ultimately futile gesture that signifies a hope that "Good" will overcome—not through any action of the group but as a consequence of some divine order. Either way, unless one already has power, apocalyptic narrative provides no effective approach to the problems of the present, no effective power. In her novel *Power,* Linda Hogan critiques both the religious and secular elements of apocalyptic narrative and the dualistic thought processes that underlie such narratives, specifically as used against the American Indian.

Apocalyptic narrative is a product of Western thought, in part, I believe, because it is a natural consequence of binary thought. There was a beginning; therefore, there must be an end. Even contemporary astrophysics falls victim to this pattern of thinking: we accept the Big Bang, and so we assume a Big Crunch, only to discover to the unease of many that the universe is accelerating and thus should expand infinitely in space and time. Apocalyptic narratives arise from the good-evil dichotomy wherein good must trounce evil once and for all in a final and convincing manner to affirm the superiority and desirability of the good. Karl Marx, in "Contribution to the Critique of Hegel's *Philosophy of Right*" (in *Early Writings*), recognizes the need of religion to posit a victorious "good" to reward the earthly suffering of the underclass. By separating good from evil, self from other, by insisting on duality, we have created an antagonism that will progress toward annihilation; if the universe is not constructed as a binary—and no evidence seems to indicate that it is[2]—then we have artificially created dualities that ultimately efface those elements in the individual and society that do not reduce easily to binary identification. It is here where Hogan seems to attack the problem as well, focusing on the varied elements of culture and identity, continually rejecting singular notions of truth and experience.

Since American culture is permeated with apocalyptic myth and the European contact with American Indians was severe, it is easy to read the effect of the conquest on indigenous peoples as apocalyptic. If we look at Kirkpatrick Sale's description of the breadth of effects on indigenous populations, we see a picture that seems taken from the Book of Revelation:

Critique of Apocalyptic Narrative

Among the diseases, new and ruinous to America, were smallpox, bubonic plague, measles, cholera, typhoid, pleurisy, scarlet fever, diphtheria, whooping cough, influenza, gonorrhea, viral pneumonia, malaria, yellow fever, dysentery, and alcoholism—perhaps . . . as many as ninety-three in all. The effect of such a high mortality [as much as 95 percent], and in such a short period of time, could have been only to shatter or distort a great part of the Indians' belief systems, disrupt their political and social institutions, discredit their medical practices and the healers among them, produce psychological disorientation and demoralization, kill off most of the elders who were the repositories of tribal history and traditional knowledge, demand the simplification of the cultural inventory and its technologies, force migration and regrouping of remnant populations often in areas far from sacred lands, and increase the likelihood of warfare either in the clash of migrating groups or in the search for new populations. (303–304)

Defining events in apocalyptic terms, however, places the American Indian in the space of victim; although that may be historically accurate, it is a space without real power. One of the difficulties in describing American Indian history is finding an appropriate language. Euro-Americans adamantly refuse to accept "genocide" or "holocaust" because that would put them in the undesired space of Nazi. The only other language we have to describe such a history is apocalyptic. The problems with apocalyptic language are that it moves culpability from the human to the supernatural and that it moves events from the historical to the mythic; mythic and supernatural language allows Europeans and Euro-Americans to shirk responsibility. Within culture, apocalyptic myths serve two functions, neither of which can provide effective help to the American Indian: apocalyptic myth provides divine justification for those with power to exert it against those without, and it provides hope for those without power that "good" will eventually triumph. Both aspects of the myth function to maintain the status quo. Therefore, for the American Indian to effect real change, he or she will have to move beyond such narratives.

Hogan's critique of apocalyptic narrative requires that we trace apocalypticism to its source, the Europeans.[3] From the voyages of Christopher Columbus, apocalyptic narrative has been driving the European encounter with the indigenous peoples of the Americas. On his third voyage, at the mouth of the Orinoco, Columbus writes, "Holy Scripture testifies that Our Lord made the earthly Paradise in which he placed the Tree of Life. . . . I believe that the earthly Paradise lies here" (*Libro* 220–221). According to the Book of Revelation, a text Columbus's *Libro de las profecías* indicates he knows well, the Tree of Life is in heaven (*Holy Bible,* Revelation 2:7, 22:14); this suggests that Columbus's focus is not backward toward Genesis but forward toward Revelation and the end of the world. During the fourth voyage Columbus further imbues his narrative with biblical and apocalyptic numerology and events, mentioning that the "seas turned to blood" (*Four Voyages* 290) during a storm that was like a "repetition of the deluge" (291). By describing the events around him in apocalyptic terms, Columbus is able to present himself as an apocalyptic catalyst. The rhetoric increases, and he claims to have found Solomon's gold mines;[4] he immediately connects this with the rebuilding of Jerusalem and the temple and claims "this builder would come from Spain" (300). By claiming to find Solomon's mines, Columbus reveals part of his intention for *his* conquest—to fund a crusade to retake Jerusalem and to rebuild Solomon's temple.[5] Although the full extent of Columbus's apocalyptic impulse does not become clear in his letters until the third and fourth voyages, the impulse is present in his other writings from as early as 1481 (*Libro* 9). These passages from the third and fourth voyages and *Libro de las profecías* show us that he actively read himself into biblical prophecy as xñï FERENS (Cristo-ferens, the Christ bearer), the one who would help bring about Christ's return in 1656—the seventh millennium since God supposedly created the earth (*Libro* 90). Emphasizing this idea, the Cuban novelist Alejo Carpentier, in *The Harp and the Shadow,* cites Columbus: "[W]ith me, the prophecy in the Book of Isaiah is fulfilled" (103).

Although few if any of Columbus's contemporaries in the Americas shared his particular apocalyptic myth, the fantasies of Cities of Gold and Fountains of Eternal Youth seem derivative from or participant in the same Edenic and apocalyptic myths.[6] In *Power* Hogan mentions two Spaniards, Juan Ponce de León (42), who was part of Columbus's second voyage and is the first recorded European to visit Florida, and Alvar Núñez [sic] Cabeza de Vaca (96), the first Spaniard to explore much of the American Gulf Coast and Southwest. Although Ponce de León may not have actually sought the Fountain of Youth, the continuous association of him with the Fountain creates a "historical" myth that nonetheless becomes part of our origins and history. David J. Weber writes, "No firsthand report supports the often-told story that the thirty-nine-year-old explorer went in search of a 'fountain of youth,' but it may contain some element of truth. The idea of such a fabulous fountain, located on an enchanted island, was deeply rooted in the lore and imagery of medieval Europe and had strong religious and sexual overtones" (33). We know Columbus's fascination with biblical prophecy comes from the lore and imagery of medieval Europe as well; is a fountain of youth essentially different from a tree of life? Weber can affirm that Ponce de León was actively in search of "gold and Indian slaves" (33). As such, he sounds exactly like Columbus: he is exemplified by slavery, gold, and an aura of religious or mythic fixation.

The other Spaniard mentioned in *Power* is Cabeza de Vaca. Although he tends to be a different kind of conquistador than Ponce de León,[7] he does facilitate the myth of the Golden Cities, the Seven Cities of Antilia, in part

Critique of Apocalyptic Narrative

because he does not exaggerate what he sees; thus Spaniards who are accustomed to reading accounts of gold everywhere assume he is hiding a great treasure:

> [S]tories had persisted that the Seven Cities of Antilia existed somewhere in the New World, and by the late 1530s evidence pointed to North America. By then, Spain's relentless explorers had exhausted most other options, and fresh rumors emerged from North America with the dramatic return of Alvar Núñez [sic] Cabeza de Vaca, whose unintentional journey gave impetus to the expeditions of both Coronado and De Soto. (Weber 42)

These stories of golden cities, fueled by the great treasures found in Mexico and Peru, tend to be traced to the story of seven Portuguese bishops who fled during the Muslim invasion of the Iberian peninsula (Weber 24); however, any reference to golden cities must be taken back further to the description in Revelation of the New Jerusalem: "The wall was made of jasper, and the city of pure gold, as pure as glass. . . . The street of the city was of pure gold, like transparent glass" (*Holy Bible,* Revelation 21:18, 21). The original El Dorado.

From the beginning of *Power,* Hogan reminds us of the continued presence of the Europeans and Judeo-Christian myth in American Indian life: "From the fossil road, near Ama's house, I can just see the tree everyone calls Methuselah. They call it that because it's been there so long with its tangled dark roots hanging on five hundred years or so. They say it's a tree the Spanish brought with them here and planted" (6). This tree is on the fossil road, which suggests it is part of geologic history, not recent "human" history. Furthermore, it is named Methuselah, a figure from Judeo-Christian myth who supposedly lived 969 years, making him the oldest biblical figure (*Holy Bible,* Genesis 5:27). To an extent, Hogan is giving the European influence and presence geologic weight, except that she does have the tree fall. Throughout the novel Hogan sprinkles references to the conquest, from horses (42) to Spanish moss (63), to continually remind the reader of the Europeans' influence on the indigenous peoples and the land. These references keep history close, if only through association.

By locating her narrative in Florida, a region conquered first by the Spanish, Hogan can participate in both American Indian and Latin American literary traditions. Hogan's historical allusions echo those in Gabriel García Márquez's *One Hundred Years of Solitude.* The Spanish Conquest haunts his novel from the very beginning through continual references to its traces:[8] "The only thing that [José Arcadio Buendía] succeeded in doing was to unearth a suit of fifteenth-century armor which had all of its pieces soldered together with rust and inside of which there was the hollow resonance of an enormous stone-filled gourd" (2). By dating this armor as fifteenth century, García Márquez traces the rust and the hollowness to the very beginning of the Spanish Conquest. García Márquez

Michael Hardin

locates the traces of Spain deep in the jungles, as if these communities had forgotten or tried to hide them and yet cannot escape their calcifying grip: "Before them, surrounded by ferns and palm trees . . . was an enormous Spanish galleon. . . . The hull, covered with an armor of petrified barnacles and soft moss, was firmly fastened into a surface of stones. The whole structure seemed to occupy its own space, one of solitude and oblivion, protected from the vices of time" (12). *One Hundred Years of Solitude* is about a conflict with time and history, about forgetting the past and the consequences of that amnesia, repeating the past. The novel ends with its own apocalypse when Aureliano Babilonia is deciphering the Sanskrit parchment that contains the story of his family and its demise:[9] "Macondo was already a fearful whirlwind of dust and rubble being spun about by the wrath of the biblical hurricane" (422). "Reaping the whirlwind" (*Holy Bible*, Hosea 8:7) is the punishment for Israel's sins, and "biblical hurricane" suggests an apocalyptic end such as Noah's flood.

Whereas García Márquez uses the whirlwind to destroy the family and the town, Hogan utilizes the hurricane to uproot Methuselah, the towering reminder of the Spanish Conquest. In Florida hurricanes are not uncommon, but in conjunction with references to the Spanish conquistadores and in the context of other apocalyptic references, the hurricane in *Power* takes on greater significance. Hogan uses a great hurricane to uproot this tree early in the novel (37), thus removing the visible burden of history and apocalypse and its entrenchment in the lives of the indigenous peoples.[10] Within the Taiga mythology, "'We were blown together by a storm in the first place.' It was all created out of storms. . . . I look about me and wonder if it was a storm that carried us Taigas here" (42–43). Unlike the biblical flood myth, which one can argue is also an origin myth, no punishment or destruction is necessitated by the Taiga myth. No destruction of a previous world is included in the myth, nor do the Taiga displace others upon their arrival. The biblical myth, stuck in binary and causal ideology, requires a destruction of one world to accompany the creation of another.

Massive storms are important symbols, from the myth of Noah to the Apocalypse, from Columbus to García Márquez and to Hogan. Hogan must critique these myths, in part because of the role in which they have functioned for Europeans and Euro-Americans but also because these myths have been appropriated by indigenous peoples. Noah's flood is important in biblical mythology because it is the first apocalyptic event, in which God destroys all life on earth except a few of each species and eight humans. After the flood the Lord tells Noah, "Never again will I curse the ground because of man, even though every inclination of his heart is evil from childhood. And never again will I destroy all living creatures, as I have done" (*Holy Bible*, Genesis 8:21). Shortly thereafter God qualifies this statement: "Never again will all life be cut off by

Critique of Apocalyptic Narrative

the waters of a flood; never again will there be a flood to destroy the earth" (Genesis 9:11). These passages foreshadow the destruction of the earth *by fire* and designate great floods—hurricanes, for example—as reminiscent of the first biblical apocalypse. This myth is incorporated into Incan "history" and recorded by the Inca-turned-Catholic Garcilaso de la Vega in 1609:

> Another fable about the origin of their Inca kings is told by the common people of Peru, the Indians of the region south of Cuzco called Collasuyu and those of the regions to the west called Cuntisuyu. They say that it occurred after the deluge, about which they have no more to say than that it took place. . . . Another version of the origin of the Incas similar to this is . . . at the beginning of the world four men and four women, all brothers and sisters, came out of some "windows" in some rocks. (47–48)

Fifty years later, when Father Bernabe Cobo is writing down his own history of the Inca, he challenges this story—not because of the belief in the flood but because the Inca were asserting that they were the original peoples: "Some confuse their origin with the descent of man, considering the Incas to have been the first inhabitants of the world. Others tell that since all men perished in the Universal Deluge, only the Incas were saved and restored the universe" (103). Columbus encounters his "biblical hurricane" on the fourth voyage: "This terrible storm had lasted for eighty-eight days and all this time I had never seen the sun or the stars" (*Four Voyages* 286). During the fourth voyage Columbus repeatedly mentions that his trials are greater than Job's (285) and suggests that he should be seen as equal with Moses and David (293); thus, by doubling Noah's storm of forty days and nights, Columbus can argue that he is worthy to be Christ's bearer.

Hogan's storm also recalls the American Indians' most famous apocalyptic myth—one that seems derivative from the Christian myth—the Ghost Dance. According to Susan Hazen-Hammond in *Timelines of Native American History*, the Ghost Dance of Wovoka (also known as Jack Wilson), a Paiute, is the product of a number of ideas circulating among the American Indians in the second half of the nineteenth century: Wovoka's father, Wodziwob (Paiute), predicted "deceased ancestors would return to guide them and turn the world into a paradise where no one would die, and there would be no distinction between the races"; Smohalla (Wanapum) said that "if Native Americans returned to their original way of life, whites would vanish"; Eschiti or Isatai (Comanche) announced he could "make people invincible against bullets, and deliver his people from white oppression" (202). Wovoka prophesied that if the American Indians performed the Ghost Dance, the dead ancestors would return and the whites would disappear. In some accounts of this prophecy, "Wovoka is quoted as saying he was Christ" (Toledo 4); according to the "Messiah Letter"

Michael Hardin

Wovoka believes Christ will come soon or is already on earth (Wovoka 845–846). In another version of the Ghost Dance prophecy, "[T]he Sioux predicted that a great whirlwind would annihilate whites, leaving Indians free to reclaim their ancient traditions and lands. Short Bull and Kicking Bear, two Sioux leaders, urged the Sioux to get the whirlwind going by donning a ghost shirt to protect them from bullets" (Hazen-Hammond 202). This whirlwind is apocalyptic in the same way Noah's flood is: it destroys the offending people. In his novel *Indian Killer*, Sherman Alexie names a white "wannabe Indian" Jack Wilson and has an American Indian (ironically named John Smith) kill him, effectively removing the Christian apocalyptic narrative from the American Indian mythos. It seems particularly important that Hogan and Alexie move beyond the apocalypticism of the Ghost Dance because it involved utilization of a specifically European mythology that did not lead to the removal of the Europeans but instead led to further destruction of Native peoples and cultures, to further victimization.

The particular apocalyptic myth that forms the basis of the Ghost Dance enters American Indian mythology more from the East Coast through the English Puritans than from the Spanish to the south. According to Stephen Stein, in his introduction to Jonathan Edwards's *Apocalyptic Writings*:

> [I]n New England a long line of colonial spokesmen—most prominently, John Cotton and Roger Williams in the first generation, the historian Edward Johnson, the poet Michael Wigglesworth, Samuel Sewall the commentator, and father and son Increase and Cotton Mather—had made the visions of the Revelation a formative influence upon the consciousness of the people. The Puritans filled their diaries, sermons, and public papers with apocalyptic discourse. (8)

Stein traces this apocalypticism to the first settlers. The proximity of the apocalypse seems strong in the Puritans. John Cotton, an early Puritan and forebear of Cotton Mather, believed "the beginning of the millennium was imminent—in 1655, to be exact" (Edwards 5); Cotton seems to be using a source similar to Columbus's. According to L. Michael White, Cotton Mather came up with four separate dates for the apocalypse: 1697, 1736, 1716, and 1717 (paragraph 11). William Bradford, in *Of Plymouth Plantation: 1620–1647*, begins with references to both the actions of Satan and the Antichrist and the "later times": "The like method Satan hath seemeth to hold in these later times, since the truth began to spring and spread after the great defection made by Antichrist, that man of sin" (4). To locate oneself in the "later times" is to assume that in the long time line of history, one is near the end; this is a relatively common designation by apocalyptic churches, especially those that claim to be in covenant with God. (This identification with the later times is taken up 200 years later by the Mormons, who self-identify as the Church of Latter-day Saints.) Bradford's fascination with the end of the world can also be found in some of the events he records—pestilence, a plague of locusts, a great hurricane, a lunar eclipse, and "a great and fearful earthquake" (260, 279–280, 302)—all of which are "signs of the times."

From John Cotton to Jonathan Edwards, the first century of Puritans in America espoused a form of Christianity that was particularly apocalyptic and engaged in constant battle with the Antichrist. In *The Bloody Tenet of Persecution for Cause and Conscience* (1644) by Roger Williams; *Ichabod: Or, a Discourse Shewing What Cause There Is to Fear That the Glory of the Lord Is Departing From New-England* (1702) by Increase Mather; *The Day of Doom* (1662) by Michael Wigglesworth; and *Wonders of the Invisible World* (1693) by Cotton Mather, among others, we can see a people committed to a covenant with God and actively engaged in spiritual and physical conflict against Evil. The Puritan beliefs that they were in special covenant with God, that they were his elect, and that the end was near contributed to an extreme intolerance of difference that resulted in numerous massacres of indigenous people, the Salem witch trials, and constant trials and expulsions for heresy (Roger Williams and Anne Hutchinson, for example).

Power follows a number of American Indian novels that openly confront and subvert the apocalyptic nature of the Europeans, both Spanish and English. In *The Sharpest Sight,* Louis Owens also includes "four- and five-hundred-year-old oaks" (4) to signify the presence of Europeans in North America. Like Hogan, Owens references the Spanish throughout the novel: "[T]hey could date their ancestors back to a seventeenth-century Spanish expedition into the New World" (100). Owens, however, alludes to the Puritans as well—from a Choctaw woman, Onatima, feeding corn to Rhode Island Red and Plymouth Rock chickens (185)[11] to a bartender, Jessard Deal, who cites Jonathan Edwards (212). Although the Ghost Dance is mentioned (254), Owens has an overtly racist, white FBI agent make the reference, effectively disqualifying it as a viable option. *The Sharpest Sight* does not provide solutions to the apocalyptic narratives but does suggest that "the whole world's out of whack and people like us Indians is the only ones that know how to fix it" (90). In *Heirs of Columbus,* Gerald Vizenor writes, "Columbus was Mayan. . . . The Mayan brought civilization to the savages of the Old World and the rest is natural. . . . Columbus escaped from the culture of death and carried our tribal genes back to the New World, back to the great river, he was an adventurer in our blood and he returned to his homeland" (9). By making Columbus Mayan, Vizenor removes the dualistic and apocalyptic elements from Columbus: a Mayan Columbus eliminates the Self-Other and conquistador-victim binaries and changes the linear, apocalyptic nature of the voyage into a return, a cyclic event.

Michael Hardin

A similar plot device is used in *The Dogs of Paradise* by the Argentinean novelist Abel Posse, who has an intellectually and technologically advanced Aztec and Inca coalition discover the Old World in 1392 and debate whether they should conquer Europe and eat "the white-faces for lunch, before they can eat us for supper" (34). Vizenor also incorporates the history-myths of Pocahontas, or Matoaka, into his novel as a way to deflate that historical moment when she supposedly begs for John Smith's life, signaling the end of the indigenous peoples of North America's last chance to expel the Europeans. Kirkpatrick Sale cites the treaty between the British and the Powhatan as signaling the end of the indigenous peoples' limited success at repelling Europeans: "never once after this defeat would the natives of America succeed in repelling and rejecting a single European colonial power" (279).

In *Crown of Columbus,* Michael Dorris and Louise Erdrich also highlight the convergence of the apocalyptic myths of Columbus and the Puritans. As Vivian Twostar and her boyfriend, Roger Williams, are preparing articles and poems for the 500th anniversary of Columbus's arrival in the Americas, they reflect on the history of conquest, especially in terms of the religious impulses behind the conquest. Although much of the novel depends on the characters' and reader's assumption that the crown will be golden or jeweled (the book's cover depicts a golden crown), the surprise is that it is the crown of thorns that Columbus has carried with him, "*this greatest treasure of Christendom*" (223; original emphasis). Thus Columbus appears again as Cristo-ferens, the one who will prepare the world for Christ's return. Although the novel's focus is on the apocalypticism of Columbus, it deals significantly with the apocalyptic movements in North America—namely, the Puritans and Manifest Destiny. *Crown of Columbus* also looks at the apocalyptic nature of the secular history of indigenous peoples since their contact with the Europeans began: "It's estimated that more than a hundred million people lived in the Western Hemisphere in 1491, and nineteen out of every last twenty of them died from things like smallpox and measles and other infections imported from overseas" (84). In a manner similar to Sale's, Dorris and Erdrich show us how "apocalyptic" the Columbian "exchange" was.

Within this tradition of critiquing apocalyptic history and narrative, Hogan names the protagonist-narrator of *Power* Omishto, "the One who Watches." As Watcher, Omishto is placed in the position of John the Revelator, who "testifies to everything he saw" (*Holy Bible,* Revelation 1:2) and records the unveiling—the *apokalypsis*—of the biblical end of the world. Hogan begins her narrative with a dream Omishto has in which the "earth was bleeding" (1), a passage reminiscent of John's vision in which "[a] third of the sea turned into blood" (Revelation 8:8) and of Columbus's fourth voyage. In contemporary English, the definition of apocalypse has changed from meaning "unveiling" or "revealing" to "imminent

Critique of Apocalyptic Narrative

disaster" or "universal destruction." Hogan utilizes both meanings—the catastrophic end and the unveiling—to emphasize her critique.

Based on Omishto's descriptions of her mother's church, it is both fundamentalist and Pentecostal; this places the mother squarely within the apocalyptic religious tradition of the first Europeans who arrived here.[12] The idea that the mother's church posits a physical heaven and hell is a frequent tenet of fundamentalist Christians: "[A]t school I have learned there's no room in [the] sky for my mother's heaven; there's no room at the center of the earth for hell, either" (106). That the church calls itself "the First Sanctified Church of the Holy Ghost" (157) indicates the privileged role of the Holy Ghost, the defining characteristic of Pentecostals. Hogan highlights the apocalyptic nature of this church through her description of the congregation: "They are good women, nice women, but even so, I don't want to be here in this somber place that tries too hard to look cheery, where everyone is waiting for the Rapture" (100).[13] Omishto cannot simply dismiss these believers because her mother is part of this group, and the women are "good." All too often binary thought requires that we reject the Other as "evil" because there is no middle term; however, Hogan rejects the binary and the apocalyptic ideology that derives from it without rejecting the people or other forms of life.

The real critique here may be the "waiting"—the passive, powerless stance of the victim, one Omishto rejects: "I am not waiting for anything. I am living" (207). Ama tells Omishto that the whites "are all waiting for Jesus to come and save them" (144). This implicates Christianity but also the Ghost Dance, given its echoes of Wovoka's "Messiah Letter." Interestingly, Omishto's mother fears Ama because "she lives as if nothing's ever come to pass, no America, no schools, no churches" (55). The mother, trained in apocalyptic narrative, reads Ama as if the Ghost Dance had occurred and all the white people were gone. The problem with both involves the hegemonic consequences of the apocalyptic narrative. Later Hogan reiterates the apocalyptic nature of the church and critiques the ideology along Marxist lines: "My mother believes there is an afterlife and when she gets there she will be compensated for her miseries on earth. She has felt the hand of God upon her and she thinks we live in the time of Revelation. She believes God will save her from sudden gusts and whirls of wind" (187). Here the mother adopts the belief that the storm is a destructive, punishing force instead of the regenerative force the Taiga propose. Hogan removes Omishto and eventually her mother from this linear, casual belief system because it is ineffective and ultimately destructive.

One of the Christian doctrines that encourages apocalyptic belief is the notion that we humans do not belong on this earth, that our real purpose is to be in heaven: "The preacher . . . believes in angels, children with wings in the sky, but he doesn't believe in what's on earth or birds; he says it's all an illusion, this life on earth, a dream, a miserable place we will one day escape into the golden streets of heaven. . . . I am in the world, the preacher says, but not of it" (40). To be in the world but not of the world is to be perpetually out of place. Countering the minister's relationship to the world is Ama: "[I]t has always been Ama's skill to live with the world and not against it" (47). "Ama" in Spanish means "landlady" or "housekeeper" but also suggests both "to love" (Sp. *amar*) and "soul" (Sp. *alma,* Fr. *âme*), as well as a clipped form of Mama. By looking at Ama's character and actions, we can see that she is the keeper of the land, the soul of the tribe, the one whose love for the tribe and the environment transcends her own welfare. Everything about Ama is grounded in both her physical and spiritual environment.

To further emphasize the difference between Ama and Mama's church, *Power* contains two references to the exodus of Moses: "The Indian land is still wet and fertile. But all the other land is poison now, like the pestilence of Mama's Bible that entered the houses as if to claim the firstborn sons" (90). Not coincidentally, the biblical metaphor is used with the poisoned land, not the Indian land, which is still life producing and life supporting. The second reference to Moses—"the bushes . . . are glowing in the dark with foxfire, after the storm. Like a burning bush in Mama's Bible" (94)—precedes her exit from her mother's house into "a chaotic, disordered world" (95). Again, both references to the Mosaic myth are negative. Within the Bible and for Christians, however, the story of Moses is all about the myth of a better reality, both Edenic and apocalyptic. Moses removes the Israelites from bondage in Egypt based on the notion that even after hundreds of years they were still "out of place." It also represents the movement to Canaan, the "land of milk and honey," itself an Edenic metaphor; within the structure of the Spanish and the English, Canaan represented both Earthly Paradise (Eden) and the sign of the Puritan Elect's Covenant with God and confirmed the overall linear structure of the divine plan, which placed them in the "later days."

Hogan connects the apocalyptic narratives of the church with their historical and current consequences for the American Indian. Omishto describes Mama's relationship with the church as especially self-abnegating: "This is salvation in the First Sanctified Church. And in the laying on of hands, she will find ways to heal diabetes, sterility, tuberculosis, even her own swollen fingers. . . . She doesn't love herself, I know this, because she believes like they tell her in church, that it was our fate to be destroyed by those who were stronger and righter" (187). From the belief in healing, Omishto connects to the church's underlying message "do not love the earthly body," or, in more secular terms, "the Self." Associating "stronger" with "righter," Omishto recognizes the nature of apocalyptic narrative to be participant in conquest. Thus instead of apocalyptic narrative providing an answer for the oppressed, it serves as a tool for the oppressor.

In *Power* the narratives of history and Christianity are woven together; although this may shock some in contemporary, secular America, we cannot forget that most of "American history"—even the present "War on Terrorism"— involves religious justification for political and social action. Vine Deloria Jr., in *Custer Died for Your Sins,* connects the two in no uncertain terms: "At one time or another slavery, poverty, and treachery were all justified by Christianity as politically moral institutions of the state" (104). *Power* begins with the statement "we just barely survived the tide of history" (6). At the end of the panther hunt, Omishto recognizes that something very significant is happening:

> It was a beginning and an end of something. I feel what it is but I don't have words for it yet. If I did they'd look like history and flowered lands and people with the beautiful ways we Taiga were said to have before it was cut apart in history. History is the place where the Spaniards cut off the hands of my ancestors. The Spanish who laughed at our desperation and dying, and I wish it didn't but that history still terrifies and haunts me. (73)

Omishto traces "history" to the arrival of the Spanish and the imposition of linear time onto indigenous reality. She also defines "history" as the horrific abuses carried out by the Spaniards,[14] who frequently justified their actions with the idea that the indigenous peoples lacked souls—an idea not refuted until Pope Paul III's *Sublimis Deus* in 1537 (Las Casas 6).[15] With all the atrocities of the conquest and the intervening centuries, perhaps Omishto is correct when, after the hurricane, she states, "Maybe we are happy to have survived" (42). After 500 years of genocide—murder, rape, dislocation, assimilation— the fact that American Indians have survived is significant; in a conversation the American Indian activist Ward Churchill told me that surviving the onslaught itself is an important accomplishment. *Survivor* is a term European Americans often discredit because it is neither conqueror nor victim; however, valuing survival limits the power of the conqueror because the "victim" refuses to cede appropriate power.

Throughout the novel Hogan counters the "mythic" arrival of the Europeans with the real effects on the indigenous peoples; the juxtaposition enables the reader to more fully understand the ultimate consequences of the Europeans' apocalyptic myths. Omishto remembers the stories of the first hints of European contact: "I remember it was a cold wind that told our ancestors the Europeans were coming before they emerged from a dense fog in ships and on horseback like four-legged people with beautiful bodies who believed false stories, that the manatee were mermaids, that they would find riches and eternal youth if they searched far enough and long enough" (179). Omishto mentions the fantastic elements: four-legged people, mermaids, and eternal youth. By citing the fantastic, Hogan reminds us of the mythic, the apocalyptic nature of the conquest; she reminds us of the myths that informed the decimation of the Americas. Of course, Hogan does not forget the "secular" justification of conquest, gold: "I think how gold was the thing that created one of those worlds and destinies, that the Americans invaded us for gold" (215). It is important that she uses the term *Americans* and not *Europeans,* thus reminding the reader that the conquest extended well beyond the Spanish to the American "prospectors" in the Black Hills, California, and Alaska—all participant in one form of Manifest Destiny or another.

Such a history can be overwhelming and can easily result in immobility. Joseph Post, one of the Taiga elders, questions his beliefs when confronted with history: "[S]ometimes he doubts all this. Not because he is a doubter or faithless, but because he has been made to feel small and impotent under the weight of history" (186). This may be one of the most daunting tasks writers of color in America face today—confronting and exposing a history of oppression without becoming victim to history itself. In that, I believe, Hogan has found a balance; history is always present—through references to Spanish moss, horses, and Christianity—without it dictating so much of the novel that the past becomes overwhelming. Alexie describes the difficulty of this position: "Your past is a skeleton walking one step behind you, and your future is a skeleton walking one step in front of you. . . . What you have to do is keep walking in step with your skeletons" (*Lone Ranger* 21–22). In much the same way Alexie's fiction is historically informed and conscious, Hogan's writing is as well. Not only does she include the Spanish who cut off the hands of indigenous peoples, she mentions the fate of Osceola's head: "The Seminole Osceola's head was placed on the bedpost of white children by their father, the physician who was with him when he died, to make them behave" (139). The American Indian, nearly eliminated by the European presence in the Americas, was still posited as the embodiment of Evil by this member of the scientific community, working under the political influence and religious sanction of Manifest Destiny.

Despite the extensive critique of Christianity in *Power,* Hogan frequently gives both Ama and Omishto Christ-like characteristics or places them within events evocative of those Christ supposedly experienced. I am not suggesting that Hogan is validating the Christian myth, merely that she is appropriating some of Christ's more mythic, archetypal qualities. To reject the entire myth could imply participation in the good-evil binary, whereas selective appropriation moves beyond the distinctions of self and other. Furthermore, rarely discussed in the Christ mythology is how he represents a blurring of dualities—he is both God and man, alpha and omega; instead, Christ tends to be read as one pole of the good-evil binary. In many ways Ama is the self-sacrificing savior figure in *Power.* Before she can execute her destiny, Ama goes through a baptism by water: "Ama dips and submerges her whole body like she's being baptized"

(63). Hogan chooses to compare this to a baptism, consciously drawing parallels to the Christ myth. The baptism is followed by the sacrifice, Ama's sacrifice of both the panther and herself: "'You have killed yourself, Ama.' 'I know it. Don't I just know it'" (67). The Christ myth ends for Ama when the tribal elders exile her, mimicking God the Father's rejection of Christ on the cross: "My God, my God, why have you forsaken me" (*Holy Bible,* Matthew 27:46). Even then Omishto says, "Ama is saving a world" (224).

Ama's "sin" is important, however, because had Ama sacrificed the panther according to the traditions of the tribe, she would have reenacted a myth reminiscent of the Ghost Dance: "A sacrifice was called for and if it was done well, all the animals and the panther would come back again and they'd be whole. The people in those days believed that all the hunted, if hunted correctly, would return again" (111). Omishto is also portrayed as a savior figure, and the most obvious moment is when she thinks she sees a woman in a tree after the hurricane: "I see a woman hanging in one of the trees. . . . Then I see it's only a dress in the tree, no body inside it. . . . Then I look down and see myself and I am naked" (38–39). In Christian terms, Omishto sees herself crucified, hung on a tree; however, this event also has currency within Taiga myth, since the hurricane is an event of origin. Without dying, Omishto is born, naked and wet, into her destiny as Ama's successor; Christ's crucifixion marks his death, the end of his human manifestation. Omishto is a Christ myth without the dualism.

As Omishto watches Ama hunt the panther, she thinks "maybe she is right. But she is also wrong . . . it is both grace and doom, right and wrong" (62); to be both grace and doom, right and wrong, is to exist outside of binary logic. Hogan uses Ama, Mama, and Omishto to expose the spaces outside binary thought to destabilize the apocalyptic structure. Although the narrative seems to privilege the indigenous, Ama argues for an alternative space: "Ama said the old ways are not enough to get us through this time and she was called to something else. To live halfway between the modern world and the ancient one" (22–23). Living between worlds creates a tenuous identity and ultimately allows both worlds to exile her. Mama also wants to be part of both worlds: "Mama's made her choices and they are different. Still, she'd like it both ways. . . . She'd like to learn from the old people, live the way we used to, but she wants it modern too" (16). Although most of the narrative may seem to devalue Mama's choice, her arrival in the Kili Swamp at the end indicates her salvation; thus her path, too, is validated. Mama represents not only a combination of ancient and modern worlds but a combination of the European—"my mother, who tries to pass for white" (20)—and the indigenous. Omishto, who watches both women, is herself a combination of modern and ancient: "I don't believe in magic. I don't believe because at school I learn there is a reason for everything. This is what separates me from Aunt Ama . . . she believes in all the Taiga stories, that they are true, that they are real" (13). Although Omishto may not believe the stories, she follows and learns from Ama; thus she incorporates these stories regardless of whether she believes them—an act that disrupts the entire notion of truth.

Besides the characters she uses to disrupt conventional binaries, Hogan challenges many of our binary distinctions, frequently associating the binaries themselves with Christianity. The name of the fictional tribe, Taiga, represents the erasure of our designations of the earth's ecosystems; *taiga,* a word that means coniferous, subarctic forests, is joined with the subtropical swamps of Florida.[16] The hurricane also erases distinctions between land and sea: "The strong winds have blown water all across the land. There are no edges, no borders between the elements because everything is water, silver and glassy. The whole ground moves and shimmers as if it is alive. . . . Heaven has fallen" (46). Concluding this passage with the fall of Christian heaven underlines Christianity's dependence upon duality and cataclysm; ironically, Hogan uses an "apocalyptic" event to critique apocalyptic narrative. Furthermore, the distinction between human and animal is blurred: "[T]he animals used to help the humans, how they would teach them the plants that were healing, sing songs for them to learn, how they would show the people the way to renew the broken world" (29). This passage is also important because this relationship between animal and human represents the ability to renew the world. Within an apocalyptic structure there is no renewal, only devastation and removal; thus shedding the human-animal split is one way to escape the apocalypse. Finally, even the nature of Oni escapes binary simplicity: "[W]e Taiga people have that word—Oni—for breath and air and wind. It is a force. Oni is like God, it is everywhere, unseen" (41). To some extent, one could argue that the idea that the Christian God breathes life into Adam and "inspires" (breathes) the Bible makes this a parallel; however, unlike the Christian God, Oni is not defined as either good or evil.

Although much of the focus of the apocalyptic critique in *Power* is directed at religious narrative, the novel clearly attacks environmentalists' apocalyptic fervor. One does not have to look far to find environmentalists describing the fate of the world in apocalyptic terms; for example, Mystic Realm—a website advocating support of Greenpeace activists—depicts McDonald's, Esso, Nestlé, and the G-8 as the four horsemen of the apocalypse. Such depictions, however, result—as all apocalyptic narratives do—in resignation or fanatic oppression.[17] After Ama has killed the panther, Omishto confronts what seems to be a contradiction: "I agree with them [environmentalists] and with treaty rights, too. How can there be two truths that contradict each other? And me. I am on both sides right now" (115). When a narrative takes on apocalyptic tones, there is no space for nuance or negotiation: it is all wrong or it is all right. Hogan goes

Critique of Apocalyptic Narrative

beyond the simple contradiction of Omishto's position and exposes the inherent colonialism in much environmentalism:

> I would like to say to them that they are right, that it is wrong to kill land, animals, that it was wrong to destroy any of it, even us, but they are the children of those who were alive from the deaths of others and so I do not look at them even though they are right; they are taking up our beliefs and judging us, and to them I am a monster because for them everything has been so easy, but they do not see themselves or know their own history. (138)

Hogan points out that frequently those who are the most vocal and adamant about environmentalism are the descendants of those who did most of the damage—Europeans and Euro-Americans; those environmentalists have the luxury of wealth accumulated through centuries of ecological conquest and then impose that morality on people without the same economic base to fall back on. I am not arguing that Hogan is antienvironmental; quite the contrary, I believe Hogan is critiquing the way Western environmentalists have imposed an apocalyptic narrative onto the environment at the expense of those who have coexisted with the environment in a much more symbiotic manner for millennia. Owens makes this point quite persuasively: "If we had not respected this world and treated it with care, we would have long ago destroyed it. You see what white people have done in only a few hundred years" (115). Ama's killing of the panther is remarkably evocative of the Makah's hunt of the gray whale off the Washington coast. Greenpeace and other groups constantly interfered in the Makah's effort to hunt one whale. Did anyone question whether the fuel burned to transport the protestors to Washington and to run the protest boats would cause more ecological damage than the loss of one gray whale? No, because the narrative was apocalyptic and thus not open to discussion.

Hogan is an environmentalist—one who reads the environment in terms of conquest, colonialism, and survival—but not an apocalypticist. In *Power* Omishto mentions that the panther is struggling while "kudzu, an exotic species that does not belong here . . . takes over everything" (79). This is an obvious metaphor for the struggle indigenous peoples face against the Europeans. At another point Omishto comments on her mother's notion of "progress": "[T]he building and the farming and sugarcane . . . were killing the deer. . . . She thinks it's the small price you pay for progress. I think it's the way to kill a world" (27). The world is changing, the ancient is confronting the modern; but instead of abandoning one for the other, Ama and Omishto seek the space between the two, the space that is neither, or the space that encompasses both.

Near the end of the novel Omishto states, "Everyone has their theory. But these are only their stories and they need their stories, even if they aren't the truth. Stories are for people what water is for plants" (227). If everyone has his or her theory, then no one theory is privileged. The veracity of a story is not as important as the story's ability to give life. An apocalyptic narrative demands privilege because it claims to have discerned a great and immediate truth that cannot be compromised. Such narratives would not merit critique if they were benign, but these narratives accompany some of the most heinous actions committed by humans. From the moment Columbus arrived in the Americas, these apocalyptic myths were part of the conquest and were used repeatedly to justify the atrocities of conquest and colonization. For the American Indian, apocalyptic narratives only perpetuate the oppression by removing agency. Hogan systematically purges these narratives so the novel ends not "with a bang" but with a song: "I dance and as the wind stirs in the trees, someone sings the song that says the world will go on living" (235). No storm, just a breeze that says the world will go on.

Notes

1. In this chapter I use Thomas Robbins and Susan J. Palmer's definition of apocalypticism as the belief that the end of history as we know it is near (4). The term includes both secular and religious connotations, which makes it ideal.

2. One might argue that the "positive" and "negative" charges of particles and subparticles would indicate a binary universe; however, the fact that these particles and subparticles can join and become "neutral"—a third state—makes such a claim difficult. Similarly, the designation of "male" and "female" might suggest a binary universe, but the more one investigates, the more one will see that the category itself is arbitrary and that when one looks at fish, plants, bacteria, and fungi, one can find life-forms with sexes ranging from one to more than ten.

3. This is not to say that the indigenous peoples of the Americas could not have had apocalyptic-type myths, but most mythologies were either suppressed or radically altered by the presence of the Europeans to such an extent that it seems safe to state that most, if not all, of contemporary culture's apocalypticism comes from Europe.

4. This myth continues into the sixteenth and seventeenth centuries. In 1653 Bernabe Cobo wrote that "[s]ome modern writers have discussed this matter, speculating about the region called Ophir, so highly praised for its wealth in the Sacred Scriptures, which the ships of Solomon navigated to and returned from loaded with gold and other riches; they concluded that Ophir was this Kingdom of Peru or another of the rich and famous provinces of America" (64).

5. For many Protestant millennialists, rebuilding Solomon's temple is the one remaining prophecy yet to be fulfilled before Christ can return. Thus Christian terrorist groups in Jerusalem are currently attempting to destroy the al-Aqsa Mosque in al-Haram al-Sharif (which is on the supposed site of Solomon's temple) or are instigating violence between the Israelis and the Palestinians that would lead to the destruction of al-Aqsa Mosque.

6. It is important to look at Edenic and apocalyptic myths as essentially the same. Within Judeo-Christian myth, time is linear and one cannot go backward; however, Christianity posits a salvation wherein the individual may end up in heaven, purified, and the Book of

Revelation attributes to heaven many Edenic elements (the Tree of Life, for example). Thus Edenic metaphors can refer to both Genesis and Revelation simultaneously.

7. Cabeza de Vaca comes to America with the same assumptions of cultural superiority, and his conclusions about the indigenous peoples are reductive, but he seems less directly participative in the enslavement and eradication of the indigenous peoples.

8. García Márquez also refers to the English participation in the conquest through references to Francis Drake (10, 422).

9. The novel becomes metafictional at this point, as Aureliano Babilonia is reading that he is reading the demise of his family and Macondo.

10. Ironically, the Methuselah tree is also the nickname of the oldest known living species, the bristlecone pine—*Pinus longaeva*—in California's Sierra Nevada; the oldest of these trees is referred to as "THE Methuselah" and is nearly 4,800 years old (see Cohen 43). Thus these Methuselah trees predate not only the Spaniards but Christianity itself.

11. This is a truly clever reference to the Pilgrims who only survived because they were kept alive by the "miraculous" discovery of Narragansett and Wampanoag corn.

12. Spanish Catholicism and English Puritanism were both fundamentalist religions at the time. Neither was particularly Pentecostal, but today the churches that are most apocalyptic tend to be fundamentalist Pentecostals.

13. The Rapture, an idea that has currency only among certain highly conservative Protestant denominations, is an event that generally precedes the Tribulation. The Rapture is based primarily on a reading of Revelation 3:10: "Since you have kept my command to endure patiently, I will also keep you from the hour of trial that is going to come upon the whole world to test those who live on earth." The idea is that Christ will return for the Christians and take them away while the rest of humankind suffers because of its disbelief for the seven years of Tribulation.

14. This does not exonerate the Americans, English, Dutch, French, or Portuguese, all of whom were quite versed in these atrocities.

15. Even the papal bull, however, did not force the Europeans to change their actions, merely their excuses; and in some cases they redirected their hatred. Whereas the papal bull recognized souls in the indigenous peoples of the Americas, the same question was not raised concerning Africans.

16. One could also read this as Hogan's emphasis on the extreme displacement of the American Indian.

17. One member of Greenpeace, Bob Hunter, writes that the early apocalyptic nature of environmentalism actually fomented within him the feeling that he was helpless to change the problems ("The Other Side of the Fence").

Works Cited

Alexie, Sherman. *Indian Killer.* New York: Atlantic Monthly Press, 1996.

———. *The Lone Ranger and Tonto Fistfight in Heaven.* New York: HarperPerennial, 1993.

Bradford, William. *Of Plymouth Plantation: 1620–1647.* Ed. Samuel Eliot Morison. New York: Knopf, 1959.

Carpentier, Alejo. *The Harp and the Shadow.* Trans. Thomas Christensen and Carol Christensen. San Francisco: Mercury House, 1990.

Michael Hardin

Cobo, Father Bernabe. *History of the Inca Empire: An Account of the Indians' Customs and Their Origin Together with a Treatise on Inca Legends, History, and Social Institutions.* Trans. and ed. Roland Hamilton. Austin: University of Texas Press, 1979.

Cohen, Michael P. *A Garden of Bristlecones: Tales of Change in the Great Basin.* Reno: University of Nevada Press, 1997.

Columbus, Christopher. *The Four Voyages.* Ed. and trans. J. M. Cohen. New York: Penguin, 1969.

———. *The Libro de las Profecías of Christopher Columbus: An En Face Edition.* Trans. and commentary Delno C. West and August Kling. Gainesville: University of Florida Press, 1991.

Deloria, Vine, Jr. *Custer Died for Your Sins: An Indian Manifesto.* Norman: Oklahoma University Press, 1988.

Dorris, Michael, and Louise Erdrich. *Crown of Columbus.* New York: HarperCollins, 1991.

García Márquez, Gabriel. *One Hundred Years of Solitude.* Trans. Gregory Rabassa. New York: Harper and Row, 1970.

Garcilaso de la Vega. *Royal Commentaries of the Incas and General History of Peru.* Trans. Harold V. Livermore. Austin: University of Texas Press, 1966.

Hazen-Hammond, Susan. *Timelines of Native American History: Through the Centuries with Mother Earth and Father Sky.* New York: Perigree, 1997.

Hogan, Linda. *Power.* New York: W. W. Norton, 1998.

The Holy Bible: New International Version. Grand Rapids, Mich.: Zondervan, 1978.

Hunter, Bob. "The Other Side of the Fence." *Eye* 10, no. 48 (6 September 2001). Accessed 10 December 2001. <www.eye.net/eye/issue/issue_09.06.01/news/enviro.html>.

Las Casas, Bartolomé de. *The Devastation of the Indies: A Brief Account.* Trans. Herma Briffault. Intro. Bill M. Donovan. Baltimore: Johns Hopkins University Press, 1992.

Marx, Karl. *Early Writings.* Ed. Quintin Hoare. New York: Vintage, 1975.

Owens, Louis. *The Sharpest Sight.* Norman: University of Oklahoma Press, 1992.

Posse, Abel. *The Dogs of Paradise.* Trans. Margaret Sayers Peden. New York: Atheneum, 1989.

Robbins, Thomas, and Susan J. Palmer. *Millennium, Messiahs, and Mayhem: Contemporary Apocalyptic Movements.* New York: Routledge, 1997.

Sale, Kirkpatrick. *The Conquest of Paradise: Christopher Columbus and the Columbian Legacy.* New York: Knopf, 1991.

Stein, Stephen J. "Editor's Introduction." In Jonathan Edwards, *The Works of Jonathan Edwards.* Vol. 5: *Apocalyptic Writings.* Ed. and Intro. Stephen J. Stein. New Haven, Conn.: Yale University Press, 1977. 1–93.

Toledo, Robert A. "Wovoka: The Paiute Messiah." *ViewZone* 28. Accessed 10 December 2001. <http://www.viewzone.com/wovoka.html>.

Vizenor, Gerald. *Heirs of Columbus.* Hanover, N.H.: Wesleyan University Press, 1991.

Weber, David J. *The Spanish Frontier in North America.* New Haven, Conn.: Yale University Press, 1992.

White, L. Michael. "Cotton Mather." In Paul Boyer, James West Davidson, and L. Michael White, *Apocalypse Explained: The Puritans.* PBS Online: WGBH. Copyright 1999. Accessed 17 November 2001. <http://www.pbs.org/wgbh/pages/frontline/shows/apocalypse/explanation/puritans.html>.

Wovoka (Jack Wilson). "The Messiah Letter: Cheyenne Version" and "The Messiah Letter: Mooney's Free Rendering." In *The Norton Anthology of American Literature*, Vol. 2. 5th ed. Ed. Nina Baym et al. New York: W. W. Norton, 1998. 845–846.

DANCING THE CHRONOTOPES OF POWER
The Road to Survival in Linda Hogan's *Power*

CARRIE BOWEN-MERCER

> May all walls be like those of the jungle,
> filled with animals
> singing into the ears of the night.
> Let them be
> made of the mysteries further
> in the heart joined with the lives of all,
> all the bridges of flesh,
> all singing,
> all covering the wounded land
> showing again, again
> that boundaries are all lies.
> —Linda Hogan, "Wall Songs," *Seeing Through the Sun*

> I am why they survived.
> The world behind them did not close.
> The world before them is still open.
> —Linda Hogan, "Tear," *The Book of Medicines*

The Possible

IT SEEMS TO ME THAT LINDA HOGAN'S POEMS AND NOVELS EXPRESS a continuity of ideas, a relationship between walls and tearing them down. If the walls between people were more like songs linking us together through our voices, the immediate physicalness of our voices traveling, moving over distances through time, then perhaps the walls—those made of concrete and steel, language and thought, and history and culture—would be less necessary. Maybe it is true. Maybe we just forgot that everything, especially the world, is open—available to all, human, animal, and plant. Mind and body, dream and waking experience, nature and culture could fuse into the spiritual if we let them. Perhaps we could see them as always having been parts of the same whole. We might feel our connection to the animals and plants around us; we might one day hear the Language that permeates all of creation, that all members of creation speak—nature, culture, human, animal, pebble, flower.

The moment in time may come when humans realize that they need not consider themselves the center of it all. We may let our guard down, notice how closely we travel through time and space with not only other humans but also all nonhumans. It could happen. All it might take is belief, hope, a new way of imagining how and why the world is. The Native American view of a human-animal-land circularity of continual conflation, what Louis Owens calls sacred "centripetal" forces at work in Native stories (172), could replace the anthropocentric Euro-American desire for walled boundaries between humans and animals and land. Walls could be torn down before being built so high that tearing them down is impossible; land destruction and animal endangerment in the name of land development and human progress could end by choice. It could happen.

Linda Hogan offers her readers such possibility in both her poetry and her novel *Power*. In the words of Catherine Rainwater, writers like Hogan offer "alternative notions of what it means to inhabit the earth as human beings" (ix). Hogan tells the story of a fictive Native American tribe—the Taiga—that has lost land, tradition, history, and life and finds itself close to extinction. She tells the story of Ama, a woman who kills a member of an endangered species of panthers to restore balance to the world, to bring hope to the Taiga who believe themselves the relatives of panthers. Ama shares similarities with the Pueblo conception of Yellow Woman. Leslie Marmon Silko says "the stories about Kochininako made [her] aware that sometimes an individual must act despite disapproval, or concern for appearances or what others might say" (71). Like Ama, who acts against tradition to restore that tradition, "Yellow Woman . . . dares to cross traditional boundaries of ordinary behavior during times of crisis in order to save the Pueblo" (70).

Within the overall narrative structure of *Power*, which reveals the emotional and spiritual development of a young member of the tribe, Omishto, who resides in the white world, we can trace the oppositional views of life held by Natives and whites with respect to what it means to be human; what forms of behavior toward land, animals, and tradition are ethical; and what matters to the survival of different people and their environments. Hogan exposes not only the inadequacy of Euro-American ideology to understand a Native ideology but also its destructive tendencies toward all ideologies that differ from it. She shows the white world incapable of moving away from Cartesian, hierarchical relationships; incapable of thinking anything but a linear sense of time and a separate three-dimensional sense of space; incapable of living outside "an orderly, chronological procession of sequential events, each 'officially' assigned its own measure of 'importance' in an attempt to avoid what might be called chaos" (Suzuki and Knudtson 177–178); and incapable of loving self, other, animal, plant, water, sky, thought, word, rock, and fish as one and the same or as equally important. Hogan exposes possibility for change in thought and behavior, a possibility that exists both inside and outside the walls of "history."

Dancing the Chronotopes of Power

Hogan constantly weaves historical "fact" into her fictional account of the struggling Taiga on a diminished section of swampland in northern Florida. Poisoned fish and unsafe drinking water are the truths of Hogan's novel. The fact that any hope for the Fountain of Youth—once sought by fourteenth-century Spaniards in northern Florida—is completely undercut in the present place and time of the novel, where a person would be lucky to find a swamp that has not been filled in with sand, is one truth in *Power*, one present "fact" that erodes one wall called progress. Hogan brings the present ecological crisis, as I think she sees it, into a fictional account of a Native American myth-tradition that needs to be (re)imagined in this time of crisis, that needs to be believed if possible. Hogan offers her readers a story to change the way they think about their relationships with each other and their environments; she gives us this story by revealing the importance of story for the perpetuation of Native American belief systems, traditions, and lives in the past—in history—when the Natives experienced Euro-American destruction and deceit, and in the present—in a fictive representation of history in process—in order to stay alive, to survive, to thrive again. Hogan shows us that change can happen, that hope and possibility for a meaningful existence still exist. Power is in this already existent possibility.

Hogan explores the intersections of lives and cultures and times and spaces. She asks us to question history as Euro-Americans know it: a linear continuum that divides one time from another and one space from another. But couldn't time and space be less distinguishable than we think? Vine Deloria Jr., in a discussion of time and space, states that "time has an unusual limitation. It must begin and end at some real points, or it must be conceived as cyclical in nature, endlessly allowing the repetition of patterns of possibilities" (*God Is Red* 71). The Euro-American history, its concept of time, is one that desires a seamless, contained story for how things were and how things are likely to be; it is based on beginning, middle, and end points of reference—always paradoxically pursuing "an ever-elusive moment [in space] 'just ahead' in time or down the road" (Rainwater 115). But these static, chronological points of reference—often referred to as the facts of history—do not allow for Deloria's concept of the dynamic "repetition of patterns of possibilities" that is tribal time itself, which encourages a paradoxical "stillness within the present moment within the immediate setting, and [a] reconnection with the past and the present rather than [a] flight toward an ever-receding future" (Rainwater 115). In short, the Euro-American spins perpetually in a circle, moving nowhere in time and space, looking ahead to find out the ending without living; the Native American stands still, moving everywhere in time and space, living. To suggest that history as the Euro-Americans see it is factual must be both incredibly painful and laughable to the Native Americans either written out of Euro-American history or written in as the savage, as the terrible "Other"—much as nature itself is still considered by many people.

Through Ama's action of killing one member of the nearly extinct golden panther species and the resulting trials that occur (the Euro-American and the tribal), Hogan dramatizes just how little and how much fact really matters to whom and when. Different types of facts matter to different types of people for different reasons. For the white people, Taiga facts are impossible to believe; how is it possible to be a panther when clearly the Taiga are human? Walls. During the white trial, Omishto thinks she cannot tell the white judge and jury the real truth because all they want are facts, like which gun was used and where Ama killed the cat (127). Walls. The whites find comfort in the lawyer's insistence that the Taiga world is different from theirs (136). Walls. And the Taiga, although knowing the destructive history of what the whites call justice, cannot believe in that justice, may not even believe in the facts of that history. The Taiga know that whites kill panthers, land, Taiga, and other Native Americans; but they also know and believe in the history that is them, their heritage of past, present, and future. They have their own justice.

During the traditional trial, Omishto realizes that some facts must be left out of her story about the killing; she must not tell about the cat's unhealthy condition because "it would cut their world in half . . . it would have been like giving them sickness and death" (166). Omishto knows truths neither side would understand; she safely holds certain facts from both sides. Omishto begins to see that both sides, because of their different perspectives from inside-outside different walls of experience, create and live within those very walls that decrease the possibility for change. Perspective frees and limits by degrees, or, as Deloria claims, "different historical arrangements of emotional energy" of different people "come into conflict" (*God Is Red* 65).

David Suzuki and Peter Knudtson correctly assert that "the way a people views the passage of time—the particular 'geometry' that they assign to time—plays a crucial role in shaping their relationship with the natural world" (177). In other words, our cultural sense of time can determine how we live in the space around us. Paula Gunn Allen says, "[T]he traditional concept of time is timelessness, as the concept of space is of multidimensionality. In the ceremonial world the tribes inhabit, time and space are mythic" (*Sacred Hoop* 147). Time and space and myth and reality are directly connected in Hogan's novel. Even though Deloria claims that "space generates time, but time has little relationship to space" (*God Is Red* 71), Hogan shows that through a lived and narrated reality-story of recurring myth in both real space and time (the actual endangerment of panthers in Florida and the past and present domination over Native tribes in America) and fictional space and time (the text), myth and reality and space and time take on the characteristics of a dynamic stillness—a repeating pattern that changes contextually—in relationship to event, place, duration, and experience.

The Taiga have the vision of all space and time—which means all history—through their belief in the relationships between the spiritual and the physical, the real and the mythic. Allen's discussion of how American Indians view their world supports Hogan's fictional representation of the Taiga's view. Allen says, "American Indian thought makes no such dualistic division [between the supernatural and the phenomenal], nor does it draw a hard and fast line between what is material and what is spiritual, for it regards the two as different expressions of the same reality, as though life has twin manifestations that are mutually interchangeable" (*Sacred Hoop* 59). Few walls exist. The Taiga have a story to listen to, to learn, speak, live, and pass on. Time circles; it is the same story. Space expands and extends; it is the same story.

Hogan tells the story of Panther Woman, whose job it was to "keep the world in balance." She "sang the sun up in the morning," and "she was there to refresh our thoughts and renew our acts." People broke the "harmony and balance" of the world, and Panther Woman, during a wild storm, slipped into another world through a hole in the sky. She followed panther into a world of "rivers on fire, animals dying of sickness, and foreign vines." The hole in the sky closed before she could return to her world, to our world. But panther, the one Panther Woman knew best, offered herself as a sacrifice so all animals and the world could be whole again (*Power* 110–111).

The Panther Woman story breaks spatial and temporal boundaries. She is the "I" of Hogan's poem "Tear," the one who guarantees her people's survival by opening a hole in the "world behind" and the "world before" (*Book of Medicines* 60). Hogan has Omishto tell the story of the myth as myth while Hogan's narrative itself is a fictive rendering of the myth as lived reality. If the myth recurs whenever the world becomes unbalanced, the term *temporal boundary* is obsolete. The myth embraces a circular time that repeats. The myth also hinges on the communication between humans and animals and the simultaneous existence of different worlds—the physical and the spiritual—which render the term *spatial boundary* obsolete. The myth-reality inside Hogan's narrative is Ama as Panther Woman in contemporary northern Florida, trying to rebalance the poisoned world like the Panther Woman before her and the Panther Woman after her.

Hogan shows her readers that, in fact, there were never any boundaries to begin with, that, as she writes in "Wall Songs," "boundaries are all lies" (*Seeing* 68). Throughout the novel we hear Omishto think that her experience is "the end or the beginning of something" (58, 73, 151). Vertigo may ensue when we hear that "time is like waves of water, with darkness becoming light, light turning into darkness," and that "there's a place in between every solid thing where creation takes place" (230, 25). Hogan invites us on a mysterious journey through mind, over matter, through swamp and sky and dust and fog, through the "eyes and ears" (3) of space and the world that "exists in layers [with] all time here at once" (215), that could possibly change the way we interact with our environments, that could increase the likelihood of our survival. We could actually see and live within what Deloria says many tribal people do: "the reality of our existence in places" rather than the "experiential and abstract interpretations" we make of our realities and our places (*God Is Red* 73). At the end of *Power* Omishto says, "I am not waiting for anything [or for Ama's return]. I am living" (207).

In each relative moment of history and each place, time *might* move horizontally and vertically until forming a circle of crisscrossing lines and arcs; space *might* expand vertically and horizontally until it reaches an infinity of embedded circles through time. Place could indeed become self—story, memory, and deed—through the experience of time and space over and over again, changing ever so slightly with each new appearance of each generation's Panther Woman who comes to regenerate "the wounded land" and its inhabitants through the creative, transformative, boundary-breaking power of mystery and actualized myth. Hogan writes that approximately thirty golden panthers are roaming the leftover swampland in Florida among housing developments, highways, and gas stations; she also writes that approximately thirty Taiga from the Panther clan remain, living above Kili Swamp near a junkyard with old car parts and mangy dogs. The animal, the human, and the land suffer—diseased and on the verge of death—in Hogan's novel. The Panther Woman myth is the only hope that becomes "fact" in *Power*'s world.

Some Reality

The last U.S. Fish and Wildlife Service count of the Florida panther numbered the total population at seventy (Lavendel 21). Their natural habitat—the swampy jungle—has been turned into small sections of natural space bordered on all sides by human "development": highways, homes, malls. The Florida panther is losing its home and its ability to roam, its security and freedom. The panther is losing itself as a species. When it crosses human boundaries—stepping onto roads and entering neighborhoods—it is run over by speeding cars and shot by human-held rifles. When the panther's world fragments—literally cracks apart—it may be easy for us to turn away as it disappears forever; we may refuse to hear the panther's screaming night song. Like Omishto says, until we realize the fragmenting world is ours as much as theirs and their songs are also our cries of mourning, we endanger the panther, every animal, ourselves, and the earth by feeling "safe" within our boundaries (*Power* 15). This mess, this loss of life, this human ignorance or sense of superiority, this speciesism is real.

Dancing the Chronotopes of Power

The boundaries we create—the ones we never cross, the ones we fight wars over, the ones that destroy—are powerful, arbitrary codes and lines, often threatening in practice, sometimes comforting in theory. The walls we build between ourselves and animals and nature and the walls we build among different cultures, genders, and classes marginalize, hierarchize, limit, and rarely protect. The collars we put around the necks of endangered animals—as the white biologists do to the panthers in *Power*—to track them throughout their lives, to help them by learning about them, likely decrease the quality of their lives. From Hogan we learn that scientifically "tracked" panthers often die because they outgrow the collars, the collars get caught on objects in the forest, and the radio waves the collars emit attract hunters (119). Hogan implies that animals and nature—intelligent and aware beings in their own right (Allen, *Sacred Hoop* 60)—are exploited as objects of scientific studies that seek facts, not relationships; that claim objectivity in the name of "helping" a species when, as Deloria says, objectivity in science is not possible when human subjectivity necessarily "clouds" perspective and offers motives for study (*Evolution* 25).

But it is difficult to change the way we interact with those around us, difficult to break boundaries, to tear down walls. We have such faith in certain things we cannot prove, like God, but we do not always have faith in things we can see and feel, like the beauty of a panther in the moonlight. We fall prey to our own ignorance; we have faith in our ability to get through one day after another without a break, a gap, a tear in the structure of our lives. So what happens when our world cracks open and we see the fragments of our existence for the very first time, realizing our "eyesight" has kept us from seeing them before? What happens when a strange, contemporary Native American woman character, who may have mysteriously married a panther at age twelve, illegally kills a panther eighteen years later? Some of us, like the whites in *Power*, will be too afraid to "face the facts," whatever they may be; some will pretend nothing happened; some will renew their belief in traditional ways, as Omishto did, while others run off to pray to a Christian God for some kind of salvation, as Omishto's mother did; some might stand up for the animal against the human, as do the white animal rights activists whose ancestors killed people like the Taiga and their land; others argue the injustice of history, like contemporary Native Americans who want treaty rights upheld for once. Some (the whites) may temporarily see the crack in the "container of their history" (*Power* 136) and face their deceitful justice, whereas others (the Taiga) may experience renewed hope for a future—although also temporary—dependent on the present as much as the past.

These temporary states I refer to are quite different from each other, however. One state locates genetic hypocrisy and guilt deep in the minds of one group, originating from their human ancestors, whereas the other locates genetic synchronicity and love in the bodies and minds of the other group, originating from their human-animal-plant ancestors. One sees and feels for moments at a time; the other feels and breathes in timelessness.

Only seventy golden panthers are left at this moment of history in northern Florida. This particular intersection of time and space shows the destruction of at least one animal and its environment. Although Deloria asserts that "the 'universe-as-object' attitude is breaking down in Western thinking, [that] scientific studies are showing that animals, which we formerly considered creatures of instinct alone, have mental capabilities and knowledge that we did not think possible" (*Evolution* 196), the golden panther and many other animals continue to be threatened with extinction as a result of the "universe-as-object" mentality. Linda Hogan takes us to this place and asks us to watch, to bear immediate witness. Hogan's young character, Omishto, wonders if it would have been "a different world if someone had believed [Taiga] lives were as important as theory and gold" (179). Power. The power to change or reenvision "reality" exists always.

Fusion of the Possible and Some Reality Through the Chronotope

In *Power* Linda Hogan explores the cracking open of a world—a fictional one very representative of the real—through the story of a young girl who not only witnesses but also physically, emotionally, and spiritually embraces the power of watching/acting, myth/reality, nature/culture, human/animal, and Native (Taiga)/transplanted (white). Not only does Hogan posit the historically documented loss of panthers in Florida in direct relationship to a fictional account of the endangered Taiga tribe—which could represent other Native American tribes in America throughout U.S. history—but she also conflates singular experience into plural, individual into communal, human into animal such that the fictional becomes powerfully mythic *and* real. In short, Hogan decenters Euro-American ideology of the boundary and marginalizes its destructive sacredness. Instead of a world in which circular clocks measure linear time and straight rulers measure three-dimensional spatial structures, Hogan exposes her readers to a Native American epistemology of time and space that involves their inseparable interaction through the circularity of experience and a lack of boundary between them. She offers a glimpse of what Allen calls "the kind of time in which the individual and the universe are 'tight' . . . knitting person and surroundings into one" (*Sacred Hoop* 150).

Euro-American science plays catch-up, however, to these long-standing Native American epistemological systems of belief. Silko even links the two in an interview: "I am . . . intrigued with how, in many ways, there are many similarities in the effect of the so-called post-Einsteinian view of time and space and the way the old [Indian] people looked at energy and being and space-time

(Silko in Coltelli 138). Einstein's theory of relativity joined space and time in a relationship based on actual, physical lived experience. And because the relationship is both intimate, to the point of being inseparable, and contextually changeable, space-time is relative and always requires a frame of reference; it changes; it is historical, political, and social. Space-time is real—the only access we have to reality. When everything becomes relative the desire for absolute knowledge and experience is thwarted, and the transcendental ego becomes a thing of the past. The systems and relationships among things, knowledge, experiences, and people become what matter in the post-Einsteinian world—regardless of whether people actually accept their world as such. Native American epistemology already privileges the systems and relationships at work in the universe—balanced systems and relationships.

But Allen warns convincingly that a crucial difference exists between "the Einsteinian understanding of matter" and American Indian thought; she believes Einstein's concept "falls short of the American Indian understanding, for Einsteinian energy is believed to be unintelligent, while energy according to the Indian view is intelligence manifested in yet another way" (*Sacred Hoop* 60). Perhaps Deloria's claim that "the *source* of many important and fundamental theories in physics is mysticism" supports Allen's claim that the American Indian sense of energy, of space and time, is intelligent—extending beyond what mathematically based concepts can completely explain (*Evolution* 57; original emphasis).

Native American experience has always relied on a "theory of relativity" and been centered upon what Michael Harkin refers to as "circular chronotypes" (or circular time relationships) as opposed to the white man's linear chronotype (or linear time lines) (97). But Harkin's chronotype does not embrace a Native American sense of space; it only considers a circularity of time, neglecting spatial and physical relationships. Most tribes believe every individual inhabiting space and time as both physical and spiritual body (human, animal, plant, rock) has an effect on the balance of the whole. Allen states, "[T]he American Indian sees all creatures as relatives . . . as offspring of the Great Mystery, as co-creators, as children of our mother, and as necessary parts of an ordered, balanced, and living whole" (*Sacred Hoop* 59).

Even Ama's white lawyer in *Power* recognizes the "balance" Ama sought to restore to the world by killing the panther. Janie Soto seeks a similar balance when she sacrifices her leg for the benefit of the animal world after seeing it disrupted by men stealing newly laid turtle eggs (*Power* 140–141). The storm is a similar vehicle for restoring balance in the world, both destroying and creating life, killing Methuselah while younger trees survive. According to Allen, it is generally believed that "a person's every action, thought, relationship, and feeling contributes to the greater good of the Universe or its suffering" (*Off the*

Reservation 42). She asserts that "when any species fails to meet its obligations to the All-That-Is, everyone suffers—human, animal, plant, and non-human kingdoms alike" (42). Native Americans tend to adhere to a theory of relationships without boundaries such that everything and everyone touches and is perpetually in flux, moving through and in time and space as one—a Bakhtinian chronotope of life.

Mikhail Bakhtin posits a time-space matrix that he calls the chronotope, which he bases on the mathematical theory that "time [is] the fourth dimension of space" (84). Bakhtin's chronotope differs from Harkin's chronotype in that the chronotope is the fusion of time *and* space, not simply a concept of circular time. Bakhtin adheres to Einstein's theory that time and space are intricately linked and that together they form a solid concept through which to engage reality. Although all philosophers after Immanuel Kant are indebted to Kant for his work on time and space, Bakhtin specifically parts company with Kant regarding his notion of the transcendent experience of time and space (Clark and Holquist 279). Bakhtin suggests that the chronotope is our immediate access to the experience of reality, that we physically live the chronotope as we move through space and time as physical bodies and as we think and feel and envision space and time with our minds—which is how space-time is often represented in Native American literature. Kimberly Blaeser describes this representation: "Native stories are seldom about separate parallel existences, but instead are about intricately linked relationships, about intersections. Spatial, temporal, and spiritual realities of Native people reflect a fluidity that disallows complete segregation between experiences of life and death, physical and spiritual, past and present, human and nonhuman" (559). The chronotope is emblematic of this "most immediate reality" (Bakhtin 82). Not only does the chronotope imply reality as lived, but it also suggests the immediacy of its lived reality. In other words, the chronotope is relative, it changes depending on its context, it is emblematic of a particular space-time, it is history, and it is always connected.

The chronotope also encourages an investigation of the relationships between "real" and "fictive" (re)presentations of reality such that it draws relationships between the world and its art. Bakhtin explicitly insists upon the use of the chronotope by both the authors of literary texts who create worlds with the categories of time and space and the critics of literary texts who want both to seek out the typology of how space and time relate to each other within the text and to understand how the text relates to its historical context (Vice 201). Paul Ricoeur claims: "All fictional narratives are 'tales of time' inasmuch as the structural transformations that affect the situations and characters take time. However, only a very few are 'tales about time' inasmuch as in them it is the very experience of time that is at stake in these structural transformations" (22).

Hogan's novel is not only "about time" but also about space and how and why people experience and relate to them. Through a chronotopic lens, the ability to shape our sense of reality, to bridge any gap between the actual and the represented in our minds, our perception, or our art is exposed. The chronotope is real, contextual, and historical; it pertains to a real space-time context that finds representation in fiction as real time and space. But however time and space are represented in fiction, they are "real" times and spaces occurring within or alongside "real" time and space.

In *Power* Hogan, as all artists do in their works, finds a specific space (the book) and time (at least the reader's present) in which to voice her conscience on Native American and Euro-American divisions of thought, traditional and contemporary ways of life, and healthy and unhealthy relationships among humans, land, and animals. She also creates other spaces and times, like all artists, within her art (even with her description of Fossil Road she creates the concept of other worlds occurring all around if we only listen) that stretch beyond the present, that move into spaces and times I could not have imagined. And with new images comes the difficult journey of bridging what we thought we knew and believed to what we may be beginning to know and believe—like Omishto, who recognizes that "believing and knowing are two lands distant from each other" (40)—which correlates with Deloria's claim about tribal people: "It [is] not what people believe to be true that [is] important but what they experience as true" (*God Is Red* 67). Omishto learns to remember to know through her experience, not just to believe through abstract supposition.

Bakhtin's chronotope can bridge this distance between knowing and believing because it is a trickster figure that dances between "worlds"—floating with its feet on the ground through an evolving temporal-spatial continuum called "immediate" history, purging the world of a transcendent view by offering all worlds at once. Michael McDowell sees Bakhtin's chronotope as a vehicle for hearing all the voices in the environments represented in literature, not just the human ones (373). So a dialogue begins among all the "people" of the universe through time and space. And it becomes more and more possible to understand Allen's words about American Indian epistemology when she says "significance is a necessary factor of being in itself," not something assigned a "fixed" position in space and time (*Sacred Hoop* 59). Ama, Omishto, Oni, Sisa, Methuselah, snakes, horses—all beings on earth—are significant through their "mere" and fantastic existence, connected together in a space-time matrix that pushes space and time into multidimensionality and boundarylessness.

According to Gerald Vizenor, trickster expert and expert trickster, the Native American trickster is a Bakhtinian dialogic (191); in other words, trickster is comic and communal, individual and tribal, whole and freestanding, signified and signifier, a contradiction, healer and destroyer, often a necessary "evil" that brings "good." Ama is a trickster figure, a chronotope (crossing the "boundaries" of all space and time) who brings her people hope for survival by fulfilling her mythic destiny of becoming Panther Woman. She lives "halfway between the modern world and the ancient one" (Vizenor 23), between the white and the Taiga worlds. She exists in the present time but also seems as if she is "from another time . . . and out of place in this world" (23). This time, because there were and will be others, Ama says she will need to do something different to get us through; she says "the old ways are not enough" (22), which is reminiscent of what Betonie says to Tayo in Silko's *Ceremony* about the present need to alter ancient ceremonies to rebalance a contemporary world full of witchery.

Because the panther, because Ama herself, must get through to the other world—to the spirit world, to the space between things where Omishto sees things grow—in order to save us and rebalance the world, she must find a way. Ama sacrifices herself for the good of her community in a cycle of mythic renewal. She exists on the boundary between individual and tribal. She is the myth and the vehicle of the myth; she is the story and the woman about whom the story is told. Ama literally brings the future to the Taiga through her psychic "deliverance" of Omishto, the next-generation Panther Woman, and through the sacrifice of the cat so Ama herself may return as the cat in four years. Omishto may one day need to sacrifice the cat she knows best—her Aunt Ama.

And even though Ama may not embrace all the characteristics of a traditional trickster figure, she is one nonetheless. She is human/animal, past/present/future, killer/killed, creator/destroyer. And the trickster, like the chronotope, cannot be understood outside her or his contextual discourse, which means Ama's actions—although seemingly destructive—must be viewed strictly from within the historical context of her world and the real world that hers represents. She lives in a world where people rush through their lives not noticing the loss of human and animal life; not caring that land is being exchanged for buildings, fences, oil rigs that are "toothpicks" to a strong wind, and citrus groves that attempt neat, artificial rows of trees. This is a world in which Omishto's mother "plants" artificial flowers in the yard because they are pretty. It is a world in which boys try to shoot a panther in a tree for fun; a time-space where people seek a scapegoat to blame for everything rather than take any responsibility themselves. *Power* portrays a fictional account of a Florida swamp and its inhabitants—the Native human, animal, and plant life—losing ground to the foreign, transplanted forms of life that seek development and material gain at all costs. If that does not reflect upon the chronotope of the here and now—the real and the present—I do not know what does.

Although Vizenor warns against the extratextual interpretation and significance of fiction in terms of being conclusive (6), Blaeser suggests that "the

Dancing the Chronotopes of Power

works of Native women especially carry a new vision as they refuse to separate the literary and academic from the sacred and the daily. . . . Writings by Native women remain infused with supraliterary intentions" (557). In Hogan's lyrical novel about a fictive Native American culture that experiences land loss, watches animals become extinct, and manages to survive, only seventy panthers are left. The Taiga are all Native life; they are the taiga—the disappearing native forest. The only hope for the panther, for the Taiga-taiga, is the Panther Woman—the trickster-woman Ama—and her apprentice-witness Omishto.

Ironically, a trickster often attempts to break free from the prisons of custom and language although custom and language are generally the only access a trickster has to a culture. In Hogan's novel the power of language—at the center of the telling of the myth by Hogan/Ama to readers/Omishto—comes in the form of its absence, its silences; and custom comes in the form of an ancient myth that must be enacted even though it seems to go completely against tradition. It is the choice of silence or not—a selective truth telling at specific times and spaces in the novel's story—that grants the main trickster figure power and leaves readers with a sense of awe, a taste of mysticism, the idea that not all phenomena are explainable or logical. Through her sacrifice Ama offers a sort of solidarity, a rising of her people's sense of community through a revision of their "history." Ama as the newly emerged version of Panther Woman saves the future of her people, of the world, at the expense of herself and her story; her chronotope—the trickster chronotope—is the highest form of truth, a half fiction acquired through actualized ancient myth. In Hogan's trickster novel, what Bakhtin might call an adventure novel, time and place are familiar to its readers; enough "everyday" detail is given to create a fictive space and time an audience can agree is acceptable, probable (real towns, animals, cars, storms). Once readers accept the probable, the possible begins to occur.

Hogan's possible becomes the intersection of myth and plot, legend and modern fiction, Native American and Euro-American narrative form—all of which are tinged with the truth. *Power* is a bildungsroman, a Native American trickster tale, a story of cultural difference and similarity; it is a story about a girl, a woman, a tribe, trials, hunting, a dying landscape, a white horse, a sick panther. But it is also a story about struggling and surviving, watching and doing, floating and dancing and walking and getting scratched—all within spaces and times that conflate into one/many, not in a transcendent but in a heterglotic way, all possible, all probable, all welcome, all just as real as any other in the chronotopicity of power. Bakhtin states that it is through the multiple chronotopes present in any novel that readers are able to arrive at "the meaning that shapes [the] narrative" (250). He continues, "All the novel's abstract elements—philosophical and social generalizations, ideas, analysis of cause and effect—gravitate toward the chronotope and through it take on flesh and blood, permitting the imaging power of art to do its work" (250). In other words, the major chronotopes within Hogan's novel allow us the most immediate and insightful access into the meaning of the narrative, which I maintain is the Panther Woman myth being played out in the present of the text. The text, by unraveling and revising an ancient myth, also offers a revision of the world as historical, present-day reality. The chronotope of survival in *Power* becomes the powerful expression of healing myth through the art of literature, but it also grows into social commentary on the abuses of human power—often through human ignorance—that continue to destroy people, animals, and land.

Chronotopes of *Power*: Nature, Myth, and Survival

Within the first few pages of *Power,* Hogan presents the strong thematic links between time and space, animals and humans, place (including nature) and experience, and language (the silent and the uttered) and power. Omishto, the young narrator, suggests that space "has eyes and ears" and that "it moves slowly, silently" (3). She also indicates that thinking about an animal results in "call[ing] out to the powers inside it" (3). And "Ama, like the rivers," seems to Omishto to have "dropped out of time" (8). Relationships between time and space are immediately drawn out. Space is alive and moving, which implies time as "the past enfold[ing] into the present" (Rainwater 106). Power is something within both language and the body; and Ama becomes panther, land, and power. The chronotope of survival that runs deep in the novel involves the chronotope of the trickster and that of a physical-spiritual journey that links human, land, and animal through story, myth, and reality.

The chronotope of survival is set forth in the linear, causal narrative of *Power* through the storm episode, the hunting scene, and Omishto's decision to return to the Taiga tribe and land. This seemingly linear narrative traces Omishto's emotional and spiritual maturation through her physical journey with Ama. But each of these sequences is interrupted by flashbacks, which independent of their content may not be worth noting. The flashbacks are especially important, however, because they are mythic and dream sequences that slowly come to be the plot of *Power.* In other words, Omishto's experiences in the present time of the novel begin to be superseded by events of the past, even events she believes did not happen to her. Allen discusses this type of narrative structure in James Welch's works by stating that he "uses dream . . . sequences as well as flashbacks to further the plot in ways that make an Indian's experience comprehensible to white readers" (*Sacred Hoop* 152). Initially, Omishto's flashbacks are about the stories Ama tells her about her people, the Taiga, but then she begins to remember dreams she had, dreams that are becoming reality in the present. So even though she remembers her dreams of the past in the present, those dreams in a very real sense are flash-forwards into the future.

Dancing the Chronotopes of Power

For example, after the storm, when being inside Ama's house feels just like being outside, Omishto remembers dreaming and her memory becomes physical:

> And I remember now that I did dream, after all. I can see a piece of that dream, and something in my chest moves. I dreamed this storm with the flying deer. That's how it feels, like I've seen this before. I remember it, and the downy fine hair on my back moves with a chill. And I remember that Ama already said, as if years ago, in another time, when she saw the deer with the broken leg, "That's the one." As if all this has happened before and could happen again. (*Power* 43–44)

Omishto's dream becomes reality, which is relived ancient myth. Her dreams are inseparable from her waking life because the two fuse, become the same, within the chronotope of her journey. Boundaries between time and space blur.

All boundaries blur in *Power* through this fusion of dream, reality, and myth and through the chronotope. In the storm, land becomes water, snakes try to enter homes, 500-year-old trees fall without a sound, and deer fly through the air as if they were supposed to. Omishto describes the power of the storm, the wind, in human terms: it has "pushing hands . . . a body" (34). The storm shows Omishto that "clouds will join together to lend each other strength" (26), a strength stronger than any human's. Omishto says, "I ache from the effort of staying on earth" (36). Omishto learns that to be on earth requires work and desire and responsibility and respect. The one thing in nature she relies upon, Methuselah, dies in the storm. After the storm Omishto notices that "stunned animals walk about unafraid of [humans]" (38), which sounds to me like possibility for change in human-animal relationships. During the hunt Ama speaks to the panther, and the panther seems to be beckoning Ama. Ama says, "Old Grandmother, I am coming" (49). Omishto follows because she is drawn to it as if she has no choice, as if it were her fate to move from being the watcher to being involved (51). We are told that a panther is born alongside Ama and that the cat is her "one ally in life" (16). We also learn that the Taiga believe the cat, Sisa, is their ancestor.

Taiga believe in the power of the Panther Woman myth because for them it is more than myth—it is lived experience, it is chronotopic. Deloria suggests that "if we . . . look at the universe as mind manifesting itself in material form, our understanding of our relationship to the natural world changes radically. We do not have inanimate, lifeless things anywhere" (*Evolution* 199). His discussion involves the way we view animals and even stones in our environment and the fact that we may have "intimate relationships" with them if we begin to see them as intelligent forms of life sharing our time and space in the world (199). In *God Is Red* Deloria says, "tribal religions find a great affinity among species of living creatures" and discusses the Sioux's reliance on snakes in their rain dances (89). In a similar vein, Hogan explores the intimate, familial, physical, and mythical relationships among Ama, Omishto, and the panther.

Ama is the present-day version of the Panther Woman; she is a trickster figure who sacrifices for the good of the community. We are told that she is "changeable," that she is both "admired and ridiculed," and that she keeps in contact with nature and the spirit world (17). She lives at the crossroads—on the outskirts of civilization and tribal land (6). When Ama hunts and kills the panther, Omishto says, "You have killed yourself" (69). No spatial or temporal boundaries to contend with; the human body fuses with the animal body until the two images become one, as in the way Omishto describes hers and Ama's shadows "moving along the wall like unformed twins of ourselves . . . making [her] think there are four of [them], like the four women who came down the road a day or so ago" (49). Ama tracks the cat the way an animal would, and according to Omishto, Ama does not look human during the hunt (51). Omishto says it is "as if they've [Ama and the panther] always known and lived inside one another" (66). The Panther Woman myth becomes the plot, the actual journey Omishto is on, and the chronotope of the myth is powerfully rendered and handed down to the next generation. The Panther Woman myth has a past; it is a story told (with certain details left out), a tradition believed in. But the myth is also the present for Ama; she lives the Panther Woman myth destined to be part of the continuing story. And Omishto enters the present story as one who hears and sees and believes the myth; she is the future of the myth, the next Panther Woman.

So the myth itself is chronotopic, extending its mystery and power through all time and space. Through the chronotope of the journey—embedded within the chronotope of the myth as actual physical and mental space covered and time spent—the mythic is made real, and "time as it were takes on flesh, becomes artistically visible; likewise space becomes charged and responsive to the movements of time, plot, and history" (Bakhtin 84). Hogan exposes a circular history of time-space embedded within the Panther Woman myth like the overlapping layers of fossils—the bones of her ancestors (animals, humans, and plants) embedded in Fossil Road.

The storm, itself a historical chronotope because it too has happened and will happen in the world over and over again through the telling and acting of the myth, shows the power of nature; the hunt, a mythic and real and unlawful chronotope because it is a ritual story intended to heal the real and because Ama acts against contemporary white law and traditional Taiga ceremony, ironically offers the world a fresh beginning that only thirty people realize; and Omishto's decision to join her tribe, a chronotope of personal importance because she grows from a confused young girl into an understanding young woman, offers her Taiga community hope for a future. As we follow Omishto on her journey, which is the chronotope of power because it embraces the mystery in all time and space, between all times and spaces—upper, lower, and beside and before, now, and after—and all the humans, plants, and animals that inhabit them, we get tossed around by the action of the word for life and breath: Oni.

The word itself has chronotopic power in the novel because it is said the loudest in the most silent of ways. Oni breathes life into the spaces between humans, plants, and animals. Oni speaks the Language of all creation. Oni is creation. Oni travels all time over all distance; Oni forms the hole in the sky through which Ama and Omishto travel, through which a panther and a Panther Woman travel, through which balance is restored to a land wounded by humans (112). Through Oni travels the memory of all time and space from the beginning of creation, which occurs always; Omishto can hear the voices of her living relatives through Oni and through them know the voices of her ancestors in the spirit world. Oni is the source of power, the thing Omishto must take into her body, must move within, not fall through. It is nature, time, space, human, animal, God (178). She moves with Oni across the land, under the sky of the Taiga birthplace, becoming what Robert Nelson calls the event of identity—an individual who "enter[s] into some working identity not only with a cultural tradition but also with a particular landscape" (2).

Omishto moves easily from space to space and time to time, through clouds and water and trees and houses upon the sacred ground that holds her ancestors. Omishto inherits Ama's inside seeing (25). She is connected to Sisa through the words that travel through Oni (178). She hears what Sisa believes: "[H]umans have broken their covenant with the animals, their original word, their own sacred law" (190). And Omishto feels what Sisa knows about God being in the animal, having "eyes that shine in the night . . . scales and fur, claws and sharp teeth, a long tail" (191). Omishto learns that "two worlds exist" and that she can "enter them both like [she] is two people. Above and below. Land and water. Now and then" (97). Truly transformed, Omishto becomes the next Panther Woman, tracking Sisa through a hole in the world, following in Ama's footsteps.

Real time collapses into mythical, ceremonial time; both times become simultaneous as the plot becomes the myth and the narrative gets expressed through the "words" of Omishto's body—she dances the chronotope of survival. The chronotope of survival is the end result Ama/Omishto create for their people at the end of *Power* by following their destiny; but it is also the continued process of living the myth, telling the story of the myth, and existing in between the space and time in the world just before and just after the storm that begins the renewal of the Panther Woman myth. Omishto enters what Allen calls a "ceremonial world" in which "time and space are mythic" (*Sacred Hoop* 147). Omishto develops "the tribal sense of self as a moving event within a moving universe," affecting every other event she encounters all around her as those events in turn affect her (147). Omishto knows the earth, her ancestry, her self in a nonintellectual way; through her body awareness, she gains spirituality. She is power and solidarity; she is the story. Through her "(re)animation" into Taiga culture and nature, Omishto witnesses the "(re)animation" of the culture and the land and the animals; and "only then is there the song, or the dance, or the story, or the ceremony that becomes the text of that vision, the *articulation* of that experience" (Nelson 7; emphasis added). Her body speaks the silence of the chronotope, the part of the story that cannot be told because it is found only by listening to the silence, to the Language of Oni passing through the trees. She dances with and for this Language, joining in its song, performing its ceremony.

Perhaps Omishto approaches what Amy Elias calls the "coyote aesthetic" or "the history just beginning to be wrote" that exists "between the spoken words and the silence together" (198). In this sense, Omishto connects the silence not all of us can hear to the words we use to either cover up the silence or explain what we don't quite understand. Omishto hears and speaks to Oni, a silent Language that writes a history so far removed, so different from a Euro-American sense of history that, as with the concept of God being animal, we have difficulty accepting it. Perhaps Omishto guards the loss of the truth of the silence that speaks, the unseen, powerful force that shadows all of *Power*. Oni. Omishto connects the personal and communal, the past and the present. She watches long enough, and then, after being caught in a web of powers between the white legal system and the mysticism of ancestral myth, she deliberately chooses how to dwell within the present "reality" of livable possibility without forgetting the other worlds next to hers. Omishto goes home to her self, to her people, to the way it was in the world before humans broke their pact with the animals, ending the novel with what Sue Vice calls a Bakhtinian "carnivalesque cyclical renewal" (223). Hogan offers readers a creative revisioning of a fractured world. She presents a relived and relivable ancient myth that gives us a sense of being present at the re-creation of the world.

Ama follows the chronotope of power, her destiny as the mysterious Panther Woman, to offer her people the chronotope of solidarity: a belief in the future—Omishto, the next chronotope of power, the next trickster, Panther Woman. Ama's act is powerfully passionate and courageous, like the acts of Yellow Woman that Silko describes as "beauty" (70), because it solidifies the Taiga's response to change. Together, as a small tribe, they decide to err on the side of following tradition to "save" that tradition. They banish Ama because they believe in her power; they believe in the Panther Woman myth, and she needs to be banished to return one day as a healthy golden panther, to live awhile in the remaining swamplands of northern Florida, to help the Taiga become strong as in ancient times and then to act as sacrifice when it becomes necessary for Omishto to become Panther Woman and restore balance again to a wounded land. Vizenor might call Ama's sacrifice a form of "mythic verism" that provides a "comic spirit through imagination and a collective sense that people prevail and survive, get along, get by" (Vizenor in Bruchac 309). Ama might be considered a "comic spirit" in the sense that as myth she returns over and over again as Panther Woman in many shapes and forms, bringing communal hope to a struggling but surviving people.

Power explores the dialogue between nature and culture, animal and human, physical and spiritual. Ama and Omishto travel through a storm-destroyed landscape, a world turned upside down, where land becomes water; they hunt and kill the animal their people not only worship but are related to; and together they enact the past and the future in the present, crossing over the road that contains the fossils of their dead-living relatives without choice and with conviction to gain and learn the power of healing, myth, and silent story. Together Ama and Omishto form the chronotope of comic survival; they occupy time-space together in a mixture of past, present, and future in an ever-changing space of land that embeds one in mud, awaiting her time to return, and invites the other to dance on the ground formed by the bones of her ancestors—turning the dust up with her feet, tasting it in the wind, Oni. Like the Native Kayapo people from Brazil, who "gather to dance in the sacred ceremonial circle . . . to preserve and sustain the structure and integrity of the entire natural world," Omishto learns to dance with and for herself, her people, and her whole world (Suzuki and Knudtson 207). Through the story of *Power*, the powerful story of mystery and myth, we might be able to understand; to feel the pain of separation from our chosen behavior toward land, animals, and other people that we might need to feel in order to understand; to feel the unquestionable connections between us all. Power resides in our recognition of this connection and in our ability to hear and tell stories, silences and all.

In "Bees in Transit: Osage County" Linda Hogan writes, "[T]here is nothing more than air between us all" (*Seeing* 60). When the possible becomes the real or the real actually becomes realized, perhaps that space-time will come when the Florida panther—when all animals and people—will count and not need to be counted. Perhaps there will be a "place where human wants will let them be," like the time "before God and guns, orderliness and clocks" (*Power* 123, 139). Hogan often takes action in the world outside her fiction to heal the wounds humans cause the earth and the earth's beings. She speaks in her book of essays *Dwellings: A Spiritual History of the Living World* about a woman who is "such a keen listener that even the trees lean toward her, as if they were speaking their innermost secrets" (47). Hogan believes the "world told [this woman] its stories" (47). I think Hogan wants us to listen to her story about listening to stories, about imagining other ways to be in this world. And I believe she wants us to live the possibilities of our imaginations so that what we often consider "out there" or "other" can become harmony in ways we have yet to imagine, have yet to remember to imagine.

Works Cited

Allen, Paula Gunn. *Off the Reservation: Reflections on Boundary-Busting, Border-Crossing Loose Canons*. Boston: Beacon, 1998.

———. *The Sacred Hoop: Recovering the Feminine in American Indian Traditions*. Boston: Beacon, 1986.

Bakhtin, Mikhail. *The Dialogic Imagination: Four Essays*. Ed. Michael Holquist. Trans. Caryl Emerson and Michael Holquist. Austin: University of Texas Press, 1981.

Blaeser, Kimberly M. "Like 'Reeds Through the Ribs of a Basket': Native Women Weaving Stories." *American Indian Quarterly* 21 (1997): 555–571.

Bruchac, Joseph. "Follow the Trickroutes: An Interview with Gerald Vizenor." In *Survival This Way: Interviews with American Indian Poets*. Ed. Joseph Bruchac. Tucson: University of Arizona Press, 1987. 287–310.

Clark, Katarina, and Michael Holquist. *Mikhail Bakhtin*. Cambridge: Harvard University Press, 1984.

Cotelli, Laura. "Leslie Marmon Silko." In *Winged Words: American Indian Writers Speak*. Lincoln: University of Nebraska Press, 1990. 135–153.

Deloria, Vine, Jr. *Evolution, Creationism, and Other Modern Myths*. Golden, Colo.: Fulcrum, 2002.

———. *God Is Red: A Native View of Religion*. Golden, Colo.: Fulcrum, 1992.

Elias, Amy. "Fragments That Rune Up the Shores: *Pushing the Bear*, Coyote Aesthetics, and Recovered History." *Modern Fiction Studies* 45 (1999): 185–211.

Harkin, Michael. "History, Narrative, and Temporality: Examples from the Northwest Coast." *Ethnohistory* 35 (1988): 90–130.

Hogan, Linda. *The Book of Medicines*. Minneapolis: Coffee House, 1993.

———. *Dwellings: A Spiritual History of the Living World*. New York: W. W. Norton, 1995.

———. *Power*. New York: W. W. Norton, 1998.

———. *Seeing Through the Sun*. Amherst: University of Massachusetts Press, 1985.

Lavendel, Brian. "Putting the Breaks on Roadkill." *Animals* (November–December 2000): 20–23.

McDowell, Michael J. "The Bakhtinian Road to Ecological Insight." In *The Ecocriticism Reader: Landmarks in Literary Ecology*. Ed. Cheryll Glotfelty and Harold Fromm. Athens: University of Georgia Press, 1996. 371–391.

Nelson, Robert M. "Place, Vision, and Identity in Native American Literature." Accessed 27 October 2001. <http://www.urich.edu/~rnelson/pvi.html>.

Owens, Louis. *Other Destinies: Understanding the American Indian Novel*. Norman: University of Oklahoma Press, 1992.

Rainwater, Catherine. *Dreams of Fiery Stars: The Transformations of Native American Fiction*. Philadelphia: University of Pennsylvania Press, 1999.

Ricoeur, Paul. "Life in Quest of Narrative." In *On Paul Ricoeur: Narratives and Interpretations*. Ed. David Wood. London: Routledge, 1991. 22.

Silko, Leslie Marmon. *Yellow Woman and a Beauty of the Spirit.* New York: Touchstone, 1996.
Suzuki, David, and Peter Knudtson. *Wisdom of the Elders: Sacred Native Stories of Nature.* New York: Bantam, 1993.
Vice, Sue. *Introducing Bakhtin.* Manchester: Manchester University Press, 1997.
Vizenor, Gerald, ed. *Narrative Chance: Postmodern Discourse on Native American Indian Literatures.* Albuquerque: University of New Mexico Press, 1989.

BIOGRAPHICAL INFORMATION AND CHRONOLOGY—LINDA HOGAN

1947	Born 17 July in Denver, Colorado
1978	M.A. in English and Creative Writing, University of Colorado–Boulder
1978	First collection of poetry published—*Calling Myself Home*
1979	Adopted two daughters of Lakota heritage
1980	Outstanding Young Woman of the Year award for Community Service
1980	D'Arcy McNickle Tribal Historian Fellowship from the Newberry Library, Chicago
1980	Five Civilized Tribes Museum Playwriting Award
1982	Yaddo Colony Fellowship
1983	Short-Fiction Award from *Stand Magazine*
1986	American Book Award from the Before Columbus Foundation for *Seeing Through the Sun*
1986	National Endowment for the Arts Fellowship in Fiction
1989	"Aunt Moon's Young Man" featured in *Best American Short Stories*
1990	*Mean Spirit* one of three finalists for the Pulitzer Prize
1990	Guggenheim Grant in Fiction
1993	Colorado Book Award for *The Book of Medicines*
1994	Lannan Award for Outstanding Achievement in Poetry
1994	*The Book of Medicines* a finalist for the National Book Critics Circle Award
1996	Colorado Book Award for *Solar Storms*
1998	Lifetime Achievement Award from the Native Writers Circle of the Americas
2001	Special Tribute to Linda Hogan in Honor of Her Contributions to Literature, the Environment, Social Justice, and Human Understanding presented by the Diversity Caucus of the Association for the Study of Literature and Environment

BIBLIOGRAPHY

Selected Primary Sources

Novels
Mean Spirit. New York: Ivy Books, 1990.
Power. New York: W. W. Norton, 1998.
Solar Storms. New York: Scribner, 1995.

Poetry
The Book of Medicines. Minneapolis: Coffee House, 1993.
Calling Myself Home. 1978. 2d ed. Greenfield, N.Y.: Greenfield Review Press, 1982.
Daughters, I Love You. Denver: Loretto Heights Monograph Series, 1981.
Eclipse. Los Angeles: American Indian Studies Center, 1983.
Red Clay: Poems and Stories. Greenfield, N.Y.: Greenfield Review Press, 1993 (contains "Calling Myself Home," 1978, and "That Horse," 1985 [by Hogan and Charles Colbert Henderson]).
Savings. Minneapolis: Coffee House, 1988.
Seeing Through the Sun. Amherst: University of Massachusetts Press, 1985.

Other Book-Length Works
Dwellings: A Spiritual History of the Living World. New York: W. W. Norton, 1995.
Intimate Nature: The Bond Between Women and Animals. Ed. with Deena Metzger and Brenda Peterson. New York: Ballantine/Random House, 1998.
Sightings: The Gray Whales' Mysterious Journey, with Brenda Peterson. New York: National Geographic Society, 2002.
The Stories We Hold Secret: Tales of Women's Spiritual Development. Ed. with Carol Bruchac and Judith McDaniel. Greenfield, N.Y.: Greenfield Review Press, 1986.
The Sweet Breathing of Plants: Women and Writing on the Green World, with Brenda Peterson. New York: North Point, 2002.
The Woman Who Watches Over the World: A Native Memoir. New York: W. W. Norton, 2001.

Bibliography

Plays

A Piece of Moon. Produced fall 1981. Oklahoma State University.

Essays and Articles

"Crossing the River: Geology as a Record." *Parabola* 23 (Spring 1998): 6–8.
"The Great Without: Humanity's Dislocation from Nature." *Parabola* 24 (Spring 1999): 21–25.
"Making Do." In *Spider Woman's Granddaughters.* Ed. Paula Gunn Allen. New York: Fawcett Columbine, 1989. 188–196.
"Seeing, Knowing, Remembering." In *A Circle of Nations: Voices and Visions of American Indians.* Ed. John Gattuso. Hillsboro, Ore.: Beyond Words, 1993. 34–38.
* "The Two Lives." In *I Tell You Now: Autobiographical Essays by Native American Writers.* Ed. Brian Swann and Arnold Krupat. Lincoln: University of Nebraska Press, 1987. 231–251.
"Who Puts Together." In *Studies in American Indian Literature.* Ed. Paula Gunn Allen. New York: Modern Language Association, 1983. 169–177.

Interviews

"An Ecology of Mind: A Conversation with Linda Hogan." By Rachel Stein. *ISLE* 6, no. 1 (1999): 113–118.
"A Heart Made out of Crickets: An Interview with Linda Hogan." By Bo Schöler. *Journal of Ethnic Studies* 16 (Spring 1988): 107–117.
"An Interview with Linda Hogan." *Missouri Review* 17, no. 2 (1994): 109–134.
"Linda Hogan." By Laura Coltelli. In *Winged Words: American Indian Writers Speak.* Lincoln: University of Nebraska Press, 1990. 71–86.
"Linda Hogan." By Patricia Clark Smith. In *This Is About Vision: Interviews with Southwestern Writers.* Ed. William Balassi, John F. Crawford, and Annie O. Eysturoy. Albuquerque: University of New Mexico Press, 1990. 141–155.
"Native American Women: Our Voice, the Air." *Frontiers* 6, no. 3 (1982): 1–4.
"The Story Is Brimming Around: An Interview with Linda Hogan." *Studies in American Indian Literatures, Series 2,* vol. 2, no. 4 (1990): 1–9.
"To Take Care of Life: An Interview with Linda Hogan." By Joseph Bruchac. In *Survival This Way: Interviews with American Indian Poets.* Ed. Joseph Bruchac. Tucson: Sun Tracks and University of Arizona Press, 1987. 119–134.
Western Voices Interview with Linda Hogan. By Brad Johnson. 2 March 1998. *Western Voices,* <http://www.centerwest.org/voices/Hogan-interview.htm>.

Selected Secondary Sources

Ackerberg, Peggy Maddux. "Breaking Boundaries: Writing Past Gender, Genre, and Genocide in Linda Hogan." *Studies in American Indian Literatures, Series 2,* vol. 6, no. 3 (1994): 7–14.
Alaimo, Stacy. "Displacing Darwin and Descartes: The Bodily Transgressions of Fielding Burke, Octavia Butler, and Linda Hogan." *ISLE* 3, no. 1 (1996): 47–66.
———. "'Skin Dreaming': The Bodily Transgressions of Fielding Burke, Octavia Butler,

and Linda Hogan." In *Ecofeminist Literary Criticism: Theory, Interpretation, Pedagogy.* Ed. Greta Gaard and Patrick D. Murphy. Urbana: University of Illinois Press, 1998. 123–138.

Anderson, Eric Gary. "States of Being in the Dark: Removal and Survival in Linda Hogan's *Mean Spirit.*" *Great Plains Quarterly* 20, no. 1 (2000): 55–67.

Baria, Amy Greenwood. "Linda Hogan's Two Worlds." *Studies in American Indian Literatures, Series 2,* vol. 10, no. 4 (1998): 67–73.

Bell, Betty Louise. "Introduction: Linda Hogan's Lessons in Making Do." *Studies in American Indian Literatures, Series 2,* vol. 6, no. 3 (1994): 3–6.

Blair, Elizabeth. "The Politics of Place in Linda Hogan's *Mean Spirit.*" *Studies in American Indian Literatures, Series 2,* vol. 6, no. 3 (1994): 15–21.

Bleck, Melani. "Linda Hogan's Tribal Imperative: Collapsing Space Through Living Tribal Traditions and Nature." *Studies in American Indian Literatures, Series 2,* vol. 11, no. 4 (1999): 23–45.

Brice, Jennifer. "Earth as Mother, Earth as Other in Novels by Silko and Hogan." *Critique* 39, no. 2 (1998): 127–138.

Carew-Miller, Anna. "Caretaking and the Work of the Text in Linda Hogan's *Mean Spirit.*" *Studies in American Indian Literatures, Series 2,* vol. 6, no. 3 (1994): 37–48.

Casteel, Alix. "Dark Wealth in Linda Hogan's *Mean Spirit.*" *Studies in American Indian Literatures, Series 2,* vol. 6, no. 3 (1994): 49–68.

Dreese, Donelle N. "The Terrestrial and Aquatic Intelligence of Linda Hogan." *Studies in American Indian Literatures, Series 2,* vol. 11, no. 4 (1999): 6–22.

Gaard, Greta. "Strategies for a Cross-Cultural Ecofeminist Ethics: Interrogating Tradition, Preserving Nature." *Bucknell Review* 44, no. 1 (2000): 82–101.

Gillian, Jennifer. "The Hazards of Osage Fortunes: Gender and the Rhetoric of Compensation in Federal Policy and American Indian Fiction." *Arizona Quarterly* 54, no. 3 (1998): 1–25.

Hoefel, Roseanne. "Narrative Choreography Toward a New Cosmogony: The Medicine Way in Linda Hogan's Novel *Solar Storms.*" FEMSPEC 2, no. 2 (2000): 33–47.

Jahner, Elaine A. "Knowing All the Way down to Fire." In *Feminist Measures: Soundings in Poetry and Theory.* Ed. Lynn Keller and Cristanne Miller. Ann Arbor: University of Michigan Press, 1994. 163–183.

Krasteva, Yonka Kroumova. "The Politics of the Border in Linda Hogan's *Mean Spirit.*" *Studies in American Indian Literatures, Series 2,* vol. 4 (1999): 46–60.

Lee, A. Robert. "'I Am Your Worst Nightmare: I Am an Indian with a Pen': Native Identity and the Novels of Thomas King, Linda Hogan, Louis Owens, and Betty Louise Bell." In *Beyond Pug's Tour: National and Ethnic Stereotyping in Theory and Literary Practice.* Ed. C. C. Barfoot. Studies in Literature 20. Amsterdam: Rodopi, 1997. 445–467.

Linton, Patricia. "Ethical Reading and Resistant Texts." In *Post Colonial Literatures: Expanding the Canon.* Ed. Deborah L. Madsen. London: Pluto, 1999. 29–44.

Moser, Irene. "Native American Imaginative Spaces." In *American Indian Studies: An Interdisciplinary Approach to Contemporary Issues.* Ed. Dane Morrison. New York: Peter Lang, 1997. 285–297.

Murphy, Patrick D. *Farther Afield in the Study of Nature-Oriented Literature.* Charlottesville: University Press of Virginia, 2000.

Bibliography

Musher, Andrea. "Showdown at Sorrow Cave: Bath Medicine and the Spirit of Resistance in *Mean Spirit*." *Studies in American Indian Literatures, Series 2,* vol. 6, no. 3 (1994): 23–36.

Rainwater, Catherine. "Intertextual Twins and Their Relations: Linda Hogan's *Mean Spirit* and *Solar Storms*." *Modern Fiction Studies* 45, no. 1 (1999): 93–113.

Smith, Andrew. "Hearing Bats and Following Berdache: The Project of Survivance in Linda Hogan's *Mean Spirit*." *Western American Literature* 35, no. 2 (Summer 2000): 175–191.

St. Clair, Janet. "Uneasy Ethnocentrism: Recent Works of Allen, Silko, and Hogan." *Studies in American Indian Literatures, Series 2,* vol. 6, no. 1 (1994): 82–98.

Steinburg, Marc H. "Linda Hogan's *Mean Spirit*: The Wealth, Worth, and Value of the Osage Tribe." *Notes on Contemporary Literature* 25, no. 2 (1995): 7–8.

Stillwell, Mary K. "Linda Hogan's 'Seeing Through the Sun': Beyond the Absolute Good." *Notes on Contemporary Literature* 27, no. 3 (1999): 11–12.

Tarter, Jim. "Dreams of Earth: Place, Multiethnicity, and Environmental Justice in Linda Hogan's *Solar Storms*." In *Reading Under the Sign of Nature: New Essays in Ecocriticism.* Ed. John Tallmadge and Henry Harrington. Salt Lake City: University of Utah Press, 2000. 128–147.

Taylor, Paul Beekman. "Woman as Redeemer in Linda Hogan's *Mean Spirit*." In *Native American Women in Literature and Culture.* Ed. Susan Castillo and Victor M.P. Da Rosa. Porto, Portugal: Fernando University Press, 1997. 141–155.

Walter, Roland. "Pan-American (Re)Visions: Magical Realism and Amerindian Cultures in Susan Power's *The Grass Dancer,* Gioconda Belli's *La Mujer Habitada,* Linda Hogan's *Power,* and Mario Vargas Llosa's *El Hablador*." *American Studies International* 37, no. 3 (1999): 63–80.

CONTRIBUTORS

BENAY BLEND received a Ph.D. in American studies from the University of New Mexico. She is revising her dissertation for the University of Iowa Press. Her research interests include Jewish women writers of New Mexico and Latin America. She has contributed chapters to several books, including *The Literature of Nature: An International Sourcebook* (1998) and *Writing Under the Sign of Nature* (2000). Her articles can be found in *Critical Matrix, Bucknell Review, Southern Quarterly,* and other journals.

CARRIE BOWEN-MERCER holds a B.A. in biology from Scripps College and an M.A. in English from California State University–Sacramento. Her master's thesis, "Women Unforgetting the Bonds That Heal: Intergenerational Memory of Environmental Ethics in Linda Hogan's *Solar Storms,*" examines the ecofeminist implications of Hogan's novel. She has also published critical essays on Emily Dickinson and Ann Beattie. She plans to pursue doctorate-level studies in Native American literature and culture, contemporary American literature, and literary theory.

Contributors

KATHERINE R. CHANDLER is an assistant professor of English at St. Mary's College in Maryland. An originating faculty member of the college's interdisciplinary Environmental Studies Program, she specializes in environmental literature. Her scholarly interests focus on contemporary nature writers including Mary Oliver and Linda Hogan. She is working on a collection of critical essays on Terry Tempest Williams entitled *Desert Sage*.

BARBARA J. COOK is a visiting assistant professor of English and Theatre at Eastern Kentucky University. She holds a Ph.D. in English from the University of Oregon and a M.A. in American Studies from Utah State University. Her dissertation, "Women's Transformative Texts from the Southwestern Ecotone," reflects the focus of her scholarly interests in ecocriticism and women's studies. Recent publications include articles on Ana Castillo, James Welch, and Harriet Jacobs.

ANN FISHER-WIRTH is professor of English at the University of Mississippi, where she teaches poetry and environmental literature. She holds the Fulbright Distinguished Chair in American Studies at Uppsala University, Sweden (2002–2003). She is the author of *William Carlos Williams and Autobiography: The Woods of His Own Nature* and of many articles on American writers. Her first book of poems, *Blue Window*, will be published by Archer Books in 2003.

MICHAEL HARDIN is adjunct instructor of English at Bloomsburg University in Pennsylvania. He is the author of *Playing the Reader: The Homoerotics of Self-Reflexive Fiction* (Lang, 2000) and editor of *Devouring Institutions: The Life Work of Kathy Acker* (forthcoming, San Diego State University Press). He has published widely in contemporary American literatures and cultures, art, and gender studies.

JENNIFER LOVE taught developmental writing courses and currently tutors in the Writing Center at Lane Community College in Eugene, Oregon. She earned her Ph.D. in rhetoric and composition at the University of Nevada–Reno in 2000 and was Fulbright Professor of American Studies at the University of Potsdam in Germany in 2001–2002. Her teaching and research interests include feminist theories of rhetoric and composition, multicultural women's autobiography, postcolonial studies, and ecofeminism.

ERNEST SMITH received his doctorate from New York University and is associate professor of English at the University of Central Florida, where he teaches courses in modern American literature. His publications include a book on Hart Crane, *"The Imaged Word": The Infrastructure of Hart Crane's White Buildings*, as well as articles on Crane, John Berryman, Alfred Corn, Alice Fulton, Allen Ginsberg, Edna St. Vincent Millay, Marianne Moore, Adrienne Rich, and other poets.

ERNEST STROMBERG is an assistant professor at the Institute for Human Communication, California State University–Monterey Bay. He completed a dissertation on the novels of Louise Erdrich, James Welch, Janet Campbell Hale, and D'Arcy McNickle at the University of Oregon. His recent publications include articles on James Welch, Sherman Alexie, and Janet Campbell Hale. He is completing a project on American Indian rhetoric.

INDEX

Abbey, Edward: *Desert Solitaire,* 56; *The Monkey Wrench Gang,* 56
Abram, David, 27, 51(n3); *Spell of the Sensuous,* 45
Ackerberg, Peggy Maddux, 18
Activism, 49, 57–58, 147
Adam's Rib, 62, 64
Affirmation, 121
Alexie, Sherman, 99, 101, 148; *Indian Killer,* 8, 142
Allen, Paula Gunn, 46, 75, 94(n6), 106, 160; on balance of world, 165–66; *Song of the Turtle,* 78
"All My Relations" (Hogan), 108
Almanac of the Dead (Silko), 99, 106, 107
Ama, 145, 146, 148–50, 158, 160, 170, 171, 172, 174, 175; as trickster, 168, 169
"The American Indian Fiction Writers" (Cook-Lynn), 100
American Indian Movement, 104

Anglo traditions, 1, 67. *See also* Euro-American traditions
Animals, 12, 19, 83; cultural role of, 124, 125, 160; environment and, 41–42; and humans, 158, 165; imagery of, 130–31; languages of, 89, 123, 128; in ritual, 171–72
Anne, 58, 59, 60
Anthropomorphism, 4, 36
Anzaldúa, Gloria, 5, 8; *Borderlands/La Frontera,* 72
Apocalyptic narrative, apocalypticism, 135; in American Indian narratives, 143–44; Columbus's, 137–38; conquest and, 136–37, 138–40; of environmentalism, 150–51, 153(n17); Ghost Dance as, 141–42; Judeo-Christian, 7, 145–46, 152–53(nn5, 6, 12, 13); in *Power,* 144–48; Puritans and, 142–43; storms in, 140–42
Apocalyptic Writings (Edwards), 142

189

Index

Arcadio Buendía, José, 139, 140
Association for the Study of Literature and Environment (ASLE), 53
Aunt Moon (Bess), 110, 112, 113, 114, 115–16, 117
"Aunt Moon's Young Man" (Hogan), 109; community interaction in, 110–11, 114–15; negotiating identity in, 116–17; spirituality in, 115–16, 118; tradition in, 112–13
Autobiography, 94–95(n9); truth in, 87, 95(n10)
Awiakta, Marilou, 19
Aztecs, 144

Bakhtin, Mikhail, 8, 112; chronotope of, 166, 167, 169–70
Balcones Escarpment, 5, 60
Bartkey, Sandra Lee, 113
Bass, Rick, 3, 56; *The Book of Yaak,* 57; *Fiber, Colter, Brown Dog of the Yaak,* 57; *The Sky, the Stars, the Wilderness,* 4–5, 53, 57, 58–60, 61; *Where the Sea Used to Be,* 57
Bats, 42, 106
"Bear" (Hogan), 130
Bees, 23, 41–42
"Bees in Transit" (Hogan), 175
Belief systems, 5; time and space in, 164–65
Berger, John, 8; *Ways of Seeing,* 115
Berkhofer, Robert, 104; *The White Man's Indian,* 98
Bevis, William, 100
Bible, 139; apocalyptic references in, 7, 135–36, 137, 140–41, 152–53(nn6, 13)
Billie, James, 12
Billy, Joe, 42, 106, 107
Billy, Sam, 106
Binary thought, 136, 150, 152(n2)
Biosystems, 12
Birds, 42; spirituality and, 20
Birds of Prey Rehabilitation Foundation, 20, 27
Bishop, Elizabeth, 125
Blaeser, Kimberly, 166, 168–69
Blanket, Grace, 39, 103, 117
Blanket, Nola, 39
Bleck, Melani, 107; "Linda Hogan's Tribal Imperative," 81
The Bloody Tenet of Persecution for Cause and Conscience (Williams), 143
Body, human, and nature, 121–23

Book of Medicines (Hogan), 50, 68, 83, 116, 125; animal-human coexistence in, 130–31; humans and nature in, 128–30; nature and heritage in, 131–32
The Book of Yaak (Bass), 57
Borderlands, 5, 72–73, 74
Borderlands/La Frontera (Anzaldúa), 72
Boundaries, 164, 168, 171; human, 162–63; temporal and spatial, 161–62
Boundary Waters, 43, 75
Bourdieu, Pierre, 54
Bradford, William, 8; *Of Plymouth Plantation,* 142
Branch, Michael, 56
Brazil, 98
Brice, Jennifer, "Earth as Mother, Earth as Other in Novels by Silko and Hogan," 47
Buell, Lawrence, 55; *The Environmental Imagination,* 54
Buffalo, 130
Bush, 48, 49, 62, 63
Bushman, 22

Cabeza de Vaca, Alvar Núñez, 7, 138–39, 153(n7)
Calling Myself Home (Hogan), 2, 123–25
Carpentier, Alejo, *The Harp and the Shadow,* 138
Carson, Rachel, *Silent Spring,* 56
Catfish Man, 60
Cather, Willa, *O Pioneers,* 55
Ceremony, 123; and community, 68–69; pan-tribal, 105–6, 108; role of, 24–29
Ceremony (Silko), 106
Cherokee, 104
Chickasaw, 22, 24, 97, 104; natural world and, 123, 124; oral tradition, 1, 2, 87–88
Child abuse, 61–62, 75
Choctaw, 104
Christianity, 144, 150; apocalyptic, 138, 142–43, 145–47, 152–53(nn5, 6); as device, 148–49; Ghost Dance and, 141–42
Chronotopes: in fiction, 166–70; in *Power,* 170–75
Chronotypes, circular, 165
Churchill, Ward, 147
Church of Jesus Christ of Latter-day Saints, 143
Cities of Gold, 138, 139–40
Cobo, Bernabe, 8, 141, 152(n4)
Coles, Robert, 23

Index

Colonialism, 5, 78, 98, 111, 151; land and, 74–75
Coltelli, Laura, 48
Columbus, Christopher, 7, 143; apocalyptic narrative of, 137–38, 141, 144
Communication, 20, 30, 87; human-natural world, 83–86, 89–91, 123–24; nature's, 81–82
Communitism, 107–8
Community, 6, 113; ceremony and, 68–69; endurance of, 125–26; healing and, 49–50; identity within, 110–11; looking and seeing in, 114–15; oil development and, 37–43, 107
Conquest, 143, 144, 153(nn8, 12, 14, 15); apocalyptic narrative of, 136–40, 147–48
Cook-Lynn, Elizabeth, 6, 101, 105; "The American Indian Fiction Writers," 100; *Why I Can't Read Wallace Stegner*, 99
Cooper, James Fennimore, 98
Cotton, John, 8, 142
Covenants, with God, 142–43
Coyote aesthetic, 174
Creation, stories of, 21, 22
Cree, 44, 97
Cree-Anishinaabe, 62
Creek, 104
Crime, violent, 14
The Crossing (McCarthy), 56
Crown of Columbus (Dorris and Erdrich), 8, 144
Crystals, 14, 109
Cultural hybridity, 72
Culture, 17, 89; endurance of, 125–26; subordinate, 113; tribal, 5, 6, 49–50, 78–79, 117
Curtis, Edward S., 98
Custer Died for Your Sins (Deloria), 147

Damm, Katerie, 68
Daniel, John, 20
"Daughters, I Love You" (Hogan), 126
Davidson, Phebe, 92, 93(n1)
Dawes Act (General Allotment Act), 39
The Day of Doom (Wigglesworth), 143
Deal, Jonathan, 143
Deep ecology, 57, 60
Deloria, Vine, Jr., 164, 167; *Custer Died for Your Sins*, 147; *God Is Red*, 171–72; on space and time, 159, 160, 162, 165
Desert Solitaire (Abbey), 56

Directness, 87, 88. *See also* Honesty; Truth
The Dogs of Paradise (Posse), 144
Domestic abuse, 61–62, 75
Donovan, Kathleen M., 75
Dora-Rouge, 44, 47, 48, 62, 63
Dorris, Michael, *Crown of Columbus*, 8, 144
Dreams, 170–72
Dreese, Donelle N., 89; "The Terrestrial and Aquatic Intelligence of Linda Hogan," 92
"The Dry Pond" (Hogan), 124
Dryzek, John, 50
Dunne, Father, 45
Dwellings: A Spiritual History of the Living World (Hogan), 4, 36, 76, 175–76; ceremony in, 24–29; ecology of mind in, 29–32; language of nature in, 81–82, 83–84; nature and spirit in, 17–20; sacred stories in, 21–24

Eagles, 42
"Earth as Mother, Earth as Other in Novels by Silko and Hogan" (Brice), 47
Eclipse (Hogan), 124–25, 134; loss and absence in, 127–28; nuclear imagery in, 126–27
Ecocriticism, 4, 55–56, 81
Ecofeminism, 83, 88, 89, 94(n7)
Ecology of mind, 17, 29–32
Ecosystems: destruction of, 82–83; land language and, 29–30
Ecotheory, 54. *See also* Deep ecology
Edwards, Jonathan, 8, 143; *Apocalyptic Writings*, 142
Edwards Aquifer, 60
Ehrlich, Gretel, 28
Einstein, Albert, theory of relativity, 164–65, 166
Eiseley, Loren, 23
El Dorado, 139
Elegy, 56, 57, 58, 65(n1)
Elias, Amy, 174
Endangered Species Act, 12
The End of Nature (McKibben), 54
Endurance, cultural, 125–26, 127
Environment, 2, 5, 9(n1), 13; balance of, 129–30, 165–66; and culture, 125–26; destruction of, 11–12, 44, 63, 82–83, 159, 162, 164; human interaction with, 30–32, 36; interconnectedness of, 47, 77–78; oil development and, 37, 38–39, 40–42; writing on, 54–57, 64–65

Index

The Environmental Imagination (Buell), 54
Environmentalism, 17, 31–32, 53; apocalypticism of, 150–51, 153(n17); environmental justice and, 44–45
Environmental justice, 44–45, 46, 50, 61
Erdrich, Louise, 99; *Crown of Columbus,* 8, 144
Ethnohistory, 101
Euro-American tradition, 70, 71, 77, 93, 151, 158, 164; history in, 159–60
Europe, 13
"Evolution in Light and Water" (Hogan), 134

Facts, 159, 160
"The Fallen" (Hogan), 131
Fat Eaters, 63
Faulkner, William, *Light in August,* 55
Federal policies, identity and, 98
Female, and community control, 6–7
Feminism, 13–14, 17, 46
Feminist theory, 84–85, 87; gaze in, 109, 111
Fiber, Colter, Brown Dog of the Yaak (Bass), 57
Fiction, 58; as chronotope, 167–70; time and, 166–67
Fire, as theme, 36–37, 41
"First People" (Hogan), 90–91
Flood, Noah's, 140–41
Florida, 138; environmental destruction in, 162, 164; as novel setting, 7, 8, 12–13, 97, 139, 140–41, 150, 159
Foucault, Michel, 8, 113, 114
Fountain of Eternal Youth, 138
Fraher, Diane, 101
Frazier, Ian, *On the Rez,* 101
Frontier, 68, 70, 72–73
Frontiers (journal), 13
Gaia theory, 13
García Márquez, Gabriel, 8, 153(n8); *One Hundred Years of Solitude,* 139, 153(n9)
Garcilaso de la Vega, 141
Gardens in the Dunes (Silko), 106
Gaze, gazing, 6, 109, 111, 113, 114, 118(n1); female, 6–7
General Allotment Act (Dawes Act), 39
Genericism, 104, 106–7
Genocide, 14, 147
"Geraniums" (Hogan), 91–92
Ghost Dance, 141–42, 145, 149
Gilmore, Leigh, 87
Glass, 14, 109, 117
Gleeson, Brendan, *Justice, Society, and Nature,* 44, 50

God Is Red (Deloria), 171–72
Gold, 138, 139–40, 148
Gold, Jess, 39, 41–42
Good vs. evil, 136, 143
"The Grandmother Songs" (Hogan), 131–32
Graves, John, *Self-Portrait with Birds,* 58
Graycloud, Belle, 39–40, 41–42, 43, 45, 103
Graycloud, Moses, 39, 43, 45, 103
Great Britain, 144
Green, Rayna, 113; *That's What She Said,* 113–14
Greenpeace, 150
Greenpeace Magazine, 54
Guaman Poma, 98
Gulf Coast, 138

"Half-Life" (Hogan), 127
Hanta Yo (Hill), 101
Harkin, Michael, 165
Harner, Michael, 14
The Harp and the Shadow (Carpentier), 138
"Harvesters of Night and Water" (Hogan), 83, 84, 129–30
Hay, John, 31
Hazen-Hammond, Susan, *Timelines of Native American History,* 141
Healing, as theme, 49–50, 76, 125
Health, 25; language and, 90–91
The Heartsong of Charging Elk (Welch), 100
Heirs of Columbus (Vizenor), 143
Heritage, 131–32
Hill, Ruth Beebe, *Hanta Yo,* 101
Hill people, 36–37, 39–40, 45
Hiroshima, 126, 134
History, 124–25; fictionalized, 2, 7–8, 12, 101; indigenous, 37, 112; political, 5, 60–61; in *Power,* 147, 148, 158–59; worldviews and, 159–60
Hogan, Marie, 61
Hog Priest, 13, 42
Home, and identity, 74
Honesty, 6, 84–85, 86, 88
Horse, Michael, 13, 36–37, 38, 42, 103, 105
House Made of Dawn (Momaday), 35, 100
Humanities, and natural sciences, 56
Humanity, interconnectedness of, 47–48
Humans: and boundaries, 162–63; and natural world, 46, 77–78, 81–84, 85–86, 89–93, 94(n7), 121–25, 128–32, 157–58, 165–66
Hunger, as metaphor, 128–29

Index

"Hunger" (Hogan), 128–29
Hunter, Carol, 101
Hurricane, as device, 140, 141–42, 149
Husk, John, 13, 45
Hutchinson, Anne, 143
Hydroelectric projects, as setting, 43–44
Hydro-Quebec, 11–12, 14, 43

Ichabod (I. Mather), 143
"Idaho Falls, 1961" (Hogan), 126, 134
Identity, 6, 67, 68, 73, 74, 98, 100, 103; creation of, 173–74; looking and seeing and, 109–10, 114–15; loss of, 111–12; negotiating, 110–11, 116–17; reflection and, 7, 63; search for, 51(n1), 75, 76, 173; self-, 132–33; storytelling and, 69–70; tribal, 99, 103–4; writing and, 71–72
Incas, 141, 144
Indian Killer (Alexie), 8, 142
Indians, representations of, 98
Indigenism, 105–6
Indigenous traditions, 13, 67, 78; survival of, 76–77
Ingerman, Sandra, *Medicine for the Earth*, 25
"The Inside of Things" (Hogan), 133
Interconnectedness: of humanity, 47–48; land-human, 77–78
Interpreters, 32
Inuit, 44
Iron, Agnes, 44, 48, 62
Iron, Angel, 46, 47, 48, 49–50, 61, 62, 44, 77; identity and, 63, 70, 75, 76; on wilderness, 64–65
Isaac, 110, 111, 114, 115, 117
Ishi, 24
"It Must Be" (Hogan), 132

James Bay–Great Whale hydroelectric project, 43–44, 62–63
Jarratt, Susan, *Rereading the Sophists*, 87
Jeremiad, 56, 57
Johnson, Brad, 2, 50
Judeo-Christian tradition, apocalypse and, 7, 135–36, 152–53(n6)
Justice, Society, and Nature (Low and Gleeson), 44, 50

Kant, Immanuel, 166
Kayapo, 175
Keres, 106
Kicking Bear, 142

Kinship, myths of, 21
Kittredge, William, 23
Knowledge, 14, 32, 46, 110; body, 26–27; human-nature, 92–93; science, 29, 44–45
Knudtson, Peter, 29, 160
Krasteva, Yonka Kroumova, 42
Krupat, Arnold, 104–5

Laguna Pueblo, 88
Lakota, 105–6. *See also* Sioux
Land, 5, 48; caretaking, 73–74; connection with, 76, 77–78; and humans, 4, 158; as storied, 68, 72
Land language, 4, 29, 30–31
"Land of Exile" (Hogan), 127
Landscape, 36, 74–75, 76
"Landscape of Animals" (Hogan), 125
Language, 68, 94–95(n9), 123; earth and, 128–29; and health, 90–91; human-nonhuman, 83–84, 85–86, 89–90; of nature, 81–83, 157
"Language and Literature from a Pueblo Indian Perspective" (Silko), 88
Lape, Noreen Groover, *West of the Border*, 67
LaRue, 46
Le Guin, Ursula, 46
Leopold, Aldo, *Sand County Almanac*, 56
Levi-Straus, Claude, 22
Libro de las profecías (Columbus), 137, 138
Light, 134
Light in August (Faulkner), 55
Lincoln, Kenneth, 125
"Linda Hogan's Tribal Imperative" (Bleck), 81
Literature, 3, 112; environmental, 54–57, 64–65; Native sovereignty and, 101–2; Native values in, 104–5; pan-Indian, 106–8; politics and, 99–100
Looking, 6; and community, 114–15; ways of, 109–10
Lopez, Barry, 19
Lorde, Audre, 75
Loss, 14; literature of, 56, 58; as theme, 127–28
"The Lost Girls" (Hogan), 133–34
Low, Nicholas, *Justice, Society, and Nature*, 44, 50

McCarthy, Cormac, *The Crossing*, 56
McClintock, Barbara, 30, 82
McDowell, Michael, 167
McHale, Brian, 117

Index

McKibben, Bill, *The End of Nature*, 54
McNickle, D'Arcy, 98; *Wind from an Enemy Sky*, 106
Makah, 151
Manifest Destiny, 112, 144, 148
Marx, Karl, 136
Mather, Cotton, 142; *Wonders of the Invisible World*, 143
Mather, Increase, *Ichabod*, 143
Matoaka (Pocahontas), 144
Matriarchy, 46, 113, 114
Matthews, John Joseph, 102
Matthiessen, Peter, *The Tree Where Man Was Born*, 56
Maya, 22, 143
Mazel, David, 55
Mean Spirit (Hogan), 2, 4, 12, 45, 97, 103, 104, 107, 117; community and enivronment in, 37–43; indigenous worldview in, 105–6; Native sovereignty and, 100–102; fire in, 36–37
Medicine, bat, 106
Medicine, Beatrice, 101
Medicine for the Earth (Ingerman), 25
Meier, C. A., 18
Melville, Herman, *Moby-Dick*, 55
Memory, 69, 127; ceremonies and, 26–27

Minnesota, 62
Mirrors, 109; imagery of, 14–15, 116; symbolism of, 63–64
"Missing the Animals" (Hogan), 125
Mississippi River, 54
Mixed-Blood Messages (Owens), 68
Mixed bloods, 44, 75; Cree-Inuit, 44; identity of, 68, 69, 73; writing and, 70–72
Moby-Dick (Melville), 55
Momaday, Scott, 99; *House Made of Dawn*, 35, 100
The Monkey Wrench Gang (Abbey), 56
Montana, 57
Mormons, 143
"Mountain Lion" (Hogan), 130
Mulvey, Laura, 8
Mundus Novus (Vespucci), 98
Murders, in *Mean Spirit*, 40, 41, 42
Mysticism, 61
Mystic Realm, 150
Myths: apocalyptic, 141–43, 147–48, 152; role of, 22, 148–49, 171–72, 173; space and time in, 160–61. *See also* Stories

Nagasaki, 126, 127
National Book Critics Circle Award, 99
National Indian Youth Council, 104
Nationalism, 107
Native American Renaissance, 2, 3, 35
Native Americans, 161; representations of, 98–99; storytelling, 87–88; worldview, 158, 159–60
Native Science Dialogues, 13, 44–45
Nature, 5, 12; balance of, 165–66; communication with, 85–86, 89–91; and heritage, 131–32; honesty, truth, and directness in, 88–89; humans and, 46, 47–48, 91–93, 94(n7), 121–25, 128–30, 157–58, 162–63; language of, 81–84; relationship with, 30–31; sacred stories and, 21–24; and spirit, 3–4, 17, 18–21
Nature Conservancy, 2
Nebraska, 55
Neck, Ona, 42
Nelson, Robert, 173
New Jerusalem, 139
New Mestiza, 72
New York City, hydroelectric projects for, 43–44
Noah, flood of, 140–41
Nonfiction, 58
Norris, Kathleen, 25–26
Novels, 2, 7; chronotope in, 167–70; time and, 166–67
Nuclear energy, 126–27
Nueces River, 59

Oelschlaeger, Max, 23
Oil, Oklahoma development of, 36–43, 101, 107
"Oil" (Hogan), 126
Oklahoma, 2, 12, 74, 104; oil development in, 36–43, 101, 107
Omar, 59
Omishto, 105, 132, 144, 145, 146, 147, 148, 149–50, 158, 160, 163, 164, 175; dreams, 170–71; on environmentalism, 150–51; journey of, 172–73; self-identity, 173–74; on space and time, 161–62, 167; on stories, 151–52
Onatima, 143
One Hundred Years of Solitude (García Márquez), 139–40, 153(n9)
Oni, 173, 174
O Pioneers (Cather), 55

Oral tradition, 68; Native American, 87–88
Osage, as focus of *Mean Spirit*, 36–43, 97, 101–2, 103, 107
Osage Star-Looking, 103
Osceola, 148
Other, self and, 136
"The Other Voices" (Hogan), 89–90
Owens, Louis, 8, 70, 72, 111, 118, 158; *Mixed-Blood Messages*, 68; *The Sharpest Sight*, 143

Pan-Indianism, 2, 6, 103, 104; literary, 106–8; in *Mean Spirit*, 105–6
Panoptica, 114
Panthers, 172; endangered, 12, 151, 158, 162, 164; hunting and killing of, 12, 147, 149, 158, 160, 165; and Taiga, 169, 174–75
Panther Woman, 161, 162, 168, 169, 171–72, 174, 175
Patriarchy, 6, 113
Pentacostals, 145, 153(n12)
People. *See* Humans
Pishofa (Picofa) ceremony, 123
Place, 162
"A Place for the Eagle" (Hogan), 128
Plants, languages of, 89
Of Plymouth Plantation (Bradford), 142–43
Pocahontas (Matoaka), 144
Politics, 107; and social issues, 113–14; and spiritual world, 11–12; tribal-nation, 99–100
Ponce de León, Juan, 7, 138
Pontiac, 104
Popul Vuh, 22
Posse, Abel, *The Dogs of Paradise*, 144
Post, Joseph, 148
Postmodernism, 85, 118
Poststructuralism, 84–85
Power (Hogan), 2, 7, 8, 12, 13, 97, 102, 105, 106, 107, 132, 163, 164; apocalyptic critique in, 136, 138–39, 143, 144–48, 150–51; chronotopes in, 170–75; Christianity in, 148–49; environmental balance in, 165–66; historical device in, 158–59; hurricane in, 140, 141; spirituality of nature in, 20–21; time and space in, 160–62, 167; trickster in, 168, 169
Powhatan, 144
The Practice of the Wild (Snyder), 29

Prade Ranch, 58–59
Private property, 5, 60
Pulitzer Prize, 99
Puritans, 153(nn11, 12); apocalypticism of, 142–43, 144

Quebec, hydroelectric projects in, 11–12, 14, 43
Quiche Maya, 22

Racism, 74
Rainwater, Catherine, 158
Red Hawk, Stace, 105–6
Red on Red (Womack), 99
Reflection, imagery of, 7, 114, 116
Refuge (Williams), 56
Relativity theory, 164–65
Religion, 136, 147, 153(n12); apocalypticism and, 144, 145, 150
Renewal, 21, 127–28
Representations: Native American, 98–99; tribal-nation, 99–100, 104
Rereading the Sophists (Jarratt), 87
Resettlement, 104
"Return: Buffalo" (Hogan), 130
Revard, Carter, 3, 102, 106
Reviews, 102
On the Rez (Frazier), 101
Rhetoric, 86–87, 94(nn2, 3, 9)
Ricoeur, Paul, 166
Rituals, 94(n6), 123; animals in, 171–72; sacred stories and, 21–22; spirituality and, 26, 27–28
"Ruins" (Hogan), 125–26

Sabina, Maria, 14, 16(n2)
Sacred: nature as, 12, 19, 20; word as, 67
Sacrifice, 149
Sale, Kirkpatrick, 136–37, 144
Sand County Almanac (Leopold), 56
Sanders, Scott Russell, 31
Savings (Hogan), 5–6, 84, 87, 94(n7), 133–34; human-nature communication in, 85–86, 89–92, 93
Schöler, Bo, 2, 116
Science, 29, 30, 56; Native, 13, 44–45; time and space in, 164–65
Seeing, 6, 173; and community, 114–15; ways of, 109–10
Seeing Through the Sun (Hogan), 122–23, 132–33, 134

195

Index

Seeking, 121
Self, 132–34; and other, 136
Self-identity, 7, 69, 70, 103; creation of, 173–74
Self-perception, 68, 69
Self-Portrait with Birds (Graves), 58
Seven Cities of Antilia, 138, 139–40
Shamanism, 14
The Sharpest Sight (Owens), 143
Short Bull, 142
Sierra Club, 2
"In Silence" (Hogan), 125
Silent Spring (Carson), 56
Silko, Leslie Marmon, 46, 94(n4), 158, 174; *Almanac of the Dead*, 99, 106; *Ceremony*, 106; *Gardens in the Dunes*, 106; "Language and Literature from a Pueblo Indian Perspective," 88; on science, 164–65
Sioux, 142, 171–72. *See also* Lakota
Sis, 109–10, 111, 112, 114, 115, 118; negotiating identity, 116–17
Sisa, 173
The Sky, the Stars, the Wilderness (Bass), 4–5, 53, 57, 61; plot of, 59–60; setting of, 58–59
Smells, and thought, 26
Smith, John, 142, 144
Smith, Patricia Clark, 116
Smohalla (Wanapum), 141
Snyder, Gary, 19, 28, 32(n1), 46; *The Practice of the Wild*, 29
Social change, environmental justice and, 50
Social justice, 17
Society of American Indians, 104
Solar Storms (Hogan), 2, 4, 5, 36, 53, 57, 60, 68, 97, 102, 105, 106, 107, 117; characters in, 61–62; environmental justice in, 43–50; on indigenous culture survival, 76–77; mirror imagery in, 14–15; nature and spirituality in, 20, 82; plot of, 62–63; self-identity in, 70, 75; spiritual and political world in, 11–12
Solomon's mines, 138, 152(n4)
Song of the Turtle (Allen), 78
Soto, Janie, 165
Soul loss, 14
Sovereignty, 100; violation of literary, 101–2
Space, and time, 160–62, 164–65, 166
Spanish, 147; conquest and, 137–40, 143
Spell of the Sensuous (Abram), 45
Spirit, and nature, 3–4, 12, 17, 18–21
Spirit animals, 14
Spirituality, 17, 18, 78, 105, 115–16, 118; ceremony and, 25–27; nature and, 19–21, 28–29; ritual and, 27–28; stories and, 21–24
Spiritual world, and political world, 11–12
Starhawk, 88
Stein, Rachel, 44
Stein, Stephen, 142
Stevens, Wallace, 57
Stink, John, 103
Stories, 72; role of, 23–24, 67–68, 151–52; sacred, 21–24
Storms, 165; apocalyptic narrative and, 140–42; as chronotope, 172–73
Storytelling, 30; identity and, 69–70; Native American, 87–88; role of, 24, 68
Studies of American Indian Literature, 3
Sturgeon, Noël, 88
Subordination, 113
Sufi, 22
Suzuki, David, 29, 160
Sweat lodge ceremonies, 25, 26, 105–6
The Sweet Breathing of Plants (Hogan), 77–78

Taiga, 8, 97, 140, 148, 149–50, 158, 159, 164; chronotope, 172–73; and panther, 169, 174–75; space and time and, 160–61
Tall, Lionel, 106
Tarter, Jim, 46, 82
Tecumsah, 104
"The Terrestrial and Aquatic Intelligence of Linda Hogan" (Dreese), 92
Texas, 5, 58–59, 60
That's What She Said (Green), 113–14
Thelma and Louise (film), 14
Theories, role of, 151–52
Time: ceremonial, 173–74; fictional narratives and, 166–67; and space, 160–62, 164–65
Timelines of Native American History (Hazen-Hammond), 141

Traditionalism, 112–13, 114, 117
The Tree Where Man Was Born (Matthiessen), 56
Tribes, literary representations of, 99–100
Trickster, 8, 167–68, 169
Truth, 6, 84–85, 95(n10), 167; rhetorical and philosophical use of, 86–88, 94(nn5, 6)
"The Truth Is" (Hogan), 132–33
"The Truth of the Matter" (Hogan), 85–86
Turner, Frederick Jackson, 70

Index

Turtles, ritual and cultural role of, 123, 124
Twostar, Vivian, 144

Values, Native American, 67, 104–5
Vespucci, Amerigo, *Mundus Novus*, 98
Vice, Sue, 174
Victimization, of Native Americans, 137, 147
Violence, 40, 41, 42, 63; domestic, 61–62, 75; opposition to, 48–49; of the soul, 57–58
Vizenor, Gerald, 8, 102, 144; *Heirs of Columbus*, 143; on trickster, 167–68

Wallace, David Rains, 26
"Wall Songs" (Hogan), 161
Water, as device, 46–47, 48
Ways of Seeing (Berger), 115
Weaver, Janice, 103, 107
Weber, David J., 138
Welch, James, *The Heartsong of Charging Elk*, 100
Western Voices Interview, 2
West of the Border (Lape), 67
Whaling, 55, 151
"What Holds the Water" (Hogan), 83, 84
Where the Sea Used to Be (Bass), 57
Whirlwind, 142
White, L. Michael, 142
The White Man's Indian (Berkhofer), 98
"Who Will Speak?" (Hogan), 128–29
Why I Can't Read Wallace Stegner (Cook-Lynn), 99
Wigglesworth, Michael, *The Day of Doom*, 143
Wilderness, 18, 64–65
Williams, Roger, 144

Williams, Roger, *The Bloody Tenet of Persecution for Cause and Conscience*, 143
Williams, Terry Tempest, 14, 19, 23–24; *Refuge*, 56
Wilson, Edward O., 21
Wilson, Jack, 142. *See also* Wovoka
Wind from an Enemy Sky (McNickle), 106
"Window in Stone" (Hogan), 121–23
Wing, Hannah, 61–62, 75
Wodziwob, 141
Wolf, symbolism of, 131
Womack, Craig S., 2, 6, 71, 100, 101, 102, 104, 106; *Red on Red*, 99
The Woman Who Watches Over the World (Hogan), 1, 21, 61, 68, 95(n10), 105
Women, cultural role of, 6, 78–79
"The Women Are Grieving" (Hogan), 134
Wonders of the Invisible World (C. Mather), 143
Word, as sacred, 67
Worldviews, 47, 158; environmental justice and, 44–45; history and, 159–60; indigenous, 105–6; Native American, 35, 105; Osage, 39–40; space and time and, 160–62, 164–65
Wovoka, 141–42, 145
Writing, 15; environmental, 54–57, 64–65; Linda Hogan's, 1–2; as mixed blood, 70–72

Yaak Valley (Mont.), 57
Yellow Woman, 158, 173
Yucatan, 22

Zia pueblo, 28
Zwinger, Ann, 28